Oakton Community College
Morton Grove, Illinois

A THEORY OF
OBJECTIVE
SELF AWARENESS

SOCIAL PSYCHOLOGY

A series of monographs, treatises, and texts

EDITORS

LEON FESTINGER AND STANLEY SCHACHTER

A THEORY OF OBJECTIVE SELF AWARENESS

SHELLEY DUVAL and ROBERT A. WICKLUND

Department of Psychology
University of Southern California
Los Angeles, California

Department of Psychology
University of Texas, Austin
Austin, Texas

ACADEMIC PRESS   New York   San Francisco   London   1972
A Subsidiary of Harcourt Brace Jovanovich, Publishers

ACADEMIC PRESS, INC.
111 Fifth Avenue, New York, New York 10003

United Kingdom Edition published by
ACADEMIC PRESS, INC. (LONDON) LTD.
24/28 Oval Road, London NW1

LIBRARY OF CONGRESS CATALOG CARD NUMBER: 72-9997

PRINTED IN THE UNITED STATES OF AMERICA

CONTENTS

Chapter 4 **Conformity: An Objective Self Awareness Approach**

Chapter 5 **Conformity: Consequences of Attribution of Error
to Self and Other**

Chapter 6 **Attitude–Behavior Discrepancy**

PREFACE

To date, virtually all theory and research using the concept of self has neglected the phenomenon of self consciousness. Instead, the primary impetus has been toward a description of the self or analysis of self concept and self esteem. It is unfortunate that the nature of self consciousness, especially its determinants, has been given light treatment, for a theoretical understanding of the phenomenon could lead to a more complete understanding of behavior in general. We place such emphasis on self consciousness because of our belief that awareness of the self as an object acts as a feedback system which forces the individual to alter aspects of himself in the direction of his conception of what a correct person should be. When self consciousness is viewed from this perspective, the person's awareness of himself must figure into any ongoing behavior. The self conscious person responds not only to external stimuli, but also to himself as a stimulus.

The purpose of this work is to describe self evaluation within the context of a new theoretical formulation. The theory addresses itself to the nature of the conditions that cause consciousness to focus on the self, and takes as its central assumption the notion that the person will evaluate himself when he focuses on himself as an object. In the following chapters we will describe the essence of the theory and extend it to a number of diverse areas, most of them falling within the category of social psychology. Our extension of the theory within the book is not meant to be exhaustive, for the theory has a rather broad scope. It can be applied readily whenever conditions cause the person to take himself as an object and his values apply to his behaviors in that situation. Clearly many of these applications can be to the disciplines of personality theory, clinical psychology and other forms of applied psychology, even though we have limited the scope of our extensions for the present.

The theoretical ideas contained herein are entirely a collaborative effort between the authors, and the order of names is alphabetical. The development and extension of the theory owe considerable credit to numerous people who have taken the time to examine the theory and criticize the ideas as they have taken shape. The following people have commented on significant portions of the monograph, and we have benefited greatly from their advice: Linda Bell, Jack W. Brehm, Thomas C. Chase, Deborah Davis, John Dietz, Charles R. Ervin, Marilyn Golub, R. Glen Hass, William John Ickes, Edward E. Jones, Jerome Mabli, Melvin Snyder, and Stephen G. West.

Chapter 1

A THEORETICAL STATEMENT OF OBJECTIVE SELF AWARENESS

In an attempt to understand why individuation might lead to conformity, and after an examination of current theories of conformity, social influence, and attitude change, we have formulated a theory on the basis of a distinction between two alternative forms of conscious attention. The theory assumes that states of awareness are directed either toward an aspect of oneself or toward the external environment, and with this distinction it becomes possible to understand numerous phenomena in terms of the self evaluation that results from attention directed toward the self. For example, we will attempt to explain how self evaluation mediates some of the processes in hypocritical or self contradictory behavior, cognitive balance effects, social facilitation, social comparison, communication sets to send or receive, and attribution. It is likely that the theory will suggest new phenomena in addition to those just mentioned, and in the course of our discussion we will extend our thinking into unexplored areas. Before any application and extension is accomplished it is necessary to state the formulation in some detail.

We have not created a new distinction in psychology by postulating that conscious attention can be divided into a dichotomy. In 1934 Mead argued

1

that the uniqueness of the self lies in its possibility of being an object unto itself, whereas no other event in the universe is reflexive in the same sense. According to Mead, when an individual's experience is absorbed or preoccupied with objects around him, the self is the subject of consciousness, but when the person gets outside himself experientially by taking the point of view of the other he becomes an object to himself. Piaget (1966) draws a distinction similar to that of Mead in discussing his concept of egocentrism. Characteristic of egocentrism are an inability to perceive self contradictory actions, an absence of a need to verify one's statements, an assumption by the individual that others can understand him, and an assurance by the person that he is correct in all matters. In contrast to egocentrism is the self conscious state which is characterized by the opposite of the traits of egocentrism. Thus Piaget has proposed a distinction between egocentrism and self consciousness which entails the ignorance of one's unique point of view or the opposite—a consciousness that one's point of view is unique, and therefore subject to error. Apparently a dichotomous consciousness is a common conceptualization among those who have discussed the self concept, although the dichotomy is not necessarily explicated by many theorists. Instead, some conceptualizations focus exclusively on the "self as object," a notion approximating the state of self consciousness or self evaluation. The distinction between self as doer and self as object, and classification of personality theorists into those who deal with one self or the other, can be found in Wylie (1968).

Given this brief background, which will be elaborated in Chapter 3, some theoretical terms will be defined. "Subjective self awareness" is a state of consciousness in which attention is focused on events external to the individual's consciousness, personal history, or body, whereas "objective self awareness" is exactly the opposite conscious state. Consciousness is focused exclusively upon the self and consequently the individual attends to his conscious state, his personal history, his body, or any other personal aspects of himself. Our distinction requires a sharp demarcation between the "self" and the "nonself," and for the present we will assume that this distinction presents no important theoretical problems. The issue of the emergence of the self, and the ability to discriminate between self and nonself, will be examined in Chapter 3.

The terms "objective" and "subjective" were chosen because they capture the directional nature of consciousness. When attention is directed inward and the individual's consciousness is focused on himself, he is the object of his own consciousness—hence "objective" self awareness. When attention is directed away from himself he is the "subject" of the consciousness that is directed toward external objects, thus the term "subjective" self awareness. Because attention is directed away from the self in subjective self awareness it may be argued that the person is not self aware in any usual sense of the term, and that is correct. But he is self aware in the sense that he experiences the peripheral feedback from his actions and various other feelings that arise from within the body. His self awareness is the feeling of being the source of forces directed outward, but he cannot focus attention on himself as an object in the world. In short, the subjectively self aware person is aware of himself only insofar as he experiences himself as the source of perception and action. These feelings, which are the substance of subjective self awareness, are experienced simultaneously with conscious attention that is directed outward.

Our distinction between two states of awareness assumes that conscious attention cannot be focused simultaneously on an aspect of the self and on a feature of the environment. When a person's attention is directed toward a consideration of his personal virtues, it is impossible at that same instant to focus conscious attention toward driving nails into a board. Mason (1961) concurs: ". . . when one channels concentration of awareness in one direction or area of experience, there is generally only a relatively vague awareness of other areas of experience [p. 27]." Polanyi (1958) is also in agreement: ". . . our attention can hold only one focus at a time . . . [p. 57]." Attention may oscillate between the internal and external, and the oscillation may be rapid enough so that attention approximates the appearance of taking two directions at once, but it is a theoretical assumption that the possibility of directed attention toward an aspect of the self and toward external events simultaneously is impossible. When applying the theory it will be convenient to speak of "increased" objective or subjective self awareness, and when such language is used, it should not be taken to mean that the objective–subjective self awareness dimension is continuous. "Increased objective self awareness" simply denotes a greater proportion of time spent in the objective state, and "increased subjective self awareness" denotes just the opposite.

Although there may be numerous differences between the states of objective and subjective self awareness, we will focus on two differences that seem to be relatively broad, and, more important, closely bound up with our theoretical formulation. The first of these differences involves self evaluation. It is assumed that the objectively self aware person will not simply react to himself impartially and in a neutral manner, but that he will come to evaluate himself as soon as the objective state occurs. The notion of self evaluation is predicated on the existence of a psychological system of standards of correctness that is possessed by each person, and we will briefly discuss the nature of standards at this point.

A standard is defined as a mental representation of correct behavior, attitudes, and traits. To cite some examples, standards of correctness for social behavior would be such criteria of etiquette as the appropriate method of making introductions, suitable dinner table conversation, and protocol at a funeral. In the case of personality traits, each individual would have certain mental representations of ideal personality traits, such as intelligence, adaptiveness, and so on. In short, all of the standards of correctness taken together define what a "correct" person is.

It is a theoretical assumption that when attention is focused on the self, there will be an automatic comparison of the self with standards of correctness, and a perceived discrepancy and resultant self evaluation will be the result to the extent that the self is not identical with the mental representation.

The person's evaluations can be along any of the multitude of possible self related dimensions. For example, once he focuses on himself as a singer (perhaps through hearing his tape recorded voice) he will evaluate himself according to the disparity between his voice as he perceives it and a voice to which he aspires, and the greater the disparity, the more negative his self evaluation. Similarly, on any other dimension where an "ideal–actual" discrepancy is possible, so is self evaluation possible provided the conscious state is objective self awareness. There will be some instances where an ideal or aspiration does not exist, but in such cases a negative evaluation can result from a contradiction; thus, whenever the person behaves in a manner discrepant from his beliefs, engages in two contradictory behaviors, or states a logical contradiction, the result will be a negative evaluation when he is objectively self aware, provided that he focuses on the discrepancy.

In summary, the state of objective self awareness will lead to a negative self evaluation and negative affect whenever the person is aware of a self contradiction or a discrepancy between an ideal and his actual state. The greatest negative affect will be experienced when a substantial discrepancy is salient for the person; thus we would expect the state of objective self awareness to be maximally painful immediately following a failure experience. But even without a prior failure, or loss in self esteem, we would argue that the objective state will be uncomfortable when endured for considerable time intervals. As the individual examines himself on one dimension after another he will inevitably discover ways in which he is inadequate, and at such a point he will prefer to revert to the subjective state.

It is obvious that self evaluation is not characteristic of subjective self awareness. In subjective self awareness, attention is directed away from the self, and because a comparison between standards of correctness and behavior will not take place, there can be no self evaluation. For example, an English teacher might say "ain't" to her class, but fail to engage in self evaluation because the focus of her attention is drawn outward, toward the condition of her class. However, she will experience the bodily feelings and so forth that are concomitant with the subjective state, but it is important to note that these feelings cannot bring about a comparison between standards of correctness and behavior. In addition to the element of self evaluation there is a second difference between objective and subjective self awareness that can be most easily described by reference to the subjective state. We have postulated that the subjectively self aware individual focuses his attention outward—toward other people, toward tasks, toward sources of entertainment, and so forth. This would imply that the person's relationshp to the environment will be one carrying a feeling of control and mastery, for it is only in objective awareness that he will think about himself as falling short of the ideal of exerting control over the environment. Provided the person does not enter objective self awareness, he will not evaluate his actions and will feel as if he is forcing his energies onto external events. In short, his experience will be that of subject, rather than object.

Rotter (1966) has drawn a distinction similar to our objective-subjective self awareness dichotomy, although he limits the distinction to the type of control the individual has over his pursuit of rewards, and rather than an analysis of the variation in a person's felt control, he has assumed that people can be categorized reliably into "internal" and "external" control categories. When the person engages in some action that is followed by a reward and does not think that he was the sole cause of the occurrence of that reward, he is classified by Rotter as one who believes in external control. This same person is likely to place considerable weight in the concepts of luck, chance, and fate. In contrast, the person who believes in internal control perceives that a reward following his instrumental actions is caused by his own behavior or other of his characteristics, and does not result through fate, luck, or chance. We would suggest that any person can feel the extremes of internal and external control provided that the states of objective and subjective self awareness are varied. Given subjective self awareness, all of conscious attention is directed toward the objects being pursued (assuming that the person is trying to obtain something), and the feeling of being the subject or author of the forces directed toward those external objects will result in a feeling of internal control. Further, the subjectively self aware person will not attend to the relative strength of his own abilities versus the strength of environmental forces; consequently he will be unable to realize the possibility that his abilities are insufficient without the contribution of environmental forces or luck.

de Charms (1968) has drawn a distinction between "Origins" and "Pawns" that parallels the internal-external dichotomy of Rotter, and as an "experiential" example of the two alternative states, he has quoted a self description of personal feelings about intellectual activities by Koch (1956). Segments of this self description that are classified by de Charms under "Pawn" (Koch's "State A") are as follows:

> I am distractable, flighty, self-prepossessed, rueful over the course of my life and the value choices it has entailed . . . My responses towards people are bumbling, inert, ineffective, rejective . . . My self-image constricts into a small, desiccated thing: I am physically unattractive, devoid of color, wit, or style. An enormous distance seems to supervene between myself and my most prized values.

The unhappy fact about State A, at least for me, is that no manipulation of "extrinsic" conditions, or augmentation in the strength thereof, seems to improve matters much. One remains a prisoner to State A until it runs its course [Koch, 1956, pp. 66-67].

We might note that Koch's state of Pawn is foremost a condition of negative self evaluation, and apparently this self-evaluation goes   hand-in-hand with a "bumbling," "ineffective" approach. We might well substitute "objective self awareness" for "pawn," for we will argue in the next few pages that the conditions creating the state depicted by Koch can be predicted and controlled, and, further, that the lack of control and negative self evaluation described by him will always accompany objective self awareness.

In obvious contrast to State A is the state of Origin, which is exemplified by de Charms in the following quotations from Koch.

The central and decisive "mark" of State B [Origin] is domination by the problem context, or, better, by a certain direction defined by the problem context—a "diffuse" but absolutely compelling direction. All systems of personality seem "polarized" into the behavior; thus the personality is either integrated or, in a special sense, simplified, as you will. In State B, you do not merely "work at" or "on" the task; you have *committed yourself* to the task, and in some sense you *are* the task, or vice versa.

. . . in State B, most of the "effortfulness" or "strain" encountered has to do not with the generation of ideas relevant to the problem context but with their decoding, fixing, or verbalization, and their selection and assemblage with respect to socially standardized requirements of communication [Koch, 1956, pp. 67-68].

In the words of Koch are two themes that are central to our conception of subjective self awareness. First, the individual feels a compelling sense of direction toward the problem such that he is the author of the progress on his work—and, in addition, he and the task are one. To be at one with the task is, of course, to be unaware of oneself as an individual entity in the environment. The nearest the person comes to viewing himself as an individual entity when in the subjective state is to feel that he is the source of energy directed toward events external to himself, in that he is the subject or origin of the relevant forces and the environment is the object. Second, Koch notes that the greatest difficulties of his State B have to do with molding his ideas into socially acceptable forms of communication. It would seem clear that the subjectively self aware person will commit numerous errors of logic, syntax, and so forth, simply because he is unaware of himself as a distinct object, hence unaware of discrepancies between his performance and desired standards.

In summary, subjective self awareness is characterized by a feeling of control over the environment, an experience of at-oneness with the environment such that the person is the subject of action and the environment the object. Objective self awareness is associated with entirely different effects, for the individual views himself as another object in the universe—not at one with the environment and not the subject of forces that move the environment.

THE SOURCES OF TWO STATES OF SELF AWARENESS

Given the distinction between objective and subjective self awareness, there are two ways to proceed to construct a theory. We could assume that people fall with regularity into these two categories, much as Rotter has assumed that people tend either to believe in internal or external control, or we can presume that both the objective and subjective states are frequently characteristic of everyone, and are determined primarily by factors in the person's present situation. It is the latter approach which we think will be most fruitful, particularly since we would like to think that knowledge of whether a person is in the objective or subjective state is more likely to be gained by having control of his immediate situation than through historical self reports.

We would suggest that the conditions leading to objective self awareness (or subjective self awareness) are nothing more than stimuli that cause the person to focus attention on himself (or on the environment). More generally, whether attention is directed inward or outward is completely determined. We assume that subjective self awareness is the primary state in that the environment is normally a strong enough stimulus to draw attention toward it, which means the self is totally excluded from attention. In order that the person become objectively self aware, it is necessary to create conditions that remind him of his status as an object in the world. Many of these conditions can be impersonal, and examples are looking into a mirror, hearing one's tape-recorded voice, seeing a photograph of oneself, or any other setting where a manifestation or reflection of the person is external to the individual and can be perceived by him. Given that perception of oneself as an object is the only requirement for creation of objective self awareness, it is not logically necessary that part of himself be "externalized" by a device such as a mirror or tape recorder. If he can focus on himself simply by examining his hand, foot, navel, and so forth, objective self awareness may result. The difficulty with the latter method of arousing the objective state is in control of the awareness: it is relatively hard to determine what causes a person to examine his appendages, but it is easy to arrange for his personal aspects to be reflected outside himself.

Among the stimuli that generate objective self awareness are other human beings and as we will see later in discussion of social comparison, social facilitation, and communication sets, an extension of the theory to other people as sources of the objective state serves as a means of understanding several notable social phenomena. The analysis of inanimate sources of the objective state is considerably more simple than the application to humans, since we think that several dimensions of the others who arouse objective self awareness are theoretically important.

For a beginning we will assume that a person can be made objectively self aware by the presence of another simply by his knowledge that the other is aware of him. If he has good reason to believe that the other is not seriously attending to him, then the presence of the other will not arouse the objective state. But when the person encounters another and believes that the other is focused on him he will begin to evaluate himself along dimensions that are cued by the situation. Which dimension will become salient will be determined through prior experience with the other person, through the situational context, or will be determined by the chronic importance of certain personal dimensions. For example, if a boy who studies the harmonica happens to encounter his harmonica teacher on the street, he may well assume that the teacher is attending to him, and, further, he is likely to assume that the teacher is contemplating his harmonica playing ability. Thus the boy will become objectively self aware and in the process will focus primarily on himself as an object that plays the harmonica, although it is entirely likely that his attention would shift to another dimension of himself, such as a chronic failure in school, provided that such a dimension is prominent in his life. As a second example, we might imagine a young woman who arrives at a party and is confronted by numerous strangers. Given that they don't say anything, and that the context is primarily oriented toward physical impressions, she is likely to become objectively self aware in regard to the goodness of her dress or body. But it is also possible that through prior experience with those at the party she would know that they are interested only in her intelligence, thus she would focus on her intellectual gifts (or deficits). Alternatively, there may be one dimension on which she feels chronically inferior, such as her social position, and even though the context may tend to focus her attention toward her physical attractiveness, her chronic concern about social class may overpower the tendency to focus on her attractiveness.

The individual is not seen by us as using the values of the other as the criteria for his self evaluation—but he can employ the dimensions that are set off by their presence. The politically conservative person will not necessarily think of his values as incorrect simply because he finds himself in the presence of liberals, but, instead, he will examine the discrepancy between his personal standards of correctness (which may be relentlessly reactionary) and carry out his self evaluation according to the perceived discrepancy between his present opinions and his standards of correct opinions. This all assumes that the individual does not immediately accept the standards of the other as his own standards. Similarly, the college girl who is a radical dresser will not come to evaluate herself in terms of the standards of the Daughters of the American Revolution when she walks into a room full of them, but she will invoke her own standards of correct dress when she imagines that they are evaluating her on the clothing dimension.

Since we have postulated that the presence of another will create objective self awareness as a result of the person's awareness of attention of the other, it is easy to conceive of social situations where subjective self awareness should prevail over the objective state. The presence of a small child who is unlikely to attend to others with any consistency, the presence of someone sleeping, the presence of someone who obviously is preoccupied with other matters such as reading profusely or talking rapidly should be weak stimuli to objective self awareness. The more attentive or potentially attentive the other person is perceived, the more power the other will have to generate the objective state.

Thus far we have focused on events that bring about objective self awareness. It is all too obvious that the subjective state, the primary state of consciousness, should result to the extent those factors are not present, because the alternative states of awareness are mutually exclusive. But there is something more that can be attempted to produce subjective self awareness, and this method entails a forcing of the individual's energies onto the external environment, away from himself. It is the passive, nonspeaking, nonacting individual who is most susceptible to objective self awareness, and one condition that should increase subjective self awareness and curtail the effect of stimuli designed to bolster the objective state is that of placing the person into an active situation. If he talks, shovels coal, skis down a mountainside, or engages in any other activity that necessitates his focusing attention on events external to himself, subjective self awareness will result. Self evaluation will be difficult since he will be aware of himself only insofar as he is the source, or the subject, of forces acting on the environment. He will experience bodily feelings, but focused attention will not be turned toward himself. Further, it is not necessary that the action totally occupy conscious attention in order to effect increased subjective self awareness. We have already discussed an assumption that objective self awareness creates a negative affect, which implies that the person will often seek out methods of moving out of that state. The individual who is passive may have difficulty in transferring his attention away from his own self, but when he is occupied with a task, no matter how routine and automatic it may be, he can easily shift his attention from himself to the task. The task provides a ready escape from the undesirable state of critical self evaluation.

MOTIVATIONAL CONSEQUENCES
OF THE TWO STATES OF SELF AWARENESS

We have offered some postulates that deal with the antecedents of the two opposing states of self awareness, but as yet we have provided little more than a description of the two states. The motivational consequences of objective self awareness depend upon the assumption that a person's awareness of discrepancy between the self and the system of standards of correctness produces a negative affect which the person then tries to avoid. There are two channels for reducing this negative affect. The first of these is as follows: Since the presence of a discrepancy produces negative affect, a reduction of the discrepancy would obviously reduce this negative affect. Since standards are relatively fixed elements, reducing the discrepancy would entail the person's movement of his actual behavior, attitudes, traits, and goals, toward the definition of correctness represented by the standard. Thus, in general the theory predicts that a person who is objectively self aware, and whose actual self is discrepant from the standard of correctness, would attempt to change his present state toward agreement with the standard.

The second and equally viable channel for reducing negative affect is derivable from the idea that the person must not only be discrepant from the standards, but must also be aware of the discrepancy, otherwise no negative affect will be generated even though a discrepancy might be present. Since objective self awareness is the only state in which awareness of discrepancy occurs, it follows that avoiding the stimuli which produce self focused attention will reduce the negative affect contingent upon awareness of discrepancy, although the discrepancy itself remains. Little more will be said in this chapter about motivational consequences, and the implications of these postulates will be pursued in later chapters along with further refinements of the theory. For now it will suffice to cite an example in the interest of clarifying the theoretical statements.

A person who is devoutly religious may understandably believe in the golden rule, although he is likely to pay only lip service to the rule if he is a businessman. If the golden rule is for him an absolute standard of correctness, he can probably get by in the business world only by denying religious thoughts six days a week or by otherwise avoiding contact with situations reminding him of the golden rule. We would suggest that these "avoidance" strategies serve to keep him in subjective self awareness as regards his religious beliefs. If, during the business week, he encounters his minister at approximately the same time he is about to close a shady transaction on a used car he will become objectively self aware with respect to his religious values and will discover in himself a serious hypocrisy. The objectively self aware state will be a most uncomfortable one, and he has two options: the hypocrisy can be resolved or he can attempt to revert to subjective self awareness. To resolve the contradiction would not be easy, and he may find himself trying to conclude that the used car he has sold is in fine condition and so on, but when this is difficult he will begin to engage in activities that will cause his attention to focus on events other than himself. We might expect to see him avoid the minister, and it would not be surprising if he sought after strenuous activity.

STANDARDS

Three components constitute the system of self evaluation; the actual or real self as manifested through behavior and attitudes, the standard of correctness by which the actual self is measured, and objective self awareness, which results in the comparison between the standard of correctness and the act itself. We should now like to focus attention on the nature of the second of these elements. Our discussion will not be concerned with why a person has any particular set of standards, but instead, will address itself to the structure of standards in general.

The most direct route to understanding the structure of a standard is to look first at the function of the standard within the entire evaluative system. We have shown through numerous experiments, which will be discussed in chapters to follow, that individuals do judge the correctness of their various self attributes when in a state of objective self awareness. What kind of structure docs this imply? Any evaluation of an object (where an object is anything that can be realized by the person, whether physical or psychological in nature) requires a second object, either real or ideational, which serves as the criterion of measurement.

To show what is meant by the necessity of a criterion, an example taken from the physical world is suitable. If a carpenter needed to pass judgment on the appropriateness of a length of wood for his cabinet, it would be necessary to compare the actual piece of wood with a second stick of wood or measuring rod that indicated the correct length. For the person to decide that his stick is too long, too short, or the correct length, he must have a criterion for judgment. If he has no such criterion object, there is no possible way to decide whether or not the actual object is of the correct length. Thus the act of evaluation necessarily implies that there be a criterion of correctness against which the questionable object can be measured.

Another example which points up the necessity of a criterion of correctness can be found in the music studio. If a music teacher is to decide whether a piece of music has been played correctly or incorrectly by one of his pupils he must have an idea of the sound of correctly played music. If he did not have this idea in mind, then he would be completely unable to say that the present performance was correct or incorrect. Again, there is the necessity of a criterion of correctness, ideational in this case, before evaluation can take place.

Thus, if a standard enables evaluation it must be a representation of correctness. As the examples indicate, the standard can be either physical or ideational in nature. A person might carry around a model of a perfect square, which he has probably seen on occasion, or he might carry around a conception of the perfect woman, which has no basis in physical reality.

The use of these standards does not assume any special training. The only ability which we assume the person must have to evaluate is the capability to determine when two objects are not identical. That is to say, when a person puts two sticks together, he knows when one is longer, shorter, or identical to the other. If this were impossible, then evaluation in the sense of determining correctness would be impossible. Since this ability is the essence of the act of evaluation, it is also necessary that the criterion object and the actual object be on the same dimension. In other words, we are suggesting that the music teacher must have a mental representation of the correct way to play the piece that corresponds to the physical reality of notes and tones, and that he could not evaluate the music through a mathematical representation of the piece but must have a tonal representation of the piece in his mind.

The process of evaluation is a direct perception of a unit that is comprised of a section of the dimension in question. This section is bounded by the actual behavior on one end and the standard of correctness on the other. The perception of this unit, or discrepancy in the case that actual behavior and the standard are not identical, is an automatic consequence of the onset of objective self awareness.

We can now state the two characteristics of a standard of correctness that its function implies. It must be a physical or ideational representation of an object on the same dimension as the class of objects to which it refers, and it must represent a criterion of correctness. Even though we have gotten this far, the notion of a criterion of correctness is still hazy. It is supposed to be some object, real or ideational, that someone considers correct, but why is one object and not another a "correct" object, and precisely how does a person come to define correctness?

Going back to our examples of the piece of wood and the music teacher, we can see that the two people involved are giving a preferred status to a particular object. The man building his cabinet measures the candidate stick against only one other length. The piano teacher measures the student's performance against only one notion of how the piece should be played. Thus, the idea that an object is taken as a definition of correctness has within it the act of imbuing a particular object with a special status. This special status comes about simply because the person finds that elements in the environment have objective qualities and properties that make them desirable or undesirable. For example, a person's standard of regular dental care shows this property of judgment about the qualities and properties of his environment. The person believes he ought to go to the dentist because he has previously reacted to the environment in such a way that a particular point on the "dental care" continuum (i.e., regular care versus no care) has come to be the most desirable. He does not simply acknowledge the existence of dentist, but he reacts to dental care as if it were desirable. The two examples we have been using also show this property of judgment of desirability. The cabinet maker who believes the piece of wood ought to be a certain size does so because he judges that the size is desirable for his purposes. The music teacher who believes the music should be played in a particular way does so because he has judged that interpretation to have qualities that are desirable. Out of all human behavior it would seem that the judgment of desirability is the only psychological event that has the effect of giving one object a preferred status over other objects. For example, the music teacher is surely aware that many different interpretations exist. If the judgments of the objective requirements of the world which result in standards did not involve evaluation, the teacher would have to pay equal due to all interpretations possible. But this is not the case. There is just one interpretation that the teacher considers superior. From our perspective this must be based upon the teacher's judgment about the desirability of the qualities of various interpretations which then leads to the selection of one as the standard of correctness.

One question that arises within this context is whether the individual attributes the standard of correctness to his own personal needs, desires, whims, and neuroses, or to the inherent qualities of the object constituting the standard of correctness. For example, if someone claims that a piece of music is played perfectly, is he saying that this music is correct by virtue of its inherent qualities, or does he mean that it happens to agree with his momentary personal tastes? Although there is no strong empirical basis for deciding this question, we presume that the person operates as though correctness resides within the object that serves as standard. If someone judges intelligence to be desirable, hence a standard of correctness, he does this by perceiving that the qualities of intelligence are desirable in and of themselves, not by casting about within his own thought processes, biases, and defenses, and concluding that from his own personal viewpoint intelligence is desirable.

Another question has to do with the origin of standards. In general, we suggest that standards come about either by the person's own judgments about the world based on his perceptual processes, or through social influence. The carpenter can judge the correctness of a length of wood either through his own perceptual processes, a method that would probably be the most likely in his case, but he could also form a judgment of correctness due to the influence of others. As will be shown in Chapter 4, the person will, under specifiable circumstances, take the standards of others as his own.

The four types of standards we have briefly discussed define in large part what a correct person is or alternatively, what a person ought to be. We have used examples that have been prescriptive, that is, they indicate what a person should be, do, attain, and believe, and as such offer the person a positive instance of correctness. The set of mental representations that pertains to traits and abilities such as kindness, generosity, and intelligence, define what a correct person should be. Mental representations of the correct goals such as education and financial success define what the person should attain. Mental representations of situationally appropriate behaviors define how a person should act under various circumstances, A fourth standard, which applies to the correctness of beliefs, will be examined in Chapter 4.

To decrease any discrepancy between these standards and actual behavior the person must act in such a way that his behaviors coincide with the standards. These standards might generally be called prescriptive, in that they operate to inform the person of which states are desirable. In contrast are "prohibitive" standards of correctness, which are expressed solely in the negative. Clearly, such standards do not give the individual as much direction as the prescriptive standards, for they demand only that particular points on personally relevant dimensions be avoided.

SUMMARY

We propose a theory of self awareness around a distinction between "objective" and "subjective" self awareness. It is assumed that the objectively self aware individual will focus attention on himself—his consciousness, personal history, or body—but, in contrast, the same person in subjective self awareness will be aware of himself only as the source of forces that are exerted on the environment. Objective self awareness may be brought about by external events that cause the individual to perceive himself as an object, and the more effective of these will reflect some aspect of himself such that he can perceive his reflection in the environment. In addition, objective self awareness may be created through the presence of others who are presumed by the person to be attending to him. Subjective self awareness is bolstered through the weakening of forces tending to create the objective state, or through forcing the individual to engage in an activity that demands that the focus of attention and energy be outward. To the degree that a person is objectively self aware he will attempt to reduce discrepancies within himself or he will avoid the conditions leading to the objective state.

For the most part our analysis will be applied to one dimension of the self when any given person or piece of research is examined, which is to say that we have not formulated a self theory in the usual sense of a self concept notion. The purpose of the theory is that of understanding the motivational consequences of objective self awareness, and there is no attempt to build a picture of the unified self, nor to delve into differences between individual selves.

Chapter 2

EVIDENCE FOR
THE BASIC PROPOSITIONS

AVOIDANCE OF OBJECTIVE SELF AWARENESS

One of the central assumptions of the theory is that negative affect results to the degree that a person is objectively self aware and is focused on a sizable intraself discrepancy. The place-kicker who has missed a crucial field goal in the closing seconds of the game possesses an intraself discrepancy of overwhelming magnitude and, provided he is objectively self aware, the negative affect will carry powerful motivational effects. In contrast, the same place-kicker whose toe has just brought his team to a world championship will experience little, if any, negative affect when his attention is drawn to his kicking ability. But no matter whether the kicker has performed an act of heroism or a fiasco, he will experience no negative affect from that event when subjectively self aware.

What are the motivational consequences of the combination of large intraself discrepancies and objective self awareness? Chapter 1 indicated that there are two: (1) attempts to reduce the discrepancy, and (2) avoidance of conditions creating the objective state. Although it has not yet been specified which of these comes first, we can indicate at this stage of the theory's development that a person will use one mode if the other is impossible. Confronted with a barrage of self-reflecting visual, auditory, and olfactory devices, the person would have little choice but to continue to focus on his discrepancies and attempt to reduce or eliminate them; but when the discrepancy is immovable, and when the stimuli to the objective state are not a necessary or permanent part of the person's environment, we would expect him to avoid those stimuli, thus reducing the negative affect.

The experiment to be reported subsequently deals with the case in which the discrepancy is a permanent aspect of the individual. To take an example of the type of situation dealt with in the experiment we might imagine a young woman who has been raised in isolation from her peers. This young woman was born with a facial birth defect, and although society at large would ordinarily condemn this defect as less than attractive, her parents have managed to isolate her from public opinion while continuously complimenting her on her beauty. On her fifth birthday her parents decide to risk exposing their daughter to the public and take her to a clothing store. Upon entering the store either of two events transpires: (1) some employees at the counter remark loudly about the hideous little girl who has just entered the store. This remark registers quite strongly on the girl, and she realizes for the first time that she may well be ugly by others' standards, and perhaps universally ugly. (2) In the other case, there are no comments about her face throughout the visit. After passing the counter the girl's parents ask her to try on various dresses, and of course this obligates her to stand in front of the store mirrors, which should be strong stimuli to objective self awareness. Depending on whether or not the girl has discovered her unattractiveness with the aid of the store employees, the mirror should bring about either of two effects: if she has discovered her ugliness the objective self awareness will carry a great deal of negative affect and she will step away from the mirror quickly, but if she has not been criticized by anyone her mirror image will evoke very little negative affect, hence less motivation to step away.

To make the example complete, we should examine what happens when there are no stimuli to objective self awareness. If the girl should stand before a mirror with a shade drawn over it, eliminating any reflection, she will avoid that situation no faster because of the store employees' prior caustic comments. This is because it is the combination of a permanent discrepancy and objective self awareness that creates an easily observable avoidance tendency; either of these elements taken alone will not suffice to generate avoidance.

Duval, Wicklund, and Fine (1971)

As in the previous example, this experiment deals with a trait that is relatively permanent, thus eliminating the possibility of discrepancy reduction given the incidence of objective self awareness. Discrepancy size and objective self awareness were varied orthogonally, and it was hypothesized that the combination of a sizable discrepancy and objective self awareness would maximize avoidance of the situation.

The experimental design required three essential components. First, there was the necessity of inducing subjects to believe that a dimension of their actual self was at a level either discrepant or not discrepant from their presumed standard of correctness. Second, objective self awareness had to be varied. Third, the experimental setting had to be designed so that the person had no easy way to reduce the discrepancy. The first requirement was met by giving subjects false feedback from a fictitious personality test which supposedly indicated the person's level of creativity and intelligence. Some subjects were given negative feedback, thus presumably creating a high discrepancy, and others received positive feedback. To stimulate objective self awareness, the design relied upon a mirror and a television camera. To enhance objective self awareness, some subjects were seated in a room facing a mirror with the camera aimed at them while others were seated facing the nonreflecting back of the mirror with the camera aimed away from them. The presence of a mirror and camera should maximize objective self awareness in that both have been used successfully to remind the subject that he is a distinct entity in the world.

The third requirement, prevention of discrepancy reducing behavior, was met in different ways. First, the dimensions of creativity and intelligence, on which subjects were given false feedback, were chosen because they are relatively permanent. An attitude can be changed by a thought. Behavior can be changed by a new intention, but creativity and intelligence are relatively fixed attributes of the person that are not readily amenable to alteration by any remedial efforts. Second, the design attempted to avoid a wishful thinking reduction of discrepancy by removing any device such as a task or reading material which the subject could even conceivably use to bolster his level of intelligence and creativity.

Following the positive or negative feedback manipulation all subjects were seated at a table in a small room either confronted with a mirror and camera or not, and they were all given the option of leaving the room at any point after five minutes had elapsed. The latency of the subject's leaving was used as a dependent measure.

Procedure

The experimenter ushered subjects into the first of two experimental cubicles to be used in the experiment after asking them to leave all books, papers, and other potential distractions outside. The experimenter then told the subject that the purpose of the first part of the experiment was to complete a follow-up study of the personality test which they filled out at the beginning of the semester.

The experimenter stated that the major purpose of the present experiment was to follow up the original questionnaire with some information about the background of students who took the measure. Before he asked the background information questions, the experimenter told the subject that because the present research would last only a few minutes, all subjects were being asked to participate in a second but brief visual perception experiment.

At this point the experimenter asked six questions concerning the person's demographic background. As the subject answered the questions, the experimenter wrote down the responses in a notebook. After the subject answered all questions, the experimenter set the stage for the discrepancy manipulation by asking the subject if she had been given any feedback about the group testing. Consequently it appeared appropriate for the experimenter to inform the subject of her score and to make a few additional remarks about the test. The experimenter continued by stating that a positive correlation exists between a person's answers on the original personality test and his level of creativity and intelligence.

At this point the discrepancy manipulation was introduced. In the low discrepancy condition the experimenter informed the subjects that their absolute score, which was related to creativity and intelligence, was 78, a score that stood in the upper 10th percentile. To emphasize the subject's relation to her class, the experimenter remarked that the average score of her class in college was at the 79th percentile. In the high discrepancy condition, the experimenter told the subject that her absolute score was 32, and fell in the lower 10th percentile of her class. As in the low discrepancy condition, the subject was led to believe that the average for her class was the 79th percentile.

Following the discrepancy manipulation, the subject was told not to worry about her score and that the test would be used only by graduate students in their research. The experimenter then said that her colleague, John Snyder, was ready to administer the short experiment on visual perception in the adjoining cubicle. The subject was then taken from the first to the second cubicle. As the subject entered the cubicle the experimenter expressed surprise that John Snyder was not there.

After the initial expression of surprise, the experimenter seated the subject. Subjects designated for the mirror condition were seated at a table directly facing a large mirror. A television camera mounted on a tripod was also directed toward the back of the subject's head. The no-mirror subjects were given identical treatment, except that they faced the back of the same mirror—a nonreflecting wooden panel—and the camera was directed toward a corner of the room. The experimenter mentioned to all subjects that the mirror and camera would be used by Mr. Snyder in his perception study.

After the subject was seated, the experimenter explained to the subject that she would have to wait since Mr. Snyder had not yet arrived. The experi-

menter proceeded to tell the subject that if Mr. Snyder did not return in about
five minutes, she should go look for him in another room of the building.
(The experimenter specified a room number.) An electric clock was displayed
prominently on the table to insure that all subjects would have the possibility
of knowing the amount of time that had passed, although the clock was not
specifically mentioned by the experimenter. After completing the story about
the waiting period, the experimenter left the subject alone.

The dependent measure was the latency of the subject's exit from the
room. Latency was measured by the interval between the moment of the
experimenter's exit from the room and the moment the subject opened the door
to leave the room. If the subject did not leave within 10 minutes, the experimenter
returned to the room and terminated the experiment, giving the subject a score
of 10 minutes. After the subject left the room, she was debriefed.

Results

The experimental hypothesis predicted that to the extent a person is objectively self aware and discrepant from his standards of correctness, he will avoid
stimuli that produce objective self awareness. As the means indicate (see Table
1), there was a main effect for the presence of the mirror ($p < .05$). To determine
the relative contribution of the individual means to the main effect, a comparison
between the means of the mirror-high discrepancy condition (6.39) and the
no mirror-high discrepancy condition (8.12) was undertaken. This comparison
showed reliable results ($p < .02$). No differences were found between the mirror-
low discrepancy (7.80) and the no mirror-low discrepancy conditions ($p > .20$).

The hypothesis also predicted that subjects in the mirror-high discrepancy
condition would tend to leave the room sooner than the subjects in the mirror-low
discrepancy condition. Consistent with this prediction the mean number of
minutes (6.39) spent in the room by subjects in the mirror-high discrepancy

Table 1

Mean Latencies for Exit from Experimental Room

	High discrepancy	Low discrepancy
Mirror	6.39[a]	7.80
	(13)[b]	(12)
No-Mirror	8.12	8.20
	(12)	(15)

[a]The values are mean number of minutes spent in the room.
[b]Ns in parentheses.

condition was less than the mean number of minutes spent in the room by subjects in the mirror-low discrepancy condition (7.80) ($p < .05$). Since the hypothesis indicated that avoidance should be maximized by the combination of objective self awareness and a large discrepancy, we might expect to find a statistical interaction. The pattern of means in Table 1 is consistent with the form of interaction that would be expected, in that the mirror-high discrepancy condition mean is greater than the others, while the other three means are very similar. However, the interaction does not reach the conventional level of significance.

Discussion

The experiment directly supports the contention that avoidance of a situation is a joint function of intraself discrepancy and the power of the situation to evoke the objective state. Holding discrepancy size at a high level (high discrepancy condition), subjects avoided the situation to the degree that they were rendered objectively self aware. Holding objective self awareness at a high level (mirror condition), avoidance was a positive function of discrepancy state. When either of these variables was at a low level, the other variable failed to create an effect.

The experiment was designed explicitly to eliminate discrepancy reduction as a means of coping with the negative affect, and it was assumed that avoidance would be most apparent under such conditions. It remains to be seen precisely what conditions determine which mode will be used, especially when the two reactions are equally possible. There is a possibility that when a person is free to either reduce discrepancy or avoid the objective self awareness-creating stimuli, his choice of mode will be determined by the nature of the discrepancy. It may be that a person will choose to reduce a discrepancy if that discrepancy can be reduced effectively, while avoidance would be found only if the efforts at discrepancy reduction are futile. This reasoning suggests that an objectively self aware person would alter a trivial, unimportant, and easily changed attitude that was discrepant from a standard of correctness, but would avoid objective self awareness-producing stimuli when the discrepancy was on a relatively permanent and important trait or ability, such as intelligence or creativity. (This analysis assumes that importance and permanence would generally be positively related.) Another way to approach the problem is from the standpoint of magnitude of discrepancy. Theoretically, the person must suffer the negative affect produced by a discrepancy even in the process of reducing the discrepancy. If the discrepancy were large, the negative affect the person would have to endure while attempting discrepancy reduction might outweigh the anticipated satisfaction of negative affect reduction. Hence, the person would adopt the mode of avoidance. However, were the discrepancy small, the anticipated positive effects of reduced discrepancy might outweigh the negative affect suffered during the process of discrepancy reduction. We leave it to future research to answer this question definitively.

Before moving on, we should note an important contrast between the present experimental procedure and the example of the ugly little girl. In the case of the girl in the store, the device stimulating objective self awareness directly reflected the trait that was salient in the situation. That is, her face was the salient issue in question, and the mirror reminded her directly of her face. In the present experiment the subjects did not see their intelligent quotient in the mirror. The success of the experiment relied upon the theoretical assumption that self-focused attention will move to the dimension of the self that is most salient in the situation. If this assumption is viable, it becomes possible to bring a person's attention to focus on a salient dimension by any stimulus that reminds him of himself, even if that stimulus bears no relation to the salient dimension. A person's concern about his intelligence could thus be brought about by the image of his face (as in the present study), by the sound of his voice, by the attention of others, or by a variety of other stimuli. We will see additional examples of this "cross-dimensional" arousal of objective self awareness in the research reported throughout this volume.

Sarnoff and Zimbardo (1961)

Although not originally conceived with objective self awareness in mind, the Sarnoff-Zimbardo experiment offers additional support for the notion that objective self awareness-arousing situations will be avoided when a large within-self discrepancy is salient. In the present case the large discrepancy consisted of a certain kind of humiliation, and the source of objective self awareness was the potential attention from others.

The experiment was conducted with the purpose of demonstrating an exception to Schachter's (1959) finding that fear leads to affiliation. In Schachter's research the fear was an "objective" one in the Freudian sense, which is to say that there was a potentially harmful and threatening event in the environment. His subjects showed an increased desire to affiliate with others, given that they expected to receive a substantial shock.

Sarnoff and Zimbardo propose that certain anxiety states can be created by stimuli that are objectively innocuous, and that this anxiety will lead to avoidance of other people because of the inappropriateness of the motive basic to the anxiety. For example, it might be argued that the sight of a nipple arouses the repressed motive to take milk from one's mother's breast, and that anxiety follows once this motive comes into consciousness; because the person is aware of the inappropriateness of his feelings about the nipple, he may well attempt to avoid others, thereby averting potential ridicule. On the basis of these arguments, taken from Freud (1949), the authors designed the following experiment to test the proposition that an individual will prefer to remain alone to the degree that oral anxiety is aroused. Our description includes only those aspects of the study that are relevant to the objective self awareness notion.

Under a suitable pretext, subjects were told that they would have to place some items into their mouths, and with this procedure oral anxiety was manipulated. Some subjects (High Anxiety) were led to expect to suck on numerous breast-related items such as baby bottles, oversized nipples, pacifiers, breastshields, and lollipops. They were told that the sucking behavior would last for two minutes. In the Low Anxiety condition subjects expected to place other kinds of objects into their mouths—whistles, balloons, "kazoos," and pipes—and only for 10 seconds.

Once the subjects were given these different expectations they were told that there would be a waiting period prior to the oral stimulation and that they could either wait alone or with someone else. The strength of the subject's preference of waiting alone or together was then assessed on a scale.

Consistent with the Freudian idea, the subjects in the High Anxiety condition evidenced a greater preference for waiting alone than did the Low Anxiety subjects. According to the Sarnoff-Zimbardo interpretation of the data, the prospect of sucking the breast-related objects brought into consciousness an unacceptable motive, which in turn created anxiety and finally an avoidance of others.

An analysis of the experimental situation in terms of the objective self awareness notion is somewhat different from the original. The two interpretations are identical with respect to the interpretation of the initial effect of the expected oral stimulation. That is, we assume with Sarnoff and Zimbardo that the subject was not happy over the prospect of engaging in that behavior; in fact, the High Anxiety subject appears to be a clear case of someone whose behavioral commitment is discrepant from his standards of correctness. Sarnoff and Zimbardo argue that the subject's realization of an inappropriate motive generates anxiety, and that such anxiety leads to an avoidance of others due to the prospect of public humiliation. The objective self awareness analysis implies an avoidance of others only because of their potential for creating objective self awareness. Theoretically, it is not the disapproval of others per se that causes avoidance, but, rather, the self disapproval that is anticipated in a public situation, such disapproval leading to the objective state.

SELF EVALUATION AND SELF ESTEEM

A central assumption of the theory is that the objectively self aware person will become increasingly self critical. Stated more conceptually, the focus of attention upon the self will force the individual to be aware of intraself discrepancies, while such discrepancies would go unnoticed during the subjective state. It is immaterial whether the awareness of these discrepancies is called self evaluation or reduced self esteem; in any case the phenomenon is identical: the more time spent in the objective state, the greater one's awareness of falling short of personal standards of correctness.

If discrepancies are noticed only in objective self awareness, it should be possible to induce someone to report larger discrepancies as he is confronted with various self-related dimensions, provided that he is confronted with conditions forcing him to focus upon himself as an object. This was accomplished in the experiment to be reported below, in which the degree of objective self awareness was varied while subjects filled out a "real self-ideal self" self esteem questionnaire.

How permanent are the self esteem changes brought about by self focused attention? There are two ways that this question should be examined: (1) If someone has indicated an increased deficit in mental ability under conditions forcing him to be objectively self aware, this admission of a deficit should carry into future situations only to the degree that he is objectively self aware in the future. Otherwise he would simply not be examining himself, and thus would find no discrepancy. But suppose he is asked about his mental ability on two separate occasions—the first time confronted simultaneously with various visual and auditory symbols of himself, and the second time with no elements reminding him of his object-like nature? Disregarding the difference between these situations in regard to symbols of himself, shouldn't the fact of asking him a question about one of his dimensions (mental ability) evoke objective self awareness? Probably so, which is to say that objective self awareness is evoked in both testing sessions. But this is not to say that the reported discrepancy will be identical in both situations, for the amount of time spent objectively self aware will be greater in the first session. The more time spent in the objective state, the more components of mental ability will be examined and the more personal experiences associated with mental ability will be called up, all of these adding into the reported discrepancy between actual and ideal mental ability. In summary, the reported discrepancy sizes brought about by objective self awareness should not be permanent, and will only be reported on future occasions to the extent that objective self awareness on those occasions is comparable in duration to the state aroused in the first situation.

(2) The second issue relevant to the question of permanence has to do with the permanence of the power of the self reflecting stimulus, rather than the permanence of the widened discrepancy. If an individual is confronted continually with any stimulus reminding him of his object-nature, there is reason to think that the stimulus will eventually lose potency. In fact, there are at least two reasons for thinking this: first, since the objectively self aware person is

motivated to avoid the conditions leading to the objective state, people generally find ways of reducing the impact of the stimulus on them. With a mirror, they might turn away, and the same is true of the glance of another individual. Confronted with an auditory reflection of themselves they might make distracting noises or attempt to occupy themselves with unrelated activities. Second, the concept of "adaptation" applies to the declining-over-time effect of the self-reflecting stimulus, given that adaptation means simply a decrease in the power of a stimulus to evoke a response.

Ickes and Wicklund (1971)

The present experiment was designed to examine the basic theoretical notion that objective self awareness creates an awareness of intraself discrepancies. Subjects were administered a self esteem scale, during which time they were confronted either with a stimulus to objective self awareness, or else a stimulus that should not have reminded them of their object-like status. The experiment was designed to examine the possibility that the self-reflecting stimulus loses its power while the subject is repeatedly exposed to it. Given these theoretical considerations, the following hypothesis was proposed: reported intraself discrepancies will increase when subjects are confronted with a stimulus to the objective state, and this effect will be most pronounced immediately after the stimulus is introduced.

Procedure

Each subject (subjects were female undergraduates) was met by the experimenter and seated in an experimental cubicle. As a cover story for the manipulations to follow, the subject was told that the study was a joint project of the psychology and the linguistics departments whose purpose was to determine which linguistic factors, if any, are good predictors of academic success. The plan of the research was supposedly to record the voices of a large sample of people, keeping the content of the recordings constant by having each person read the same short selection. The recordings were to be evaluated by several faculty members and graduate students in the linguistics department who would rate them on various dimensions and then correlate these ratings with the subjects' GPAs and college entrance exam scores to determine which factors best predict future success in college.

In line with this story, the subject was asked to sign a release statement to the registrar, giving permission for her college entrance exam scores and her GPAs through the following year to be used as experimental data. Following this introduction the subject was required to make a four- to five-minute tape recording of a rather abstract selection in an introductory philosophy text. The instructions given by the experimenter were as follows.

What we want you to do is to read the selection as naturally as possible, speaking about as rapidly as you would, say, in a telephone conversation with a friend. Once you start recording I won't be able to erase, so if you make any mistakes in your reading, don't worry about them; just correct yourself and continue the reading through to the end. Here is a copy of the selection we want you to read. Please wait until I've introduced you on the tape and then begin.

The experimenter introduced the subject by name on the tape and then began recording her reading of the selection. When the recording was finished, the experimenter continued:

Since our study is so short, Dr. Wicklund of the psychology department has asked us to have our subjects fill out a "Real-Ideal Self Questionnaire." You probably filled out one similar to this at the beginning of the semester, but now we would like you to fill it out somewhat differently to help us see if a difference in procedure makes a difference in the responses people give.

The subject was then informed about the nature of the two questionnaires she was to fill out. She was told that each questionnaire would consist of 20 pairs of adjectives, and that she was to indicate her "real" self on one questionnaire and her "ideal" self on the other questionnaire. The two questionnaires were identical, each one consisting of 20 bipolar adjectives with a line of 20 dots running between each pair. The following is an example:

Courteous . . . . Rude

The entire list of adjective pairs is as follows:

Courteous	Rude
Skilled	Unskilled
Competent	Incompetent
Pleasant	Disagreeable
Creative	Unimaginative
Honest	Dishonest
Careful	Reckless
Trustworthy	Untrustworthy
Kind	Cruel
Independent	Dependent
Courageous	Cowardly
Generous	Selfish
Tolerant	Intolerant
Considerate	Inconsiderate
Sucessful	Unsuccessful
Well-liked	Disliked
Industrious	Lazy
Sensitive	Insensitive
Optimistic	Pessimistic
Intelligent	Stupid

The order of presentation of questionnaire items was counterbalanced, such that half of the subjects received them in the Courteous-to-Intelligent order, and half received them in the Intelligent-to-Courteous order. This was necessary because the hypothesis implied a sequential effect, and counterbalancing enabled us to examine the sequential effect independent of differences among individual items.

At this point in the procedure the experimenter indicated to the subject that she would leave the cubicle while the subject filled out the first questionnaire, but before leaving she gave her the following instructions in order to manipulate objective self awareness:

The subject was then asked to listen to either a playback of her own voice (High OSA), or to a standard recording of the same selection "made by another girl this morning" (Low OSA). The instructions were to "just give your opinion when I get back." The experimenter then switched on the appropriate tape and left the cubicle. After listening outside the door until the tape had ended, the experimenter returned to the cubicle and administered the questionnaire a second time.

Parenthetically, we should note that as an exploratory manipulation half of the subjects were given the OSA manipulation while filling out the first questionnaire, and half while filling out the second, but since this variation had no effect we will not discuss it further.

Results

The basic data from each subject consist of two scores on each of 20 scales, one score representing her ideal self, the other the real self. Each subject's self esteem level was computed by simply taking the difference in scale points between the real and ideal, independent of the direction of difference. The absolute difference as a measure of self esteem follows from the theoretical notion of discrepancy between actual (real) state and the personal standard of correctness (ideal).

It will be recalled that the order in which the items was presented was counterbalanced, and no interaction was found between order of presentation and experimental condition ($p > .20$). Therefore, we can proceed to the data relevant to the main hypothesis.

As shown in Figure 1, the mean discrepancy scores varied between approximately four and six points on the 20-point scales. As would be expected, the overall discrepancy in the High OSA condition was somewhat greater than that in the Low OSA condition, but the difference did not reach significance ($p > .20$). Since the hypothesis dealt specifically with sequential effects, we should examine those, and as is evident from Figure 1 the difference between conditions was maximal for the first few items, as predicted. If the hypothesis

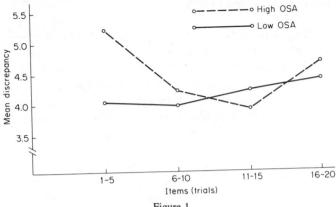

Figure 1.

holds statistically, there should be a differential linear trend over the 20 items such that the mean discrepancy scores are initially greater in the High OSA condition than in the Low, with this difference between conditions decreasing toward the end of the 20 items. The appropriate test of this hypothesis is the interaction betwen OSA and linear trend over items, which is significant ($p < .05$). We might note that the interaction between OSA and quadratic trend over items is also significant ($p < .02$). An examination of Figure 1 indicates that the differential quadratic trend is due essentially to the considerable change in slope in the High OSA condition at approximately the sixth item.

As further evidence for the hypothesis it should be noted that the self awareness effect for the first five items was reliable ($p < .01$), but that the corresponding differences on the remaining clusters of five items failed to approach significance ($p > .20$).

The experiment directly supports the basic theoretical assumption that awareness of intraself discrepancies ensues in the state of objective self awareness. This finding has implications for self esteem in general, for it could be that extreme self criticism only results after prolonged focus on the self. Another obvious implication has to do with the effects of subjective self awareness, discussed more fully in Chapter 9. To the degree that a person experiences the negative affect associated with self criticism and failure, any device that would place him predominantly in the subjective state should be welcomed.

The sequential effect operated as expected, and the phenomenon should be a useful adjunct to the theory, assuming that it manifests itself in future tests of the theoretical ideas. As discussed earlier, the effect could be due either to the person's attempting to remove himself from the objective state once confronted with the self-reflecting stimulus, or the effect could be called "adaptation," independent of the specific psychological or physiological mechanisms basic to adaptation.

Morse and Gergen (1970)

Using changes in self esteem as their main dependent variable, Morse and Gergen manipulated the social desirability of a stimulus person's characteristics and found that exposure to a person with highly desirable characteristics ("Mr. Clean") led to decreased self esteem, while exposure to an undesirable person ("Mr. Dirty") tended to produce an increase. The authors interpreted these results as supportive of the theoretical notion that social comparison processes can mediate changes in self concept.

Morse and Gergen noted a subsidiary effect, but one that is central from our standpoint. Each subject in the Morse and Gergen study was rated for his similarity to the stimulus person. If the subject was in the "Mr. Dirty" condition, he was rated with respect to his physical similarity to Mr. Dirty, and if he was in the "Mr. Clean" condition, his similarity to Mr. Clean was rated. Morse and Gergen correlated change in self-esteem with similarity to the stimulus person and, surprisingly, they found that self-esteem increased to the extent that the subject was similar to the confederate, while self-esteem decreased when the confederate and subject appeared dissimilar. The result makes perfectly good sense according to an analysis of deindividuation within the context of objective self awareness theory.

The theory implies that any situation forcing the individual to be aware of himself will bring forth the objective state, and included among such situations are cases where the individual is distinct from his surroundings. If a person blends completely into his background, he cannot stand out physically, and it follows that objective self awareness will be less frequent (cf. Festinger, Pepitone, and Newcomb, 1952; Singer, Brush, and Lublin, 1965; Zimbardo, 1969). If someone is in the presence of similar others, it is difficult for him to view himself as a distinct individual, relative to the case when he is surrounded by people radically different from himself (see Chapters 4 and 9). Extending this line of thought to the Morse-Gergen experiment, it is reasonable that the subjects in the presence of a dissimilar other were objectively self aware a good part of the time—hence their lowered self-esteem, and it is also consistent that those who confronted a similar other were relatively less objectively self-aware—thus higher self-esteem.

In summary, both the Ickes-Wicklund experiment and Morse-Gergen experiment demonstrate the phenomenon of lowered self esteem resulting from objective self awareness. The interesting contrast between the studies is that a self-reflecting stimulus was basic to the objective self awareness effect in the former study, while immersion among similar (or dissimilar) others created the objective self awareness in the Morse and Gergen study.

Chapter 3

THE ORIGIN AND NATURE OF OBJECTIVE SELF AWARENESS

Many writers and psychologists have attempted to explain how self consciousness comes into being. For the most part, such explanations have assumed that something about social contact is responsible for bringing about self consciousness, but they have never fully explained the mediating states of the process whereby the child first gains self knowledge. In this chapter we have attempted to construct a more complete explanation than previous writers, and admittedly our proposal is at this stage completely theoretical and without a great deal of direct research support. Nonetheless, such an explanation is necessary given the absence of satisfactory systematic accounts of the beginnings of self consciousness. We would only hope that our conjectures are sufficiently specific that they are open to confirmation, modification, or refutation by appropriately designed research.

A theory that attempts to understand self consciousness must contain two elements. First it must develop some idea of what the self is and how it comes into being. Second, the theory must posit the mechanism by which the person becomes or is aware of the self. This latter explanatory construct may also include conditions and circumstances under which the self awareness occurs. The most prevalent approach for dealing with these two problems is what could be called "social origin theory." The essence of this position, that self and self consciousness are social in origin, is the assumption that the person's original

29

psychological makeup lacks some essential component that is necessary for selfhood and self consciousness, and that this component is supplied in the interaction with the social other. In psychology this approach has been most forcefully articulated by Mead (1934) and Cooley (1954). We will take Mead as an example.

In *Mind, Self, and Society*, Mead argues that selfhood cannot be constituted by a person's subjective or "feeling" awareness of himself. He illustrates this assertion with an example about a person who is running down a road. The argument is that the moving individual has a feeling or rudimentary awareness of his body but that this awareness does not constitute a genuine self. To ascend to true selfhood Mead believes that the person must detach his awareness from its seat inside the organism and then assume a point of view that lies outside the organism proper. If a person gains an exterior vantage point and then looks back at himself, self and awareness of self occur simultaneously.

Mead thinks that the unassisted individual lacks any innate ability to externalize his point of view. This is where the role of the social other comes into play. The person cannot externalize his point of view by himself but he can establish an empathic relationship with the social other. The consequence of this link between the individual and the other person is to provide the individual with an opportunity to see himself through the eyes of the other person. For Mead, this empathic relationship embodies a genuine self, that is, it causes a self to come into being for the first time, and provides the vehicle through which the person can become self aware in the future.

In Mead's psychology of self consciousness, taking the role of the other is the key phrase. Taking the role of the other is as if the person enters another's head and observes himself through the other's characteristic ways of perceiving and evaluating the world. If the other thinks the person is a buffoon, the person will also see himself as a buffoon.

Thus the content and substance of the self is made up of the perceptions and evaluations of the social other. As far as the incidence of self awareness is concerned, Mead implies that a person cannot be self aware unless he is able to take the role of someone else. He often uses the phrase, "getting outside oneself experientially." Since he means this literally, introspection in isolated surroundings would be an impossibility within Mead's framework.

The way in which Mead views the phenomenon of self consciousness implies two qualitatively distinct forms of consciousness; an original type of consciousness, and a consciousness which is the result of a unique interaction and combination of two separate consciousnesses. The original consciousness is a feeling or rudimentary awareness of the organism and the world whose function is the facilitation of the organism's manipulations of the environment. Self consciousness is impossible in this state. Second, there is the type of consciousness which is not consciousness of the other but, rather, a transmutation of the other person's consciousness of oneself into one's own. From any point of view the rudimentary consciousness and empathic consciousness are qualitatively different; this assumption is completely unnecessary within objective self awareness theory.

Mead's version of self consciousness is a social learning relationship between social entities that comes about only when one person adopts the viewpoint of another toward himself. The theory of objective self awareness takes exception to Mead's thinking and social origin theory in general in postulating that self consciousness occurs because consciousness can focus its attention on the self in the same way that attention is focused on any other object. In no way do we assume that the individual is dependent upon the point of view of the other in the sense that Mead intends. If the object-like nature of the self has been discovered and stimuli in the environment are such that consciousness turns in the direction of the self, the person will become objectively self aware.

The major step that the objective self awareness theory of self consciousness takes beyond Mead's theory is the assumption that the components or elements of self consciousness are indigenous to the person's original psychological structure. To be self conscious a person does not have to borrow either the substance of self or an external point of view from another person. Consciousness of self is not different from consciousness of any other object. Just as a person is innately capable of the awareness of the various things in his environment, he is innately capable of the awareness of the object that is his self.

In order to analyze self consciousness from the standpoint of objective self awareness, several general assumptions must be made about the nature of consciousness and self. As far as consciousness is concerned, objective self awareness theory postulates that the individual has one innate consciousness with directional properties. As indicated earlier, we assume that this consciousness can focus upon any object. Furthermore, we assume that consciousness will focus on a particular element if the stimuli that control the directionality of attention direct consciousness to the region of the environment where this element resides.

The conception of two alternative states of self awareness entails separating the possible foci of consciousness into two separate regions: consciousness focuses on the self in objective self awareness and focuses upon whatever is not the self in subjective self awareness. Thus, there are not two qualitatively different consciousnesses but two distinct foci for one type of consciousness.

Objective self awareness theory also defines "self" in a particular way. The self is not an entity that is developed or comes into being through taking the other's viewpoint, nor is it a subjective phenomenon accessible only to the individual. Instead, self is an object-like entity that exists from the moment that the person is conscious of internal and external stimuli and, as such, is present to any other's awareness.

Given the postulated nature of self and consciousness, we assume that at any time during the person's life, objective self awareness can result provided that the person knows the object nature of the self, and conditions are appropriate for the focusing of consciousness in the direction of the self.

With the preceding remarks we have attempted to demonstrate that our analysis of consciousness and of the self departs from that of Mead and possibly from other self theorists whose analyses have followed precedents established by Mead. The central points of discrepancy between the theory of objective self awareness and Mead's conception are the following: we assume only a single consciousness, with directional properties such that it focuses either toward or away from the self, while Mead postulates two distinct consciousnesses. Second, we assume that the individual possesses a self from the moment of consciousness, while Mead's analysis suggests a self built incrementally out of taking the role of the other. Given this point of view toward self and self consciousness, we will devote the remainder of this chapter to the following questions that arise when consciousness and self are treated as indigenous to the individual's psychological makeup. (1) Precisely what is meant by our concept of self, and in what sense does the self exist from the moment of consciousness? (2) Given that every person has the potential for objective self awareness at a very early age, that is, he has a self and directional consciousness, does objective self awareness emerge spontaneously? (3) If not, what are the conditions that make objective self awareness possible?

THE SELF

On the basis of the extant body of psychological literature dealing with the concept of self, it is clear that there is no unanimity in the definition of the term. However, one notable consistency among many of the definitions is with respect to the hypothesis that there are two separate and distinct selves. Mead draws a distinction between the "I" and the "me." The "I" is an actor in the present, whereas the "me" is the "I" reflected upon. The "I" has consciousness in the sense of awareness of sensations or feelings of self and the external field but does not have the true self consciousness associated exclusively with the "me." Similarly, Wylie (1968) draws a distinction between the self as doer, and the self as a passive entity. de Charms (1968) discusses the aspect in which self appears as an origin, and the aspect in which self appears as a pawn manipulated by external forces. The origin or controller is active and has a sense of control of the environment. The self as pawn is controlled by the environment. Piaget (1966), who will be particularly relevant to the later discussion, distinguishes between the child who is able to take the point of view of the other and the egocentric child. Thorpe (1966) maintains that there are three significant characteristics of self: a feeling of unity, an awareness of internal sensibility, and an awareness of one's individual existence in the world. His description does not explicitly bifurcate the self, but the characteristics of unity and internal sensibility correspond closely to the "I," doer, origin, or egocentric self; and knowledge of one's individual existence to the "me," passive self, pawn, or nonegocentric individual.

In examining past efforts at formulation of the self we discover that we have not just one, but two selves to contend with: first, self as associated with an action complex which includes perception of proprioceptive and external stimuli, thinking, and an extension into overt behavior; and, second, a self which is nonacting and reflected upon as opposed to serving as the source of perception, and which is distinguished by a feeling of distance between the perceiver and the perceived self. We would agree that there appear to be two separate selves, one active and one passive. However, we must take the position that this categorization exists in appearance only.

While the self may appear to be of a dual nature under different circum-stances, just as a color may appear in two different hues under varying lighting conditions, the theory takes the position that there is just one self, which may be called a "causal agent self." This self is a psychological structure with observable manifestations, and its functions are simply the usual functions of any organism: perception, thinking, and action. Clearly these elements of the self are manifest early in the child's existence, albeit in a primitive form. Since this "causal agent self" of objective self awareness theory is synonymous with perception, thinking, and action, we assume that this self is indigenous to the organism. It does not arise from social interaction or biological development. It exists from the moment the child lives. But this is not to say that the individual is objectively self aware at an early age, for the fact of a person's possessing a self structure identifiable by others in no way implies that he is aware that it is an object. As we will suggest below, the child attains the capacity for objective self awareness only when he learns that self is an object in the world.

Given that consciousness may be viewed as a monotypic phenomenon and that the self may be defined as the causal agent of the organism that is associated with perception, thinking, and action, the definition of subjective and objective self awareness becomes a simple matter. Objective self awareness is the state in which the causal agent self is taken as the object of consciousness. Subjective self awareness is the state in which the causal agent self is not the focus of consciousness. But how do we account for the fact that other investigators have identified two types of self instead of our one? We would argue that the states of subjective and objective self awareness have secondary characteristics which produce the effect of a dual self identified by other theorists. For example, in the "objective state," the self would appear as passive because it is being reflected upon by consciousness. The reflected upon organism is rendered immobile insofar as behavior requiring volition is concerned because volitional mobility requires that conscious be directed outward, toward the organism's goals. The consciousness of the objectively self aware organism is in a sense removed from the organism and reflects upon past thought and actions of the causal agent self. Mead describes this state literally as one of being outside one's self experientially, or examining oneself from the vantage point of another person's mind. We disagree with the notion of "taking the role of the other," but the feeling he describes of being outside one's self does coincide with our theoretical notion. The experience is similar to that which comes from examining a movie or photograph of oneself. The person understands that the entity he observes is himself, but contemporaneous consciousness is not situated within the causal agent self being observed; instead, consciousness is focused on the historical causal agent as it has performed, thought, and perceived in the past. In short, the causal agent self has figuratively come outside itself and focuses upon itself in retrospect.

In objective self awareness theory the self may also appear impotent or trapped by the forces of its environment, as the quotation by Koch (Chapter 1) and de Charm's term "pawn" so aptly describe. This impotence or immobility take place for essentially the same reasons as stated above: the causal agent self is effectively (although only figuratively) removed from the organism as the organism exists in the present and separated from the organism as the organism appeared in the past. The actions of the causal agent self have become locked in the immutability of the past. The action occurred and can now be reflected upon, but obviously the contemporaneous causal agent self, in reflecting on previous behaviors, can do nothing to alter them. The self in the present can change the interpretation of that behavior but it cannot recall the organism to a position in time where the error can be erased. Its only power is to resolve to irradicate those discrepancies in the future, or to attempt to remove itself from the conditions creating objective self awareness. Nor can the person deal actively with the external forces confronting him in the present. Consciousness is turned toward the self to the exclusion of the external environment, making the task of dealing with present external exigencies impossible. How could a person deal with the forces around him or pursue a chosen course through those forces if he were unaware of his external environment?

In contrast to the appearance of passivity and impotence engendered by objective self awareness, the self under conditions of subjective self awareness regains its potency. When the person is externally focused, the causal agent self guides the organism through perception, thinking, and behavior. In this state the organism's consciousness is directed outward and is concentrated upon whatever activity—perceptual, thinking, or behavioral—is the focus of the causal agent self. The causal agent self works unobserved by itself and directs the organism toward its goals in pursuit of satisfaction of needs. The fact of directing one's self gives rise to the feeling quality of "origin," as described by de Charms. For conscious attention not to be focused upon the causal agent self means that physical limits of capacity and ability are essentially eliminated from the organism's consideration, resulting in a feeling of control or power.

An experiment by Duval and Ritz (1971) was designed to demonstrate this general notion that the self is preceived differently in the two states of awareness. The dimension chosen for study was the person's perception of his control over the process and outcome of his interactions with the external world.

Subjects for the experiment were seated either in front of a mirror or were not. After seating the subject, the experimenter asked her to perform a simple task—rotate a turntable with her index finger while keeping the finger as still as possible on the surface of the turntable. The experimenter then asked the subject to practce rotating the turntable. At this point the experimenter left the room. At the end of two minutes the experimenter returned to the room and told the subject that unknown to her the turntable was attached to a machine which recorded the extent of the movement of her finger over the surface of the turntable during the warm-up period. The experimenter then told the subject either that her performance was scored as erratic (the erratic condition) or as constant (constant condition), erratic meaning that her finger moved a total of at least three centimeters from its original position, while a performance score of constant indicated that her finger moved less than three centimeters. After this feed-back, the experimenter further explained that the turntable was also connected to a device which, for the part of the time during the warm-up trials, was producing minute changes in the speed of the turntable. The effect of this externally produced variation in the speed of the turntable was to produce a movement of her finger that was totally beyond her control. The subject was further told that this externally controlled movement could have either bad or good effects on her overall performance. It could have caused her finger to move erratically or it could have compensated for some of the erratic movements of her finger; the latter effect contributing to a performance scored as constant. Thus, in effect, the cover story of the experiment was designed to lead the subject to believe that her overall performance, whether erratic or constant, was partially the result of the movements of her finger she had control over and partially the result of movements of her finger that she had no control over.

After explaining the operation of the turntable, the subject was asked to estimate the degree to which she had had control over her performance during the two-minute warm-up period and the degree to which the performance was controlled by the device connected to the turntable. This measure was taken by asking the subject to estimate the amount of the two-minute period the machine had been controlling the movements of her finger. The results showed that the objectively self aware subjects (those who performed in front of a mirror) estimated that the machine controlled their performance a greater percentage of the time than did the subjectively self aware subjects (those who performed without the presence of the mirror). No interaction between the erratic performance and constant performance feed-back condition was found.

The conclusion we draw from this experiment is that the objectively self aware person perceived the causal agent self as having less control over the outcome of an interaction between self and environment than does the subjectively self aware person. Theoretically, this perception of loss of control is produced by the person's preoccupation with self as object when he is in the objective state of awareness. With consciousness turned toward the self, to the exclusion of the external world, the line of communication between the causal agent self and external reality is temporarily eliminated. This disconnection of the causal agent self's contact with the world makes it impossible for the person to constantly monitor the environment for stimuli changes and control his behavior accordingly. Thus, in the objective state of awareness, the perception of self as a pawn or as impotent is a veridical perception of the state of the causal agent self. With the causal agent self's perception of the world and volitional control over action blocked by the introversion of consciousness toward self, the person is at the mercy of the forces around himself and cannot in fact exert control over his outcomes.

We have postulated that the organism at birth has the necessary mental equipment to be self conscious. He has a causal agent self that perceives, mediates those perceptions, and moves the organism to action. The consciousness-attention can in principle take the causal agent self as an object of that attention. But in practice the child is not objectively self aware despite the fact that the presence of the capacity to be so can be verified by an outside observer. That the child is not objectively self aware is demonstrated by Piaget's (1966) early experiments on perception in children. In one experiment a child was positioned on one side of a table opposite another person. A set of blocks was arranged so that some were closer to the child than others. The other person, being opposite the child, was of course nearest the block that was furthest from the child, and vice versa. When the child was asked which block was nearest the person opposite, he responded by naming the block nearest himself. Had the child been objectively self aware in the experimental situation he would not have committed the error of assuming that the other's point of view was equivalent to his own. With consciousness focused upon the self the child would have been reminded that he was a unique entity in the world, and it would have been apparent to the child that the self has a particular point of view. Thus the child would have grasped that he was seeing the blocks from a point of view to be discriminated from that of others.

WHY DOES OBJECTIVE SELF AWARENESS
NOT EMERGE SPONTANEOUSLY?

If the child can in principle be objectively self aware and is not, the question is why? It is our contention that the child cannot focus attention inward upon the self because he has not yet differentiated the causal agent self as a separate object in the world. The child certainly has a type of awareness of himself, but it is not the awareness of self as an object. The mere facts of possessing a causal agent self and of having the ability to focus attention around the environment do not of necessity include the knowledge that the causal agent self is an individual and separate object. Since consciousness can only focus upon something which is an object, the child will not be able to take his self as an object until he learns or discovers the object-like nature of self.

The proverbial case of the man who cannot see the forest for the trees is a good illustration of the difficulties which prevent the child from spontaneously recognizing himself as an object. However, to get the full value of the aphorism we must tease a precise meaning out of the general statement.

A person will be unable to perceive that a group of trees makes up a forest only under certain circumstances. If a person is positioned two hundred yards from the trees so that he can see where they begin and end, he will perceive the aggregate of trees as a forest. In psychological terms, a person will see any aggregate of individual elements as an object, that is, a unity, if he is in a position to perceive the boundaries or limits of the aggregate. Thus the person stationed so that he can see the boundaries of the aggregate of trees will perceive the aggregate as a unit called a forest. In light of this consideration, the aphorism must have the following intended meaning. The person will miss the forest for the trees only when he is at a position where he cannot see the limits or boundaries of the trees. This implies that the person must be immersed in the individual trees before he will fail to grasp the bounded, object-like nature of the aggregate. The young child finds himself in the same relationship with regard to self as the man in the middle of a group of trees is to the forest. He is immersed in the self to the extent that he is incapable of the awareness that the individual elements of action, thought, and feeling constitute a higher order unity. Like the man in the middle of the forest, the child implicitly sees the self extending to infinity. And like the man, the child cannot focus attention upon the unit-object that is the self because he is not yet in a position to be aware that the self is a differentiated, object-like entity in the world. In the remainder of this chapter we will take the position that the possibility of objective self awareness is contingent upon a special type of enounter with the environment in which the child learns that his causal agent self is a bounded unit, that is, an object. Until such a recognition, the child's immersion in the self precludes the possibility of self-focused attention.

The problem of the ability of the child to be conscious of the self as object will be framed in terms of the differentiation or nondifferentiation of the causal agent self as an object, the former being sufficient for objective self awareness, the latter associated with a state of chronic subjective self awareness. However, this question of the differentiation of the self is not simply to determine how and when the child becomes aware that perception, thinking, and doing take place in general. Piaget's experiment on perception in children shows that the egocentric child is aware of his consciousness in some general sense, otherwise he could not even answer the relational question, "which block is closest to you?" In this connection Sartre (1968) points out

> . . . if my consciousness were not consciousness of being conscious of that table, it would then be consciousness of that table without consciousness of being so. In other words, it would be a consciousness ignorant of itself, an unconscious—which is absurd. [p. 11].

Thus, we would grant that the child is aware of his own consciousness well before he differentiates the self. Instead of asking when consciousness is aware that it exists, which may be a question beyond psychology, we have put the problem in terms of how the child comes to differentiate the causal agent self, that is, comes to knowledge that the causal agent self is a separate entity.

Before going further, it should be noted that knowledge of the causal agent self as a separate entity in the world should not be confused with knowledge of the specific characteristics of the causal agent self. Every individual will have a unique "accurate" self description. One person may feel that his causal agent self is kind, intelligent, but unemotional. Another may conclude that he is thoughtless and egotistical. But despite a person's tendency to carve the causal agent self into categories, all causal agent selves have one characteristic in common: they are separate and unique entities. Whether a person perceives the causal agent self to be generous or miserly, it is a particular entity. Thus, when we speak of differentiating the causal agent self, we mean attaining knowledge of that one characteristic, uniqueness, common to all causal agent selves.

In approaching the problem of transition from a state of prediscovery of the causal agent self (chronic subjective self awareness) to a state in which the causal agent self is known (objective self awareness), it is tempting to assume that the failure to differentiate the causal agent self is the failure to differentiate the body from the nonbody environment. Heider (1958) states that psychologists generally agree that in the early part of the life there is a lack of separation between the ego, as associated with the body, and the environment. Wylie (1968) and Kilpatrick (1941) concur with this statement in suggesting that a person learns that he is separate from other persons and objects by experiencing discontinuities in his perceptions of other objects and persons, and by failure to be able to manipulate them at will. The approach taken by these three authors implies that the absence of self consciousness is due to the failure of the individual to distinguish himself physically from the environment, and, of course, if their claim were correct, self consciousness could occur once the child had learned this distinction. Wylie provides a general paradigm for this learning process.

The child bites on a block and bites his finger, and the experience for the child is different when the finger is bitten than when the block is bitten. When this learning process has continued for some period the child apparently winds up with something that is uniquely different from the sensations of handling physical objects around him. By extension, one might argue that the individual could become self conscious, in the sense of being aware of the causal agent self, simply through distinguishing one component of his self (the body) from his surroundings. Although we do agree that the knowledge of the body's relationship to self is important in the exercise of objective self awareness, the evidence of at least one author implies that knowledge of body is not responsible for the initial event of discovery of the causal agent self. Piaget states that long after the child is conscious of its body as belonging to the self in a unique way, the processes of thought, communication, and perception remain egocentric, or unaware of their own perspective.

We suggest that consciousness does not have its origin in body differentia tion, for that argument would assume an overlap between body and the causal agent self either in structure or function. When Heider states that the ego confuses itself with the environment, the implication is that the ego can end this confusion and, in the process, can gain self knowledge by determining what in the physical environment genuinely belongs to the self. Such an assumption is contradicted by Schilder (1950), who reports direct observation of manifestations of a lack of isomorphism between body and self. In one study, his subjects were asked to close their eyes and imagine their physical appearances. They reported that the body they were visualizing was strangely empty. It was visualized as disconnected from the self, incomplete, and lifeless. Schilder suggests further that the person's body image is actually created by the ego instead of the body image embodying the self. Similarly, Mead makes the following statement:

> The parts of the body are quite distinguishable from the self. We can lose parts of the body without any serious invasion of the self. The mere ability to experience different parts of the body is not different from the experience of a table. The table presents a different feel from what the hand does when one hand feels another, but it is an experience of something with which we come definitely into contact [p. 136].

Both Schilder and Mead argue against the identity of self and body, thus they add credence to the proposition that an awareness of the body cannot in and of itself lead to objective self awareness.

In the language of objective self awareness theory, the causal agent self is the perceiver, thinker, and mover, while the body is simply the instrument of expression for the self. The causal agent self may be revealed to itself through the movements and appearance of the body, but only to the extent that the person has already discovered that the causal agent self is an object. For example, the person who has already differentiated his causal agent self may be aware that he has carried out certain actions. In retrospect he is able to reconstruct his own motives for the movements because he assumes that his causal agent self is the moving force behind the movements. Until the causal agent self is discovered, the individual's observation of his past bodily movements will not call forth an awareness of self, and as Piaget has noted, the child will neither show an ability to assess whether or not his behavior was generated out of volition, nor will he even be clear about whether or not he was responsible for a certain idea or behavior.

Two points have been made so far. First, the child is not automatically aware that the self is an object, and thus cannot be self conscious. Second, his physical differentiation of his body from the rest of the environment does not constitute differentiation of the causal agent self. But how does the child come to the realization that his causal agent self is an object-like entity? To answer this question the properties of childish consciousness must be fully understood.

The assertion has been made that the child does not know that he is an object in the world. From Piaget we learn that the primary characteristic of the awareness of the child who is not self aware is what may be callled absolutism. The term is used to indicate that the child has an unquestioning acceptance of the functions of the causal agent as being completely correct. Piaget describes the peculiar nature of childish consciousness in his *Judgment and Reasoning in the Child*:

> Anyone who thinks for himself exclusively and is consequently in a perpetual state of belief of confidence in his own ideas will naturally not trouble himself about reasons or justification [p. 137].

Further, Piaget maintains that ". . . the child, ignorant of his own ego, takes his own point of view as absolute . . . [p. 197]." Piaget illustrates this absolutism by describing four behavioral and perceptual patterns characteristic of the egocentric child that we mentioned earlier, but which now take on an added significance: (1) The child has absolute belief in his ideas; (2) He believes that everyone else understands everything that he says; (3) He is incapable of recognizing self contradictions; and (4) He believes everyone sees events from his point of view.

The child's state of absolutism can be compared to the adult attitude of egotism which has several of the same perceptual, thinking, and behavioral patterns as that of the egocentric, subjectively self aware child. The point of contrast between the two states is that the egotistical adult is aware of beliefs, points of view, and behaviors different from his own, while the child lacks this awareness. The consequence is that the adult maintains his complete belief in his point of view, ideas, and behaviors by declaring that while his is a distinct point of view, he is correct and others are wrong when they disagree. The child, on the other hand, believes in his ideas and point of view not because he affirms his ideas as correct (which would indicate a knowledge of the possibility of being wrong) but because he does not conceive of the existence of alternative viewpoints. Thus the child who does not know of himself as an object tacitly assumes that his perception and thinking are universals, that everyone sees the world exactly like he does. The child does not understand that self is an object because self for him implicitly extends beyond any boundaries.

The state of absolutism is the necessary consequence of the child's failure to differentiate his causal agent self. If there is no knowledge of the causal agent self, then perception, thinking, and behavior must be perceived by the child as nondifferentiated phenomena, identical for everyone and thus universal. What the child sees, he believes everyone else sees. But the converse of the relationship between failure to differentiate the causal agent self and absolutism is also true. The maintenance of the state of subjective self awareness in which the causal agent self is not differentiated depends on the maintenance of the child's implicit belief in the universality of perception. The child can continue failing to differentiate the causal agent self only as long as his implicit belief in the universality of perception is not contradicted by events in the environment. This brings us to the central point in our discussion of the transition from nondifferentiation to differentiation of the causal agent self. The child will differentiate the causal agent self as a unique object in the world and become capable of self consciousness only when his assumption of the universality of perception is contradicted by a demonstration that perceptual, mediational, and behavioral processes different from his own do exist, thus pointing out that each person's perception is a bounded, object-like particular, and not a universal. The following is intended to illustrate the transition from an awareness that operates as if it were universal to an awareness that deals with itself as a particular.

Heider discusses the effects of the clash of differing points of view in his discussion of attribution of percept to person or object. He notes that

> . . . the cause of a difference resides within the variant condition rather than in the condition common to diverse instances. For example, if an auditory stimulus is constant and several individuals perceive it, if one person cannot hear what everyone else hears well, then his impression that the speaker's voice is too low will be attributed to himself as the variant. . . .
> In the Asch experiment the variant factor is quickly located in the deviant subject—everybody else sees that the two lines are equal while the subject sees one as longer than the other. Therefore, the subject becomes suddenly aware that what he sees has to do with himself in an idiosyncratic way [p. 69].

Although Heider was speaking specifically about how a person judges whether or not his perception is correct, the example also demonstrates the outcome of a condition in which the individual is faced with a differing perception of the world. When a disagreement between perceptions is evident, each person is forced to the awareness that the perceptual process is a particular, hence the person acquires the knowledge that his point of view is unique. Just as a person is unaware of the variable of oxygen-no oxygen until there is a shortage of oxygen in the immediate atmosphere, the child will become aware of himself as a limited and bounded object only when an instance opposite his point of view is presented to him.

WHAT CONDITIONS BRING ABOUT
THE EMERGENCE OF OBJECTIVE SELF AWARENESS?

The necessary condition for differentiating the causal agent self is that the child becomes aware that there are perceptions, thoughts, and behaviors that differ from his own. By developing the issue in terms of gaining knowledge of the "objectivity" (as opposed to content) of the causal agent self, we are free to posit a process consisting of the child's repeated experience of different points of view, behaviors, and thoughts. This learning process eventually leads him to a complete differentiation of the causal agent self. Explaining how the child knows that his causal agent self is different from the self of the other requires the assumption that the child has the ability to judge when two objects are different. Without this ability the child could obviously never recognize the boundaries of the causal agent self and would never overthrow egocentrism. However, if this perceptual mechanism operated under all conditions, the question of the differentiation of self would be answered. Whenever the child came into contact with any opinion, thought, or behavior different from his own, he would automatically differentiate that aspect of himself. As it is, the child will recognize that his and another's behavior conflict only if certain conditions are met. In the next several pages we will attempt to spell out the nature of these conditions.

An example illustrating the primary conditions for the operation of the differentiating mechanism may help at this point. Suppose a person attempts to decide whether or not two inked designs are identical. The method that he will most often use is aimed at achieving the simultaneous cognition of both designs. First he stares at one design to fix its image in his mind and then looks quickly at the second design. If he can retain the one image while looking at the second he will be able to determine whether one design differs from the other. The overall effect of the operation is to bring both differing elements into the same cognitive dimension simultaneously. His purpose could be accomplished more directly by laying the transparency of one design over the other. When this operation is carried out either directly or by successfully combining the two elements in a single mental act, the person will notice any difference between the two objects. This conclusion assumes only the ability to discriminate, an ability we will take for granted.

We are suggesting that the perceptual mechanism enabling the child to differentiate any two objects (in our present case his own point of view from another's) is automatically engaged when certain conditions are met. These conditions, implicit in the previous example, are as follows: (1) for the child to differentiate himself there must be another entity who has a differing point of view; (2) the two differing points of view must concern the same object; and (3) the child must be aware of the antipodal opinions simultaneously. If these three conditions are satisfied, the child will realize that the other is not himself, thus beginning the process of self differentiation.

In our example, the person was attempting to create the conditions that would have allowed him to test for differences he suspected were there. The child would never deliberately use such a scheme to test for differences since he would never suspect a difference in the first place. Since the child has no motivation to seek out differences, the cause of the child's differentiation of himself as an object in the world must lie in certain naturally occurring interactions he has with the environment. In general, any interaction between himself and the environment that meets the three conditions mentioned above will engage the child's differentiation mechanism. Once the perceptual mechanism is activated, the child will come to recognize that he is not the other. Whether or not any given interaction between the child and the environment will cause differentiation is determined by (1) the conditions necessary for the operation of the differentiating mechanism and (2) the substance of the causal agent self. The child's recognition that something else differs from himself on a physical dimension will not cause differentiation of self. The self is perception, thinking, and doing. This being the case, an interaction leading to differentiation must in some way offer opposition to the child on the crucial dimensions of his self. The physical difference between the child and a chair is simply irrelevant to the whole process.

The necessity of bringing the child into opposition with something that either perceives, thinks, or acts places severe limitations on the kinds of interactions which have the potential for differentiation. Ignoring nonhuman species of animals, a potentially successful interaction must contain another person; or, alternatively, the interaction must generate an opposition between the child's own perception, thinking, or doing at one point in time and those same processes at another point in time. Accordingly, out of all the contacts the child has with the world, we are left with just two possibilities: (1) The child could differ with a previous opinion. By examination of reality he changes his opinion about some object and notes a contrast with the earlier. (2) The second possibility is disagreement with the perceptions of another. It now remains to see if either or both of these alternatives satisfy the requisite conditions for activating the perceptual differentiating mechanism.

Contact between the Child and the Physical Environment

The first situation assumes that the child is restricted to contact with a purely physical environment. Examining this interaction, we will find that the self's perception will never be faced with an instance of a simultaneously occurring and differing point of view in encounters with that environment. The following situation may illustrate this point. Let us say that a child approaches an ill-tempered cat for the first time. His perception of the cat is initially positive since he is attracted by its fur and movement. But when he touches the animal, it scratches him. The situation deals with what we are calling two different or mutually exclusive perceptions. The adult with knowledge of the causal agent self and faced with the same situation easily comes to the conclusion that the first perception was different from the second, and that the cat is not a play object because it is vicious. The subjectively self aware child, however, will assume that both perceptions are correct and will not realize that his first perception is different from the second. Piaget calls this childish method of dealing with perceptions "juxtaposition," and relates it to the temporal nature of mental activities.

There is evidence indicating that mental functioning is temporally ordered. This means that separate mental events follow each other one after the other, are ordered in time, and do not occur simultaneously. The person looks at the table and then at the chair. The person follows the developing steps of an idea one after the other or changes from one idea to another. This proposition applies to the mental activity of the child. He sees the cat as friendly and then as vicious. Since the two mental events happen sequentially and not simultaneously, the child will not recognize the contradiction between differing perceptions and will lump all perceptions of a particular object into a whole. Piaget says,

> Any two or three characteristics can simply be combined without any consideration for the consistency or lack of consistency between the elements . . . each judgment is therefore juxtaposed and not assimilated to the judgment that precedes. Finally, the child merges the two judgments into a single whole, but this whole constitutes a mere juxtaposition, not a hierarchy [p. 223].

Thus, the subjectively self aware child can hold and even oscillate between two contradictory perceptions without realizing the contradiction. This propensity to order mental events in time in turn enables the child to differ with his own evaluations from moment to moment without any one perception being seen as inconsistent with the others. In other words, the conditions in which the child differs from his own opinion about some object would appear to be insufficient to cause differentiation.

Even though the child juxtaposes his perceptions, it would seem that he could not ignore reality indefinitely. If the child does not bring his conception of the world into equilibrium with that world, then surely he could not survive. Put another way, if the child does not rid himself of the juxtaposed friendly-vicious conception of the sometimes dangerous cat, he runs a distinct chance of being scratched to death.

In spite of this common sense reasoning, a close examination of the nature of the physical environment reveals that it is incapable of forcing the bringing forth in a person of an awareness of self contradiction. The sole correctional procedure for juxtaposed perception in the case we are discussing would be to force the child to deal with contradictory perceptions simultaneously. Since the child's mental functioning is temporally ordered, forcing the fact of the inconsistency of his notions upon him would require the intervention of the environment in such a way that the child would be forced to deal with the two points of view, vicious and friendly, simultaneously. But the physical environment is incapable of posing this kind of contradiction, since the child has a perception that fits either a vicious or a friendly cat.

To illustrate this point, imagine that the cat is trying to force the child to recognize his contradiction. The cat knows the child thinks he is friendly, so he becomes vicious. The child responds with a new perception, the vicious cat. Since our cat is basically imaginative, he becomes friendly toward the child, in an effort to force a contradiction upon him. Unfortunately for the cat, the child already has a perception to fit this category of behavior, the friendly cat. Since the child does not realize his internal contradictions, he can shift back and forth from friendly to vicious depending upon the actual circumstances. The cat is powerless to force the fact of a contradiction on the child because, by nature, the physical environment cannot communicate any state other than its present one. To force the child to deal with friendly and vicious simultaneously, the cat would have to be vicious (or friendly) and, at the same time, indicate to the child that the one state was in opposition to the other. The physical environment does not possess the ability to indicate any state other than a noncontradictory contemporaneous state and, therefore, is incapable of forcing the child to deal with the two perceptions simultaneously.

As a possible candidate for forcing differentiation of the causal agent self, we can eliminate the condition in which the child interacts with the physical environment. As our previous discussion indicated, the child's internally differing perceptions fail to meet the requirement of simultaneity. Because his mental events are temporally ordered, the child juxtaposes these perceptions and fails to grasp the inconsistencies between them.

Contact between the Child and the Social Environment

While the physical environment and the child's internal contradictions fail to bring forth objective self awareness, the child's interaction with social others meets all three conditions. By way of review, these three conditions are the following: (1) the presence of another viewpoint; (2) the difference in point of view concerning the same object; and (3) a simultaneous awareness of the opposing opinions. If the child and the other are attending the same object but come to different conclusions about that object, the first two conditions for the operation of the differentiating perceptual mechanism are satisfied. Furthermore, if the parent communicates his perception to the child in such a way that the child perceives the two opposing opinions simultaneously, the third condition is also satisfied and the child will recognize that his opinion is not unusual.

Thus it appears that the social theories of Mead, Piaget, and others did in fact identify an important element by insisting that something about social contact brings on self consciousness.

Situations that contain a disagreement between the parent and child occur with enough frequency to provide the child ample opportunity to differentiate himself. In fact, a major characteristic of the child's early life must be the conflict in attitude between himself and his parents. He likes this or that; they have the opposite attitude. However, this type of interaction must have several additional properties if the child's self differentiation is to be the eventual result.

The first criterion the parent's communication must satisfy is meaningfulness. The parent may gesticulate, shout, or do elaborate pantomime, but these actions will be of no consequence in terms of creating objective self awareness unless the child understands the attitudes behind the gestures. The origin for the evaluative meaning of actions, gestures, and words lies in the affective impact these items have upon the child. He learns to interpret behavior toward himself on the basis of pleasure and pain. If an action or set of actions causes him pain, the child will infer that mother or father has a negative attitude toward him at that moment. If the parent's actions cause him pleasure, the child will infer a positive attitude. From this basic communication the child will build a vocabulary of action, consisting especially of the evaluative meanings of action. The repeated association of words or expressions that have no immediate physical consequence will expand the set of behaviors that have meaning for the child. The facial expressions and words associated with pain will come to indicate a negative attitude. Similarly, the smile will take on positive connotations because it is associated with actions that bring pleasure.

At first only the actions that have the child as their object will have evaluative meaning since meaning occurs through internal sensation. As soon as the child learns the meaning of certain gestures and actions by experiencing the effects of those actions he will generalize the meaning of others' behavior to objects that are outside of him. After the child learns the evaluative meaning of being punished he will generalize the meaning of punishment to other objects. When the mother punishes the dog the child will infer that the mother's current attitude toward the dog is negative. If she pets the dog, then the child will infer a positive attitude.

Once the child has learned the evaluative meaning of certain actions, gestures, and words, the possibility of a conflict between his attitudes and the other's attitudes arises. As a realistic example let us take the case of opinion between the child and the parent over the value of the child's excrement. Suppose that the child is in his crib occupying himself by playing in his feces from which his mother is attempting to remove him. Assuming that the child enjoys playing in his excrement, there is the possibility of a clash between his and his mother's attitudes. He smiles and generally has a good time. The mother grimaces, frowns, and acts thoroughly upset. Since we grant the child the ability to distinguish when one event is not another, we would argue that he automatically differentiates his point of view from the mother's given that he has an awareness of the mother's negative gestures at the same time that he responds to the object positively. The gestures of disgust indicate an attitude that the child will differentiate from his own attitude of liking or enjoyment.

An example that may be closer to adult experience is the following. Suppose that two people are attending a play. One person likes the play and the other does not. As person A, smiling and enjoying himself, turns to B who is frowning and scowling, A will immediately know that he and B disagree about the merits of the play. He may not be able to interpret the precise meaning of B's gestures, but he does know that B's opinion of the play is not his opinion. The same situation exists for the child.

Often the parent's actions will be directed toward an object of the child's attention, and at other times the parent's attitude will be directed at the child's actions. If we replace the feces of our first example with the actions of the child, we again have a conflict between the child's attitude and the attitude of the parent. The child might mark the living room wall with crayons or throw marbles at an expensive vase. When the mother scolds the child or spanks him, the child will be forced to realize that the mother's attitude toward his actions is different from his own.

Since we have insisted that the child is subjectively self aware and cannot take himself as the object of attention, it might seem strange that we have suggested that the child has an attitude toward his own actions. But to assume that the child has no implicit attitude toward his own behavior would mean that the child was not only unable to take himself as an object, but also that he was unconscious, which is untenable. When the child crawls toward the glass sculpture, he has a positive attitude toward his behavior, otherwise he wouldn't carry out the act. The important point concerns the child's assumption of a universal thought process extending from his own. The purpose of our discussion is to indicate the manner in which he comes to realize himself as distinct, not to describe how he comes to be aware of himself in general.

Before a parent can successfully communicate a difference in opinion to the child, the communication must be in terms that are meaningful to a child. In addition, the communication must concern the same object to which the child is attending. If the mother communicates her attitude to the child after the child has lost interest in the original object, the communication will cause no conflict and no differentiation. To return to the earlier example, suppose that person A in the theater audience is not paying any attention to the play. Instead, he is daydreaming or wondering how he is going to pay the rent. As he turns to person B who is still grimacing and scowling, he understands what B feels toward the play, but that knowledge is not sufficient to cause a differentiation. B's attitude is merely irrelevant to A's. This irrelevancy of the communication also describes the mother's communication to the child when the child is attending to a different object. The child may understand what the mother's attitude is, but since it is on a dimension different from his train of thought, such a communication will not engage the differentiation process.

The third condition the parent's communication must satisfy is simultaneity. The child will tend to juxtapose the parent's opinion and his opinion unless the child is made aware that the two opinions are occurring simultaneously. Suppose that a child perceives a particular object in a positive way. The parent arrives and indicates to the child that the object is not suitable for play. Having learned the meaning of the parent's gestures toward the object, we can readily grant that the child understands that the parent's attitude is negative. But as in the physical setting, the child avoids the recognition of the differences between his and the parent's attitude because he juxtaposes the two opinions. It is both a play and a nonplay object. As indicated earlier, the reason for this juxtaposition lies in the temporal ordering of the child's mental events.

In juxtaposition the child sees an object as x and then as y. The unavoidable time gap between the two perceptions makes the juxtaposition possible. There is x and then (denoting a time lag) a y which is added to the x to make a whole. Psychologically, this whole represents "x or y," or alternatively "x and y."

Piaget discusses this process in describing a small boy's perception of life. In the example, the boy has said that life is defined by self movement and the fact of having blood, but he does not multiply these elements (logically) as the adult does. Instead he considers them separately and one at a time.

Duss says that the sun is alive because it moves forgetting that it has no blood. Or even if in limiting cases the child thinks of this second clause, it will not disturb him in his affirmation that the sun is alive (though bloodless) so long as he keeps the idea of self-movement before his mind. In a word, logical multiplication does not take place, and the factors involved are not compounded; each works separately on its own . . . among very young children (up to the age of 8) two conditions cannot be held before the mind simultaneously and not even collected into a single mental act [p. 161].

In the case of the parent and child, any verbal communication runs the risk of allowing a time-gap between the child's focus of attention upon the target object and his awareness of the parent's attitude. If the child does not have his own attitude in mind at the time he receives the parent's communication, the child will treat the object as both x and y. To prevent this juxtaposition it is necessary to eliminate the time gap between the two perceptions. This forces the child to deal with both perceptions simultaneously. Only if this can be accomplished will the full set of circumstances exist under which the child will become aware of the difference between the two attitudes.

The three conditions a communication must meet if it is to cause the child to differentiate himself are the following: (1) it must be meaningful to the child; (2) it must concern the same object to which the child is attending and must be different from the child's attitude; and (3) it must be conveyed to the child in such a way that he perceives his attitude and the other's attitude as occurring at the same time. There are three media through which the parent can convey an attitude to the child: direct contact (corporal punishment), gesture, and verbal command. Each of these encounters its own separate problems in satisfying the three conditions. Before the child learns the meaning of gestures and verbal commands, the only way the parent's communication can satisfy all three conditions is to be in terms of direct contact. This is the only possible solution at an early age because no other form of communication is meaningful, assuming that the child learns the devaluative meaning of gestures and expletives by experiencing the painful or pleasurable effects of the actions associated with the two forms. By the same token, the parent's actions in early years must take the child as their object. Actions taken toward any other object, even direct action, will mean nothing to the child until the child has experienced the effects of those actions.

Even after the child has learned the evaluative connotations of certain gestures and words, direct contact remains a more certain mode of communication to the child. The gesture and spoken word always run the risk of allowing the child to juxtapose the two disparate opinions. Direct contact assures simultaneity because it inevitably eliminates the time-gap between the two perceptions. The pain that indicates a negative attitude occurs at the same time the child is maintaining his own positive attitude. Consequently, the differentiation process is automatically triggered, resulting in the child's recognition of the differences. Until the child is old enough to comprehend verbal commands, a negative consequence in the form of punishment is the surest way of communicating an attitude to the child in such a way that he will apprehend the other's position and his own simultaneously. However, this does not mean that we advocate early and severe punishment of the child. The reasons are varied. On the one hand, it is difficult to say that the consequences of differentiation are always positive. Immersion in the self and its absolutist point of view may act as a buffer between the child and the vicissitudes of reality. If that implicit source of comfort is rudely snatched away from the child, the same thing could happen as when his favorite blanket is taken away from him; an acute state of anxiety. If adults have difficulty in dealing with the possibility of perceptual incorrectness, the same problem in large doses might well be insurmountable for the young child. Experience with the environment that promoted a gradual differentiation seems the wisest course of action.

A second objection to unrestrained punishment as a differentiating device is the possibility that such action may achieve unacceptable results. If punishment is employed it must be carried out in such a way so that the child's attention is not distracted from the object of dispute, otherwise no real conflict of opinion will be apparent to the child. Further, the process of differentiating the causal agent self demands repeated confrontations of the child's and parent's opinion. If the punishment is such that the child develops a strong avoidance response to the parent, no continued communication of differences is possible unless, as Lewin points out, the parent places a barrier around the child. While this might force the child to receive the punishment, theoretically such a barrier could too early divert the child's attention from the original object. In view of these considerations, the use of punishment must be controlled if the parent is to effectively communicate his opinions. The child must be prevented from leaving the field during punishment but not distracted from the object of his attention by the severity of the punishment.

While qualifying the conditions under which punishment will effectively communicate the existence of a different point of view, we must also point out that punishment, if too strong, can actually prevent recognition of a difference in point of view while seemingly having been successful in communicating that difference. Suppose that the child initially sees an object as suited for play. The parent enters the situation and communicates his point of view that the object is a nonplay object, accomplishing this by punishing the child. However, in this case the parent's punishment goes beyond communicating a different point of view, and through association with the object elicits a new response from the child. Because the child associates strong punishment with the object, it now becomes a nonplay object as far as he is concerned. This change eliminates the conflict between himself and the parent. The parent sees it as nonplay object, and so does the child. But without conflict over differing attitudes, no differentiation can result. Therefore, punishment must not be so severe and overwhelming that it brings the child to agree totally with the parent and forego his own desires. The child must maintain his desire for the object as a play object while the parent communicates his difference in point of view to the child. In the process of differentiation of the causal agent self it is not the change of the child's evaluation, but rather his understanding that a difference in opinion exists, that is crucial.

By punishment we do not necessarily mean corporal punishment. Any action the parent takes toward the child that involves physical or psychological punishment, removal of reward, threat, and so forth, can potentially communicate a negative attitude to the child. We do not suggest that any particular form of punishment would be optimal, because the constraints applied must fit the situation in such a way that the child will feel conflict over whether or not to continue his previous behavior.

If a differing point of view is communicated to the child in such a way that it engages the differentiation process, the child will be faced with the realization that different perceptual processes do exist. As he becomes aware that his causal agent self is a unique entity bounded on all sides so as to produce a differentiated unity, objective self awareness becomes an increasing possibility. Through repetition of this difference of opinions, the child will come to fully differentiate the causal agent self as a separate and distinct entity in the world. Consciousness will then have an object upon which to focus when certain stimuli present in the environment direct attention to the self. For the child the infinitude and absolutism of complete immersion in the self is ended. He has become an object to himself.

It is difficult to fully convey the child's new experience of himself as object. The mature person differentiates his causal agent at an early age, giving up egocentricism and the claim to perceptual universality. We are so used to treating ourselves as objects that it is sometimes hard to imagine the self in any other way. However, the adult is never totally differentiated. Situations continue to occur in adult life which repeat the child's differentiation process on a smaller scale.

The child's beginnings in objective self awareness are comparable to the experience of a stranger in a foreign country. Just as the child acted as though he assumed a universal consciousness, the traveler from America (or anywhere else) all too often appears to assume universal customs that are coincident with those back home. Because the traveler acts as though culture is a universal constant, he is also unaware of possible conflicts between his culture and others, just as the egocentric child was unaware of the possible clashes between his viewpoint and those of others. As the visitor comes into contact with the local customs, he finds himself in conflict, especially when the legal correlates of the local customs threaten him with imprisonment, ostracism, and other punishments. Once he experiences the contradiction of the alternative customs his own culture should begin to assume an object-like status. Once a person's culture is an object, consciousness-attention can focus on that culture, or himself as a carrier of culture. Witness the increased self awareness exhibited by many visitors returning from a foreign country. Previously they never considered that using the fork with the right hand was a particular method of eating. Now they can focus on using the right hand. The contact with a differing set of behavioral assumptions has caused the person to become objectively self aware with respect to his own culture, to see it as one distinct culture because it has been brought into conflict with another distinct culture. In a very real sense, this is what happens to the child, except that the child differentiates a much larger portion of the causal agent self.

An Emerging Self Concept

As experience with differing points of view accumulates, the child will slowly realize his causal agent self as a distinct entity in the world. As we have said, once the person has knowledge of a distinct causal agent self, he has gained the ability to be objectively self aware, and prior to this discrimination there was no specific self upon which to focus consciousness. With repeated instances of objective self awareness, the child will gradually come to focus on himself in many respects, and once he has had considerable experience with focusing on himself it becomes a simple matter for him to transfer his focus from one aspect to another. Further, through repeatedly incurring situations that cause him to examine dimensions of himself, he will come to build up a unified conception of himself, a conception that will constitute a comprehensive causal agent self that has numerous perceptions, customary mediating or thinking processes, and countless behaviors. As this conception develops, a stimulus that reflects just one aspect of himself will have the power to make the person objectively self aware of the unitary self, just as reminding a person of an instance of a concept will often call forth in his consciousness the concept itself. Once he is aware of the concept of the self, he will then come to focus on those dimensions of self that happen to be salient in the situation. The implication is that a person who sees his own visual image may become objectively self aware with respect to an opinion, a physical characteristic, an ability, a way of thinking, or any other characteristic dimension of the causal agent self.

A COMPARISON WITH MEAD AND PIAGET

This chapter began by stating the opposition between the social theories of the development of self consciousness and the objective self awareness account of the phenomenon. The purpose of this section is to explicate some of these contrasts.

The principal point of disagreement between our analysis and those of the social origin theorists was whether or not the elements of self consciousness were indigenous to psychic structure. The social origin theories answered negatively and objective self awareness theories answered affirmatively. On this point we believe there is little ambiguity. The child has a self and the self is an object. The child's consciousness can focus on any object. However, it is also clear that the child initially does not know that his self is an object and cannot be objectively self aware. As it turns out, we rejected the social other as source of self consciousness but did not totally eliminate the role of the social other in the development of self consciousness. The analysis of childish consciousness, the substance of self, and the conditions under which the child will recognize that another's thinking, perception, or behavior is different from his own led to the conclusion that contact with a differing other is the sole circumstance in which the child will achieve knowledge of the objectivity of the self.

In this light, social origin theory and objective self awareness are not totally incompatible. Both emphasize the crucial role that presence of a social other plays in the process. Having presented an interpretation of how the social other enters into the development of self consciousness, we would take time to analyze Mead and Piaget on this point more carefully.

Mead

Briefly, Mead holds that a person becomes self conscious by taking the point of view of another, and in so doing he leaves himself experientially and can view his own consciousness as if it were an object. Self consciousness for Mead is defined strictly in terms of knowledge about one's self gained by self examination from the point of view of another. We would suggest that Mead's hypothesis is correct insofar as the presence of another may cause an individual to take his self as an object, but we fail to see the logic of his analysis of the development of self consciousness. In assuming that the person has only to take the other's point of view to become self conscious, Mead neglects the distinct possibility that the subjectively self aware child is not cognizant that there exists another point of view. Knowledge of another's point of view presupposes that the person is aware that he has his own differentiated point of view, otherwise the person would assume that his perspective is shared by all others. As we have maintained, the child does act as though his perspective is shared by the world. Thus, if a person is able to take the point of view of another as Mead proposes, he must already be aware of himself as a distinct entity, which is to say that taking the other's perspective could not bring about self consciousness. Taking the point of view of another is possible after differentiation of the self occurs, not before. For Mead's hypothesis to operate it would be necessary to find a mechanism whereby the individual could take the other's perspective prior to self consciousness, but we find it difficult to understand what would constitute such a mechanism.

Piaget

Piaget has also developed some interesting hypotheses about the development of self awareness. He has concluded that consciousness of the ego results because self consciousness is a necessary adaptation to the environment:

For in so far as he is thinking only for himself, the child has no need to be aware of the mechanism of his reasoning. His attention is wholly turned towards the external world, towards action, in no way directed towards thought as a medium interposed between world and himself. In so far, on the other hand, as the child seeks to *adapt himself to others* [italics ours], he creates between himself and them a new order of reality, a new place of thought, where speech and argument will henceforth hold their sway, and upon which operations and relations which till then have been the work of action alone will now be handled by imagination and by words. The child will therefore have to become conscious to the same extent of these operations and relations which till then had remained unconscious because they were sufficient for the purposes of action [p. 213].

The result of adaptation to others is what Piaget refers to as the "logical point of view," or the "objective point of view," which is self conscious as opposed to egocentric. It is argued that the development of the logical point of view is a result of participation in social intercourse. Piaget proposes that the habits of discussion and social life are necessary for development of the logical point of view. But what are the qualities of discussion and social life that lead to self consciousness? He says first, "Never without the shock of contact with the thought of others and the effort of reflection which this shock entails would thought as such come to be conscious of itself [p. 144]." From this statement we learn that contact with the thought of others causes reflection. Piaget continues by noting the reason social contact creates reflective thinking: "Surely it must be the shock of our thought coming into contact with that of others, which produces doubt and the desire to prove [p. 204]." Thus it is the desire to prove to the other person the correctness of one's beliefs that forces the individual to seek verification by reflecting upon his thoughts, such reflection being synonymous with self consciousness. But precisely what happens in the contact with others is not clear from Piaget's discussion. At one point Piaget states,

We are constantly hatching an enormous number of false ideas, conceits, Utopias, mystical explanations, suspicions, and megalomaniacal fantasies, which disappear when brought into contact with other people [p. 204].

Is it that one person tells the other that he does not believe him, or that he is crazy? Or is it that the first person proves to the second the incorrectness of his notions? Piaget is simply vague at this point. Whatever happens in the process of self consciousness, the desire for proof amounts to a need to show others that one is correct—it is not the need to show oneself that one is correct that leads to self consciousness.

Apparently self awareness is brought about in the process of the socialization of thought, which entails learning to prove and verify one's own thoughts through developing the habits of discussion in a social context. But now a question arises. If the egocentric child is by nature not interested in communicating his thoughts to others or actually understanding their thoughts, why does he ever participate in the type of social activity that leads to the logical point of view? The solution resides in Piaget's postulate of a social need to successfully communicate to others and to share their thoughts, a need that counters the egocentric forces pushing the child away from social encounters. Unfortunately Piaget's system is not as simple as one need (for social encounters) overpowering the directions established by egocentric thinking. There is a missing link, an apparent contradiction in the system for which we see no solution. The problem is as follows.

The success or failure of the development of self awareness is based upon a social need to communicate successfully with others and to share in their thoughts. This need is necessarily posited as a separate region which does not come into contact with or influence egocentrism. In fact, Piaget equates the predominance of egocentrism in children with a lack of social need and implies that once social needs develop, egocentrism will decline. The inconsistency in his framework comes from his assertion that the child can continue to be egocentric while possessing the particular social need outlined. Because Piaget argues that the egocentric child believes everybody understands him and that he is understood by everyone, it is difficult to understand how the child could at the same time develop a need to communicate successfully. If he is truly egocentric, he must already be convinced that he does communicate successfully, for he operates as though there is a universal perception and universal point of view.

Summary

In general, the strength of objective self awareness theory in comparison to Mead and Piaget is that it recognizes an essential step in becoming self aware—the differentiation of the causal agent self, that both others neglected. By neglecting this point both authors wind up formulating the development of self awareness in terms of special classes of external stimuli that only cause objective self awareness to occur once the self is differentiated. Taking the point of view of another (becoming aware that another is observing), as discussed in Chapter 1, is a separate class of stimulus that causes consciousness-attention to focus upon the causal agent self. As we have shown in several experiments, mirrors, television cameras, and tape recorders simulate the human situation and are just as effective in causing consciousness-attention to focus upon the self. Contact with the ideas of others is another class of stimulus that will cause objective self awareness if the condition is added that these ideas must be different. The impact such differences have in creating objective self awareness is well documented in the Asch experiments. Whether they conformed or not, all subjects indicated in the postexperimental interview that they were strongly aware of themselves and their perceptual processes. This will be further elaborated in Chapter 4. Becoming aware of being observed and contact with the different ideas of others are both important situational variables that cause objective self awareness, but they are not related to the development of the ability to be self aware. As we hope to have demonstrated, this development must entail the differentiation of the causal agent self as a separate and particular entity in the world. Only if differentiation is successfully established can any stimulus, whether the class suggested by Mead or Piaget or some other form, cause oojective self awareness.

Chapter 4

CONFORMITY: AN OBJECTIVE SELF AWARENESS APPROACH

The first three chapters have endeavored to develop a broadly based theory of behavior based upon the idea of two states of consciousness. This chapter departs from the previous design in that we are now ready to apply the theory to concrete behavior. The set of behaviors that will occupy us in this chapter falls within a range of response generally known to psychologists as conformity behavior.

WHAT IS A CONFORMITY SITUATION?

The purpose of this chapter and the next is to explain, in terms of objective self awareness theory, why conformity occurs. The first step this objective requires is a definition of conformity. As a general definition, we will understand conformity to mean a change in the person's attitudes, beliefs, or behaviors in the direction of the differing attitudes, beliefs, or behaviors of other people who are present in the same situation. This definition accomplishes two related things. It defines what behavior the theory will try to explain and it indicates that the theory will try to explain this behavior only when the behavior occurs in certain circumstances. In other words, our definition of conformity indicates the theoretical objective. We will attempt to explain why attitude change and behavior change toward the opinions and behaviors of others (the dependent variables of the theory) occur in a situation consisting of (1) two or more people who (2) hold opinions about the same object but who (3) differ in their opinion of this object.

Defining conformity as we have makes some obvious but important distinctions. The theoretical explanation developed in this chapter is not meant to apply to behaviors that are not attitude change, even though such behaviors are found in a conformity situation. If a man is in a conformity situation and increases his desire to achieve a certain goal, the theory as it deals with conformity does not apply. Conversely, the theory is not meant to apply to attitude change unless such a change occurs in the prescribed conformity situation. If a man changes his attitude in a direction that happens to coincide with another man's attitude but in a situation that is different from the defined conformity situation, the theory does not apply.

By defining conformity as a particular behavior in a prescribed setting, we know in general what phenomena the theory will attempt to explain. However, Asch (1961) indicates that difficulties may arise if conformity, as we have defined it, is treated as a phenomenon with just one psychological basis. He says that conformity is not a psychological category, but an external classification which may include heterogeneous phenomena. We take this to mean that conformity defined as the attitude change toward another in the appropriate situation is a general description of a class of human behavior that can be caused by several separate and independent factors. According to Asch, a psychologist who observes what looks like conformity on two separate occasions would be unable to conclude that only one motivational system was responsible for the behavior in both instances. The conformity behavior might have been caused by factor A or factor B, or both together. Without further information about the situation, it would be impossible to tell.

If Asch is correct, conformity can be caused by forces that cannot be related to each other within a broader theoretical framework. This means that there cannot be one single answer to the problem of why people conform and that a single theory of conformity is an impossibility. The issue this raises is how to differentiate the conformity behavior that objective self awareness can explain from other kinds of conformity that the theory cannot explain. The clearest solution for this difficulty is to subdivide conformity into separate categories according to characteristics of the situation in which the attitude change occurs, assuming that each category implies a single explanation. Objective self awareness theory can then be applied to the appropriate category with the expectation of achieving a complete explanation. Thus, in light of the heterogeneous nature of conformity, the objective of this chapter must be modified slightly. Instead of trying to explain all conformity behavior in terms of objective self awareness, we will attempt to use the theory to explain why conformity occurs only in a particular situation, leaving the conformity that occurs in other situations to other theories.

CATEGORIES OF CONFORMITY

Conformity can be divided into two major categories: conformity in a coercive situation and conformity in a noncoercive or minimal situation. The distinction between the two categories is that conformity in a coercive situation is conformity in the presence of a tangible threat of punishment or promise of reward, whereas conformity in a minimal situation is conformity in circumstances where there are people with different opinions about the same object, but no threat of reward or punishment. Although it is not always perfectly clear, we believe that all conformity behavior takes place in either the coercive situation or the minimal situation. Since these categories seem to imply single causal explanations, two theories should satisfactorily explain all of conformity.

Conformity in a Coercive Situation

The situational classifications of conformity assume that some property of the circumstances stimulates conformity by interacting with a specific motivational system in the individual. In the case of conformity behavior in a coercive situation, the important situational factor is the presence of persons who can pose rewards and/or punishments for others in the situation. This situational factor interacts with the desires of others present to gain the rewards or avoid the punishments of the powerful other. Conformity occurs given two conditions: (1) the person holding the rewards and punishments indicates that his rewards can be gained and/or his punishments avoided through conformity to his opinions, beliefs, or behaviors, and (2) the person who desires the rewards of the other decides that he can gain his objective by conforming to the other.

French and Raven (1959) provide a general paradigm for the coercive situation. They indicate that individuals in a group may possess reward power in the sense that X mediates rewards for Y or coercive power in which X mediates punishments for Y. If X insists that Y conform to gain rewards or avoid punishments, Y will conform. This basic approach to conformity is characterized by an emphasis upon the necessity of the presence of a person who holds tangible rewards or punishments and a person who desires those rewards or wishes to avoid the punishments. Under this category we could also subsume the theories of Byrne (1961) and Jones (1964).

Conformity in the Minimal Situation

Noncoercive conformity is unique in that it occurs in situations where there is an apparent absence of any pressure toward conformity. Kiesler (1969) makes the following point:

> It is not necessary for "group pressure" to be explicitly transmitted to be effective. . . .
> For example, in several experiments (such as Kiesler, Zanna, and De Salvo, 1966), the
> subject knows only that he disagrees with the group on an important topic or norm [p.
> 238].

Sherif (1935) makes the same point in reporting that subjects were influenced simply by overhearing the opinions of people they never met nor could reasonably expect to meet. The question of conformity in the minimal situation is best summarized in the following way: Why does one man conform to another when he has little to gain by doing so and little to lose by not doing so? There have been several credible solutions to this problem.

As in the case of conformity in a coercive situation, classifying conformity in a minimal situation as a distinct phenomenological category assumes that some feature of the particular situation interacts with some motivational system to produce attitude change toward another. There are several extant theoretical attempts to explain conformity under these circumstances which employ various situational properties and motivational systems.

Sherif assumed that the basic drive which led man to conform under noncoercive conditions was the desire for a stable mode of response. Understanding this as a primary need, Sherif believed that stimulus situations lacking in stable perceptual anchors, that is, certainty of perception, frustrated the drive for a stable way of responding to the environment and caused the person to seek the necessary anchorage in other ways. For Sherif, one of the primary sources of such anchorage was in the opinions of others. Thus, if a person was lacking in certainty of perception, he would use the opinions of others as additional situational indicators of the true perception. This would result in the movement of his perception in the direction of the others.

Another theory of noncoercive conformity was introduced by Festinger (1950, 1954). He hypothesized that the person had a drive to have correct opinions and abilities and that correctness of abilities and opinions was largely bound up with the extent to which others shared a belief or ability. From this initial postulate of social reality, Festinger reasoned that a difference of opinion within any group would exert pressure on all members of the group to achieve unanimity. These pressures toward uniformity would be manifested in persuasive intragroup communication and in the actual attitude change of involved individuals toward each other.

In 1957, Festinger suggested that his earlier notions of social comparison and informal social influence be integrated into the theory of cognitive dissonance. In the section of "A Theory of Cognitive Dissonance" dealing with

social influence processes, he suggested that difference of opinion between the
two persons resulted in dissonant cognitions. Since these cognitions produced
a state of tension, the individual was motivated to change his opinion toward
the other or the opinion of the other toward himself, or to seek supporting
cognitions in the form of others who held a similar opinion.

More recently, Rappoport (1965) has suggested that conformity can result
from the mere existence of differing opinions. He states that:

> In the latter case (noncompetitive conflict), however, we assume the primary cause (of
> conflict) to be discrepant cognitive processes: cooperating persons may think differently
> about their mutual problem [p. 323].

Rappoport does not give us any explanatory principle per se, but assumes that
something about mere difference of opinion between the two people can bring
about conformity.

We have briefly looked at two categories of conformity and some theories
associated with each one. Objective self awareness theory will be applied to
conformity only under noncoercive conditions, leaving coercive conformity to
other explanations. Looking at the theoretical approaches to noncoercive conformity, we see that with the exception of Sherif, who selected the opinion object
as the important situational factor, these explanations are built upon the interaction
between the situational factor of a difference of opinion and some psychological
variable. The application of objective self awareness to conformity will follow
a similar course. Defining the phenomenon to which the theory addresses itself
as conformity under noncoersive conditions we will attempt to explain why
one man alters his opinion in the direction of another by developing the interaction
between the mechanisms of objective self awareness and the presence of a
difference of opinion.

A PRELIMINARY OUTLINE

We believe that psychologists who have concerned themselves with explanations of conformity in the minimal situation have not suitably answered a funda-
mental question which is as follows: Why does a person alter his existing beliefs
and behavior at all? People depend to an enormous extent upon the validity
of primary sensory data and the resulting concepts into which their mediational
processes organize that data. It is not at all obvious that people would readily
relinquish existing beliefs and behavior simply because someone else disagreed
with them or tried to influence them. To do so would indicate that they had
less than full confidence in the faculties upon which their negotiation of the
environment depends. In light of the dependency relationship between a person
and his perceptions of the world, we would argue that a person, in
the absence of coercive forces, will change his beliefs, attitudes, or behaviors

only when forces present within his situations cause him to believe that his beliefs, attitudes, and behaviors are in error. Once a person believes that any of his perceptions of the world or behaviors toward the world are incorrect, those self attributes will become unstable, that is, ready for change.

Since the presentation of the theory attempts to follow the natural course of events that lead to conformity, this chapter will demonstrate how the interaction between the differences of opinion and objective self awareness can cause a person to believe that his opinion is in error. Chapter 5 will show how a person's belief that his opinion is in error leads to conformity.

The objective self awareness account of how a person comes to believe that his opinion is in error begins with a simple premise. The presence of a difference of opinion between two or more people will produce what will be called the error of the contradiction.

THE ERROR OF THE CONTRADICTION

In Chapter 3 we proposed that the origin of objective self awareness depended upon conditions that forced the child to realize that his belief was different from the belief of another person. But what state of awareness exists after the child becomes aware that his opinion is x and the other person's opinion is not-x? Or in the terms of the present chapter, what happens after groups of two or more individuals perceive themselves as differentiated into separate positions on the basis of their differing opinions about an object? Do the members of one subgroup simply accept the fact that they are different than the others? We think not. It is our contention that whenever a person is aware that opinions x and not-x are simultaneously occurring, he will also be aware that there is some difficulty or error associated with the simultaneous existence of two beliefs that contradict each other. For example, if two persons are looking at the same object and one says that it is blue and the other says that it is red, we believe that each person's awareness that opinions x and not-x are occurring will be accompanied by the awareness that something is "wrong," "amiss," or "out of joint."

The following excerpts which support this contention are taken from the Asch studies on minorities of one. These examples will poignantly illustrate the feelings and cognitions that a person has after he becomes aware that two opinions, x and not-x, exist simultaneously. Asch (1952) begins by saying,

No subject disregards the group judgments. Although the task calls for independent judgments, virtually no one looks upon the estimates of the group with indifference or as irrelevant. . . .
He (the subject) notes immediately the convergence of the group responses, his divergence from them, and the contradiction between these.

There are many other structural relations that the subject comprehends. . . . (1) that the issue is one of fact; (2) that a correct result is possible; (3) that only one result is correct; . . . . It is on these grounds that the critical subject senses there is something wrong. . . .

The immediate reaction of most critical subjects is one of varying degrees of puzzlement or confusion. . . . The subjects search for a principle of explanation. . . . There is something wrong, but they cannot say what it is. . . . Lending strength to the dilemma is the sense of irreconcilability of the disagreement, the realization that two vectors that should be identical are starkly contradictory [pp. 461–465].

In addition to his qualitative data, Asch also reports data from an attitude questionnaire administered to all subjects which asked, "Would you say you were concerned about the disagreement?" Eighty-two percent of the subjects answered this question affirmatively.

Asch's data, both conclusions and specific examples taken from his subjects, make it clear that the psychological processes do not stop after the individual becomes aware that there are two contradictory opinions present within the group. In fact, it would seem that awareness of the fact of a difference of opinion is just the beginning. In Asch's conclusions he notes that the subject realized that he held x and the group not-x, that he was seeing differently from the group, and then became confused, felt that there was a difficulty, a dilemma, that something was wrong. Although Asch does not specifically use the term, we feel that "awareness of error" aptly describes the psychological state of the subjects he describes.

The phenomenon of error which occurs after the awareness of the contradiction can be summed up thusly. A person's awareness that two opinions x and not-x are occurring simultaneously will have as a component element the awareness that error is associated with the contradiction. To repeat an earlier example, two people are looking at an object. One says, "Isn't that an attractive shade of blue?" The other looks astonished and states that the object is red, not blue. Now it is the first person who looks askance at his friend. We believe that each person's awareness that his companion has a contradictory perception of the object creates an additional cognition that something about the contradiction is in error. Before each person came to discover that his opinion was at variance with the other opinion, the environment was routinely organized into the normal configuration of perceivers as ground and exterior environment as figure. It can be described as a tensionless, perhaps even quiescent state of awareness. To the persons involved, there is simply an unambiguous object sitting on a table. Then there is the sudden awareness of a difference of opinion. The attitudinal homogeneity of the two people is shattered and reorganized into opinion x and opinion not-x, and a sense of wrongness pervades the entire situation.

The reasons why the awareness of a contradiction produces awareness that error is associated with that contradiction are obscure. Asch may be correct in asserting that people assume that everybody confronts the same objective environment and that contradictory perceptions mean that someone is in error. Festinger may be right when he says that two cognitions, one of which is the obverse of the other, produce a state of tension which in turn might be felt as error. At any rate it is the phenomenon that is important to the present analysis and, for the moment, not the reasons for the existence of that phenomenon.

The error of the contradiction is the first crucial ingredient in the objective self awareness approach to conformity. Originally we argued that in the absence of coercion a person would have to believe that his opinion was incorrect before he would alter that opinion. At that time we had not as yet indicated what the source of that incorrectness would be. Now we see that any conformity situation includes error as an intrinsic property of its organization. Any time there is a difference of opinion between two or more people, all individuals in the situation will become aware that there is an error associated with the simultaneous presence of opinion x and not-x. With the source of error firmly in hand, our analysis of conformity can proceed.

The next step is to determine what the person does with the error of the contradiction once he becomes aware of it. Two possibilities immediately present themselves. (1) The person's awareness of error acts as a stimulus to further mental activity. (2) The person's awareness of error possesses no properties that stimulate further action on the part of the individual. We will take the former position to wit: the person's awareness of error has certain characteristics that automatically engage or stimulate the attribution mechanism such that the person will attribute the cause of the error to something in his total situation which of course includes himself. Substantiating this assumption requires two steps. First we must determine what properties of an event engage the attribution process. Second, we must determine whether or not the awareness of error, as an event, has these properties.

CHARACTERISTICS OF EVENTS THAT
ENGAGE THE ATTRIBUTION PROCESS

The twofold question is, what characteristics must an event possess before a person will attribute the occurrence of that event to something in the environment, and does awareness of error have these characteristics? In his review for the 1967 Nebraska Symposium, Kelley writes,

> The (attribution) theory describes processes that operate *as if* the individual were motivated to attain a cognitive mastery of the causal structure of his environment. Indeed, Heider explicitly assumes that "we try to make sense out of the manifold of proximal stimuli [p. 193]."

Kelley is suggesting that the motivational component of the attribution process is a need or desire to understand and perhaps control the environment. This idea implies that an event must possess at least one characteristic before it will engage the attribution process. Since the person's motivation for causal attribution comes from a desire to understand and control, only those events beyond immediate understanding will bring the causal attribution process into play.

The second question is whether or not the error of the contradiction is beyond immediate understanding. Clearly it is. If a person wants to understand and control the environment, this need should be acute when the person realizes that something in the situation is wrong, amiss, or in error. The strength of the need for an explanation of this error, which Asch has documented, supports this hypothesis. Thus we conclude that awareness of error does have one characteristic which will cause a person to want to find the cause for its occurrence in the environment.

Attribution theory has indicated a second distinct characteristic which an event must possess before the person's desire to understand the environment by attribution is engaged. In addition to being beyond immediate understanding, the event must represent a change in the environment. Heider (1944) says the following:

> Making a first approach to this analysis, we may say that the origin and change which is attributed to the origin form a unit, that is to say, the change "belongs" to the origin [p. 358].

Thibaut and Riecken (1955) have incorporated the process of attribution of causal relationships into a theory of social causality. They state that

> the relationship between perceived control and acceptance can also be stated in terms of the perceptions of social causality. X perceives that his influence attempt (instrumental communication) "causes" a compliant change in behavior or attitudes in Y . . . [pp. 113–114].

They continue by asserting that any change in Y's behavior in a direction conforming to X's instrumental communication may be perceived by X to have been caused by himself. Jones and Davis (1965) develop the idea of causal attribution in their theory of correspondent inference. In this paper, they employ sufficient reason. The inference of an attribute serves as a sufficient reason for the behavior if it accounts for the occurrence of an act to the reasonable satisfaction of the perceivers. From the Jones and Davis point of view, the occurrence of an act would be described as an effect which must then be related to some cause. Refining what qualifies as an effect within the theory, they say, "Stated in the broadest terms, they (effects) are discriminable changes in the pre-existing state of affairs that are brought about by action [p. 225]."

In essence, each theorist assumes that an event which will stimulate the person's attribution mechanism must represent an alteration in any previous state of affairs. If a person were faced only with a static, nonchanging environment, his causal attribution processes would never be engaged. For Heider there is a unit relationship between an origin and a change, for Thibaut and Riecken, a change in a person's behavior, and for Jones and Davis, a change in the preexisting state of affairs.

The error of the contradiction qualifies as a change in the environment. As we pointed out in a previous example, the shift from nonawareness to awareness of the existence of contradictory opinions produces an abrupt introduction of the presence of error into the situation. At one moment there is no hint of difficulty, and then at the next moment there is the distinct awareness of wrongness being associated with the contradictory opinions.

We began the discussion of attribution theory by arguing that the awareness of error qualified as the type of event or effect that engaged the attribution process. The evidence that has been presented in the last several pages substantiates the assertion. Whenever there is a contradiction, the person will be motivated to attribute the error of this contradiction to something in the environment. Where does this conclusion leave us? Since the source of the error is associated with the contradiction and the contradiction is associated with the two opinion positions held by the two subgroups, the range of the possible sources for the error is limited to the people who hold the two positions. This state of affairs offers two possibilities. Either the person will attribute the error to himself or to the other. But can we go further than this? Can we predict when a person will attribute the error to himself, and when to the other?

ATTRIBUTION OF ERROR TO SELF OR OTHER

In an experiment by Duval (1971) it has been shown that an objectively self aware person is more likely to attribute the source of a given event or effect to himself, while the subjectively self aware person is more likely to attribute the source of an event to the other. The experimental results indicate that this finding obtains regardless of the favorability (negative or positive) of the outcome. The complete experiment is presented in the fifth chapter, but it might help to review briefly some of its structure and results.

The study involved giving the subject several hypothetical situations constructed so that he could attribute responsibility for the outcome either to himself or the other hypothetical person in the situation. The following are two of the hypothetical situations.

Imagine that you pull up behind another car at a stoplight. The light turns green but the car in front of you does not move. As you pull out around the car, the other driver turns right and runs into you. To what degree did your actions cause the accident and to what degree did the actions of the other driver cause the accident?

Imagine that you have selected and purchased a race horse. You enter the horse in a major race and hire a good jockey to ride him. The horse wins first place. To what degree did your actions cause the victory and to what degree did the actions of the jockey cause the victory?

Each subject was given a set of five hypothetical situations, either negative or positive in outcome, and was asked to estimate the degree to which his behavior caused the event in question. The results of this experiment are clear cut. The objectively self aware subjects tended to attribute more of the cause for the event to themselves than did the subjectively aware persons.

The theoretical justification for this experiment is stated in the following way:

When the situation is so constructed that either the person or the other can be responsible for the outcome, the locus of causal attribution is determined by the direction of attention. If attention is directed at the self, attribution of causality will be to the self. If attention is directed at the other, attribution of causality will be to the other [p. 3].

Three experiments reported in Chapter 9 further support this notion.

The conclusion we draw about attribution of error is this. If the person who is aware of a difference of opinion focuses attention only upon himself, he will attribute the error posed by the contradiction to himself. If he focuses attention only upon the other, he will attribute the error posed by the contradiction to the other.

Through the notion of the error of the contradiction and the concept of causal attribution we have reduced the problem of conformity behavior to the terms of objective and subjective self awareness. If the person's attention is focused on the self, he will attribute the error of the contradiction to his opinion, such opinion then becoming unstable. If the person's attention is focused on the other he will attribute the error to the other. Presumably his opinion would remain stable. If we could predict where attention will focus in any given group situation, we would then be able to predict whose opinion would become unstable.

FACTORS CONTROLLING THE FOCUS OF ATTENTION

In order to understand the forces that control the direction of attention within a group where differences of opinion are occurring we must begin with some clarifications about the behavior of consciousness. The core assumption of objective self awareness theory is that the directionality of consciousness is determined. The attention of the organism is not considered to be under the control of will, or some similarly noncausal concept, but is assumed to be causally determined by certain forces in the environment interacting with the properties of consciousness. Thus at any given moment, the direction of a person's attention to one object instead of another, to himself as opposed to the external world, or even to certain dimensions of himself, is assumed to be predictable on the basis of knowledge of the existing configuration of forces and stimuli that effect the directionality of consciousness. Let us see if we can understand these forces.

As we argued in Chapter 3, the child has repeated experiences in which he comes up against different opinions. Through this contact he eventually fully differentiates the self as object in the world. But the development of self as object should not be construed as implying that the person is constantly objectively aware. Differentiating the self means only that consciousness may take the self as the object of its attention. In other words, the child in a predifferentiated self condition cannot take the self as object because no such object has been differentiated from the whole. Once the self is differentiated, however, it merely assumes a place among all the other objects within the situation. In this sense the person may take either himself or other entities as objects of attention.

SCOPE OF AWARENESS

Given that the nonegocentric adult lives in a world of objects, one of which is himself, we must first note that the directionality of attention will be determined solely by the configuration of objects that lie within the person's immediate scope of awareness. Now what do we mean by immediate scope of awareness? If blinders are placed upon a person, his immediate scope of awareness is defined by the field which lies within the boundaries imposed by the exterior constraints (assuming of course that all senses but the visual are blocked). The person's immediate scope of attention is, therefore, the totality of what he could see within the range of vision as restricted by the blinders. If the blinders were removed, the person's immediate scope of attention would be the room in which he is sitting. Thus, in general, the person's immediate scope of awareness is defined by the limits upon awareness, such limits being imposed by the particular situation.

The notion of scope of awareness is important in that it places boundaries upon the field that controls the direction of consciousness. The direction of a person's attention is not controlled by the configuration of all the objects in the universe, but rather by the configuration of objects that lie within the immediate scope of awareness. Giving due weight to this theoretical proposition is particularly important when the question is whether or not attention will focus upon the self or the not-self.

In the context of experimentation upon objective self awareness, we have observed that the subject is usually unaware that he constitutes an object in the field until we remind him of the fact with some particular type of stimulus. We account for this phenomenon by saying that the person's objective self is not normally in his immediate scope of awareness. We have alluded to this fact by calling subjective self awareness the primary state of consciousness.

If the person's self is normally not in his scope of attention, what consequences does this fact have for our conceptual model of the determination of directed-attention? It means that the self as an object does not figure in the determination of the direction attention takes until the person's immediate scope of attention is widened to a field which includes the self as an object. Only after the person is reminded that he also is an object in the world is objective self awareness even possible. Obviously, our approach to conformity is in difficulty unless the situation in which differences of opinion occur reminds the person in some way of his status as an object in the world.

Chapter 3 argues that when a child comes in contact with a differing opinion, he realizes, under certain conditions, that his opinion is not the opinion of the other person. Through this process the child differentiates his causal agent self as a distinct object. This event, which makes objective self awareness possible in the first place, continues to have psychological ramifications even after the person has a definite concept of himself as an object. When the adult encounters a differing opinion, behavior, or trait, he, just as the child, is forced to recognize that his opinion is not the opinion of the other. Since complete differentiation of the self has already occurred, this momentary differentiation on one dimension serves to call to the person's mind the previously formed concept of the object status of his self.

By reminding the individual that he is an object, differences of opinion serve to widen the person's scope of awareness to include himself. Now that we have the person included as one of the objects in the field which determines the directionality of attention, let us turn to the laws that predict where attention will be directed within a given field.

In Chapter 3 the states of subjective and objective self awareness were compared to a Gestalt figure in which two separately organized areas of the environment (referred to as a field from now on) alternately became the figure or the ground. Subjective self awareness represents the case in which the not-self is the figure. That is, it is the object in the focus of attention, while the self is the ground, that is, is not at the focal point of attention. In objective self awareness the relationship between the not-self and the self is reversed: the causal agent self is at the focus of attention and the not-self is perceived as ground. Originally the Gestalt figure was used to illustrate the dichotomy which we believe exists between the two states of consciousness. Presently we will assert that the laws that determine whether or not an area within a Gestalt configuration is focused upon are the laws that determine whether consciousness will be directed to the causal agent self or to the not-self.

Although a fully elaborated set of principles for attention is not available, the work of the Gestalt school, particularly that of Koffka (1935), gives us one clear statement. In a field which has stimulus properties such that perception organizes that field into two or more segregated regions, attention will focus upon the "stronger" region of the field. What does Koffka mean by "field," "segregated regions," and "stronger"? By "field" he means something

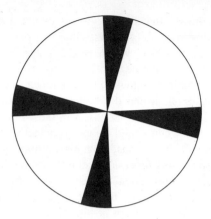

Figure 2.

roughly similar to our notion of scope of awareness. A person's perceptual field is simply all the objects and spaces which are present to the person's awareness. If a person were enclosed within a room, his field would be bounded by that room and would include all the objects in the room; thus, when Koffka says that the field is divided into two or more regions he is talking about the perceptual area that makes up the person's immediate scope of awareness being divided into two or more regions.

Koffka uses the notion of segregation to indicate that a person will organize the elements or microstructure of any given field into a particular pattern on the basis of the similarities and dissimilarities that exist within that field. The first law of this perceptual organization is that all elements in a given field that have similar properties will be grouped into units. His second law indicates that units that differ from each other will be perceived as segregated from each other. Figure 2 illustrates this law of similarities and dissimilarities. In this example, the field is segregated into two regions based on similarities and dissimilarities of color. Regions A and B are seen as units because there are color similarities in the microstructure in those particular regions of the field. Regions A and B are seen as separate because of their dissimilarities in color. Although we are using color as the major unit-forming property, Koffka clearly intends that similarities and dissimilarities on any dimension will be perceptually organized in terms of segregated units.

Knowing what a field is and how a field is organized into segregated units, we can now approach the final element in the statement concerning the direction attention will take in a given field. In general Koffka uses the notion of "stronger" to indicate a relationship between two segregated regions of a field. By calling one area of the field "stronger" he means that this area possesses stimulus properties by virtue of its relationship with the rest of the field, and that these stimulus properties cause attention to focus upon that area. To illustrate what is meant by "stronger" or "weaker" areas of the field, we offer the following example in which the field is dichotomized into two separate areas.

Let us say that a person goes to an art museum. As he enters a particular gallery his attention is drawn to one painting after another. After a while his attention may settle on one or two paintings that he wants to contemplate in depth. During the entire sequence of exploration and then fixation, the individual's scope of awareness is limited to the not-self and the direction in which consciousness focuses is determined only by the configuration of objects in the not-self. Now let us interject another person into the situation whose function is to stare at our art critic. As our original gentleman gazes about the room, his attention encounters the stare of this other person. This event expands the art critic's scope of awarenesss by forcing his consciousness to focus on the self, causing him to recognize that he also is an object in the world. However, even with the person's scope of attention expanded, the self as object must compete with other objects in the environment for the attention of consciousness. Let us assume in this case that for the art critic, the paintings exert a much stronger pull on his attention than he himself does. Consequently the person's attention is redirected toward the art gallery and he becomes subjectively self aware again. Once the art critic has returned his attention to the not-self, he is again likely to encounter the stare of the second person. Again he returns to momentary objective self awareness and again the stronger stimulus of the environment draws his attention back out. This oscillation may continue as long as the second person continues to stare at the art critic, or the potency of the stare may diminish over time because the art objects are so prominent that they override the weak tendency to focus on the self.

Let us now change the situation slightly so that the art critic's self is defined as "stronger" than the not-self. To accomplish this strengthening of the figure of the self, all that is necessary is to include a factor that makes the causal agent self seem very prominent to the individual in relation to the environment. Let us assume that the art critic has a scar which he considers very unattractive and that the scar is sufficient to strengthen the self so that it is stronger than the not-self in drawing attention to itself. Now, when he notices the man's stare, and is reminded of his status as an object, his causal agent self is a stronger figure than the not-self. Consequently, attention remains fixed to the self instead of being redirected to the not-self. Whereas in our previous example the forces that direct the focus of consciousness were flowing toward the art gallery, the forces are now flowing toward the causal agent self, and the art critic is much more likely to remain objectively self aware given the widening of his scope of awareness by the initial focus of attention upon the self. This of course does not mean that he will be eternally self aware. The appearance of a strongly figured object in the area of the not-self can realign his attention toward the not-self. Still, if no such "strong" object arises or the person takes no action, our art critic will remain objectively self aware.

The example indicates that attention will be drawn to what Koffka calls a strong area of a segregated field. As we saw, an area's weakness or strength depends upon its relationship to the other areas of the field. Under certain circumstances, the art critic was the strong area of the field. Under other circumstances, the not-self was the strong area. The question is, can the relationships between the separate regions of the field be specified so that predications can be made in advance about which region of a given field will be stronger and which weaker? Indeed Koffka offers us a specification which is germane to a group where there are differences of opinion. He says,

> Here we have a law intrinsic to the organization itself: if the conditions are such as to produce segregation of a larger and a smaller unit, the smaller will, *ceteris paribus*, become the figure (stronger); the larger, the ground (the weaker area) [p.191].

Having specified relative size as a relationship which makes an area strong or weak, Koffka elaborates;

> It is clear that the smaller the area of the figured part in a constant field, the greater its relative energy density with regard to the ground part. . . . This implies that there are degrees of *figuredness*, (strength) which we could define by the ratio of the energy densities, which indeed depends upon the ratio (size) of the areas [p. 193].

Thus Koffka gives us the general notion of relativity of size. The smaller one area of a field is in comparison to a second area of a field, the greater the force exerted upon attention to direct itself exclusively to that area. Figure 3 demonstrates this law with figures used by Koffka in his experimentation. As the ratio of the white to black increases from 1/1 to 1/20, attention is more

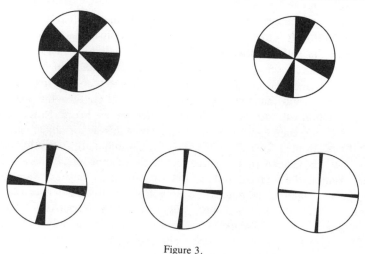

Figure 3.

strongly drawn toward the smaller or "stronger" area of the field. Now that we have a law that tells us something about the conditions that cause attention to be directed one way or another, let us see if it is any help in predicting where attention will focus in a given group.

Our problem is this: we know that a difference of opinion between two or more people causes the person to be aware of an error associated with that contradiction. From the principles of attribution theory we know that each person in the group will attribute this error to something in the environment. From the hypothesized relationship between focus of attention and attribution we know that if the individual member is subjectively self-aware he will attribute the error to something in the not-self area of the field. If the person is objectively self aware he will attribute error to himself. Thus if we could apply Koffka's law of directed attention to the structure of a group, we should be able to predict where attention will focus and thus predict where the error will be attributed.

GROUP CHARACTERISTICS AND
THE FOCUS OF ATTENTION

An important stipulation must be laid down before we apply Koffka's law of relative size to a group. In the following analysis, the individual's scope of awareness will be limited to the members of the group. We will henceforth pretend for the sake of simplicity that the only factors that affect the direction of attention are within the social field that is composed of the individuals that make up a given group. Clearly this simplification does not represent the complete state of affairs since nonsocial objects exert influence upon attention, but it is defensible on the grounds that the nonsocial field or context is the same for everyone in the group. Even more importantly, this assumption rules out the possibility that social entities not included within the immediate social field can effect the direction of attention. Later we will correct this simplification and deal with the case in which the effective social field includes social entities not present in the immediate group.

Our problem is to apply Koffka's rules to a social field where there are differences of opinion. This must be done in two parts. First, we might recall Koffka's rules of unit formation and segregation that operate in a field. In essence his formulation says that the person will organize elements that are similar to each other into unitary field areas and that these homogeneous units will be segregated from each other on the basis of differences. To illustrate this point he offers the analogy of a drop of oil placed in water. Because the various particles or elements of oil are similar to each other they tend to form a unitary area within the field. The water also tends to form a unitary part of the field which is segregated from the oil by the differences between the oil and water. If this law seems rather obvious it is probably because it fits the reality of cognitive organization very well. At any rate, the application of this principle to the group where there are differences of opinion is straightforward. Similar elements that exist within the groups will form unitary parts of the whole. These areas of similarity or homogeneity will be segregated from one another if one unitary area is different from any other unitary area. This means that in the simplest case where the group is polarized around two opinions, those individuals holding either position will perceive themselves grouped into a homogeneous zone of the field that is separated from the individuals holding the differing opinion. (It might be noted in regard to the forces of separation that Koffka was concerned about what kinds of apparent differences between homogeneous areas of the field created actual segregation in cognitive organization of the field. This issue presents no problem for the application of the law of differences and similarities to groups in which a difference of opinion exists because, as we saw in Chapter 3, a person directly experiences the incompatibility of his opinion with the differing opinion of the other.) Thus, for any group where there are differences of opinion, participants in that group will organize the field, consisting of the total aggregate of individuals comprising the group, into segregated areas of homogeneity based on similarities and dissimilarities of opinion which exist within the field.

Once the law of similarities and dissimilarities tells us how a social field will be organized it remains to determine where in the field attention will focus. Relying upon our earlier discussion of the stronger-weaker area distinction and focus of attention, we can now reach the conclusion that if any individual in a group is a part of one of the two segregated areas of the group-field that is the strong area of that field, the initial incidence of objective self awareness which widens the person's scope of attention to include himself will be followed by a prolonged focus of attention upon the self. By the same reasoning, individuals who are associated with the area of the field that appears as the weaker area of the field will also tend to focus attention upon the stronger area of the field rather than upon themselves.

Determining which segregated area of a field will be strong and which is weak is the second phase of applying Koffka's principles to a group. The primary law that pertains to the notion of stronger and weaker areas of the field is relative size. Koffka tells us that the smaller one area (A) is in comparison to the second area (B) of the field, the more attention will be pulled toward A. Thus it would seem plausible to apply this law to a group, that is, a social field, and conclude that in a group divided into two homogeneous areas on the basis of opinion similarity and opinion differences, the smaller one subgroup is in comparison to the second group, the stronger the tendency for the attention of all individuals in the group to be focused upon the smaller subgroup. Let us look at this application of the law of relative size more closely.

As we argued earlier, a group of individuals can be considered a social field. The elements that would totally constitute such a field would be the individuals within the group, each individual representing one element. Since the total size of any field is equal to the sum of the elements within that field, the size of a social field is equal to the sum of the individuals in the group. Given this definition of the size of a total field, it follows that the size of any subdivision of the field is a function of the proportion of the total number of elements found within each subgroup. Thus we reach the following conclusion: the ratio of the sizes of two subdivisions, which is essential to Koffka's law of relative size, can be computed on the basis of the number of elements found within each subdivision. In the case of a social field this value would correspond to the number of individuals found within each subgroup. To illustrate this point we can consider both a physical field and a social field.

The size of the field in any Gestalt figure can be represented as the sum of the individual elements in the field which Koffka refers to as the microstructure of a field. Let us assume that a field has a thousand elements in it. Then if the white portion of the field contains 750 elements, and the black, 250 elements, the ratio of the two subdivisions would be 3:1. Similarly, the size of a social field can be represented by the sum of the elements, the elements being individuals instead of points. If there were 15 individuals holding one opinion and five holding the other opinion, the ratio of the two areas would be 3:1. According to the law of relative size, the smaller area in both examples would draw a person's attention. The white area in the Gestalt figure would be focused upon, and the five individuals holding the same minority opinion would also be the focal point.

Thus the law of relative size applied to the group tells us where attention will focus. When a group is polarized into two separate subgroups with within-group similarity and between-group dissimilarity, the smaller that one subgroup is in terms of area compared to the other subgroup, the greater the tendency for attention of all group members to be directed at that subgroup. In other words, the members of the smaller group will increase in their tendency to be objectively self aware while the members of the larger group will increase in their tendency to be subjectively self aware.

We are now in a position to draw the final link between attribution of the error of the contradiction and focus of attention within a group. As we said earlier, causal attribution will follow the focus of attention. In the model describing the effects of differences of opinion upon the directionality of attention within a group, we see that attention will be directed toward the stronger area of the field. Further, the relative strength of the areas is determined by the law of relative size. Our conclusion must be that the members of the smaller subgroup, who we will call the minority, will be objectively self aware and will attribute error to themselves. Members of the larger group, who we will refer to as the majority, will be subjectively self aware and will also attribute the error of the contradiction to the minority position.

In order to get an overview of the concepts and relationships we are using, we offer the following example. For the sake of simplicity, the hypothetical situation will include four people and two opinion positions. Let us assume that these people meet in an experimentally familiar type of conformity situation in which there is to be group discussion on a particular issue. By means of a ruse, the experimenter leads the four people to believe that three of them have an identical position on the issue and the other has a strongly divergent opinion. According to the model developed thus far, the individual's awareness of the difference of opinion has two effects. The awareness of the two opinion positions causes all individuals to organize the group-field into segregated units, the three making up one unit, and the individual the other unit. Simultaneously with the new field organization each person becomes aware of the error associated with the contradiction posed by the presence of the two mutually exclusive opinions. Now begins the second stage of the process. When the members become aware of the existence of the difference of opinion, they broaden their scope of attention to the entire social field, which includes themselves. At this point the organization of the group field into areas of greater and smaller size comes into play. According to our model the individuals in the minority will become objectively self aware, and the individuals in the majority will focus attention upon the minority. From the theory of attribution we know that the locus of attribution of the error of the contradiction will be determined by the relative amount of time spent in either objective or subjective self awareness. To the extent that a person is focused upon himself, he will attribute the event in question to himself. To the extent that his focus of attention is directed toward the other, he will attribute the event to the other. Applied to our hypothetical example, this rule indicates that the individual who makes up the minority will tend to attribute the error of the contradiction to himself and that the majority will also tend to attribute the error of the contradiction to the deviate.

Our analysis of the mechanisms underlying conformity began with the notion of the error of the contradiction. After establishing that awareness of error would engage the attribution process, we sought a principle that would indicate where the person would attribute the error. By drawing on Koffka's principles of strongly and weakly figured regions of a field, it was determined that consciousness would focus on the smaller of the two subgroups. Drawing the diverse elements of the model together, it was predicted that the error of the contradiction would be attributed to the minority opinion position by both the majority and minority.

However, before tackling the consequences of attribution of error to self or to the other, we must qualify our position on the relationship between relative size and focus of attention.

THE LOCUS OF ERROR DECISION AND UNCERTAINTY

Up to this point we have assumed that attention in a divided opinion group was focused entirely in the direction of the strong area of the field. This was an oversimplification necessary for purpose of exposition. In reality, the person's attention will oscillate back and forth between the strong and weak areas of a divided field, social or otherwise. This presents a slight problem for our model since it is presumed that the attribution of error is a strict function of the focus of attention. If attention is focused alternately upon two areas, then error will be attributed to both of those areas. Translated into the hypothetical situation of three persons against one, the strict application of this rule means that attribution of error would occur partially in the wrong direction. The individual will spend some amount of time focusing upon the group and attributing error to the group; the group will spend some amount of time focusing upon itself, and attributing error to itself. To allow for this oscillation of attention between self and other we need to introduce a new principle which predicts the proportion of any given time span which the members of the group will spend in self focused and other focused attention. This principle can be stated as follows: The proportion of time which attention will focus on the strong area of the field and on the weak area of the field is a function of the ratio of the subgroup sizes. In a group divided into a size ratio of 3:1, the group members' attention will be focused upon the "strong" area of the field approximately 75 percent of the time and upon the "weak" area approximately 25 percent of the time. The deviate would be attributing the error to himself 75 percent of the time and to the majority 25 percent of the time. Likewise, the majority will attribute error to the minority 75 percent of the time and to itself 25 percent of the time.

This more subtle understanding of the behavior of attention in a social field calls for some modifications in the conceptual model. We can no longer say that the error of the contradiction is totally attributed to one area of the field. We must now speak in terms of a process through which the person determines whether the error belongs to himself or to the other, given the presence of data which indicate both are in error.

The motivational force behind the entire attributional process is the need to control or understand the world. The sudden awareness of error engages the attributional process which then continues until a cause for the error is determined. Looking at it from the group member's point of view, he sometimes thinks he is in error and sometimes thinks the other is in error. He will be in a state of tension until a decision is made. We would argue that such a decision will be reached through some information processing system that handles all such situations involving contradictory data. In other words, the mind includes a system corresponding to a set of rules. These rules determine the yes-or-no, self-or-other decision where there are data to support both conclusions. This system is judgmental, probably has no motivational energy of its own, and is brought into the service of the drive states that require an either-or conclusion. This system would serve the man who needs a car but sees both good and bad points in each automobile he examines, or the man who sees himself in error part of the time and the other in error part of the time.

In order to predict the either/or decision, which in the present case we will call the "locus of error decision," we need to know the principle on which the hypothetical decision system operates.

Anderson's (1965) model of impression formation hypothesizes that people arrive at evaluative judgments of target stimuli by averaging the quantity and evaluative intensity of the differing sets of information available. If a subject is presented with two highly favorable and two moderately favorable adjectives that describe a target person, he will form a less favorable impression of the person than if he were presented with two highly favorable adjectives alone. In an experiment designed to test this model, Bossart and DiVesta (1966) found that the higher the ratio of positive to negative adjectives describing a target person, the more positive the subject's evaluation of that person. If the subject was presented with a set of positive and negative data about the target person in the ratio of five positive adjectives to one negative adjective, his impression was more favorable than the impression of the subject who received descriptive information in a ratio of two positive to one negative, which in turn was higher than the impression of the subject who received data in the ratio of one positive to one negative. We would argue that the principle which Anderson sets forth for impression formation is the rule by which any set of contradictory data is handled by the individual, and is directly applicable to the problem of predicting the locus of error decision. For instance, the data indicating the other was in error could be substituted for the positive adjectives in the Bossart and DiVesta experiment. Similarly, the data indicating that the self was in error could be substituted for the negative adjectives. The result of this substitution would be the prediction that as the ratio of other/self increased, there would be an increasing tendency for the locus of error decision to locate the error of the contradiction in the other. Conversely, if the substitution were reversed so that the data indicating error to self replaced the positive adjectives, the prediction would be just the opposite. As the ratio of self/other increased, the person's tendency to locate the error in himself would increase.

The Anderson model requires that the contradictory data be quantified. This presents no problem, since the data of error to other versus error to self are quantified by the length of time the individual spends in a particular mode of consciousness. If an individual spent three times as much time in objective self awareness as in subjective self awareness, the ratio of the self/other data would be three to one. Thus the averaging model of impression formation generates predictions for the locus of error decision in any given social field. If the ratio of the majority/minority were 10/1, the prediction would be that all members would locate the error in the minority and with greater intensity than if the ratio were 2/1.

Applying the rule by which a person will make his locus of error decision entails a decision about the crucial ratio at which the impression will flip from other to self, or vis-a-versa. At the ratio of 5:1 or 3:1, or even 2:1 it is fairly certain that the locus of error will follow the predominant set of data, whether to self or other. It is more difficult to say anything certain about the ranges where the two sets of data converge towards equality. At a ratio of 1:1 or 1.5:1 we feel on shaky grounds in making a clear prediction. For the present, however, we will assume that the crucial ratio is 1:1. If the data are arranged so that the ratio is 1.2:1 (self/other), the person will decide that the error of the contradiction belongs to him. At 1.2:1 (other/self), the person will see the other as incorrect.

UNCERTAINTY

The averaging model of impression formation implies that a person forms impressions of varying intensity depending upon the ratio of the divergent data. The typical scale used in Anderson's experimentation is one involving the degree of favorableness usually ranging from very favorable to very unfavorable. It is predicted that a person exposed to four highly favorable adjectives and one moderately unfavorable adjective will form a more favorable impression of the target person than will a person exposed to four highly favorable adjectives and three moderately unfavorable adjectives.

How are we to take the intensity of impression into consideration in our model? Since we are dealing with a dichotomous variable, self and other, the concept of "uncertainty" is more applicable than intensity. A person will always decide that either he or the other is in error, but the decision will be held with more or less uncertainty depending upon the ratio of the contradictory data. For example, if one person spends 80 percent of the time focused on the other and a second person spends only 60 percent focused on the other, both people will decide that the other is in error but the first will hold that decision with more certainty than the second.

The justification for the concept of uncertainty lies in both reasoning and experimental evidence. Since Anderson's averaging model is a fairly good predictor of impression formation, we know that the individual uses both sets of data in arriving at his conclusions. This implies that in the case of an either/or decision, the person does not forget, deny, repress, or in any other way obliterate the evidence that is contradictory to the direction the impression takes. A person who spends 80 percent of his time focused upon the other still remains cognizant of the data that indicate he himself is in error. We feel that this awareness of data that is contradictory to the decision will serve to make a person uncertain about the validity of that decision, and, further, that this uncertainty is an inverse function of the ratio of contradictory data. Thus, to the extent that a person is exposed to data that are inconsistent with the decision, he will be uncertain of the decision.

The previous assumption about the relationship between the ratio of contradictory data and level of uncertainty is taken from choice certainty theory. In an elaboration of the Mills and Ross experiment (1964), O'Neal and Mills (1969) state that

> Certainty that an action is best is assumed to be determined by the proportion of cognitions favoring that action; the higher the proportion, the greater the certainty [p. 348].

The theory also holds the converse to be true. A decreasing proportion of favorable to unfavorable cognitions about an action decreases certainty about that action. Barker (1946) found that uncertainty is greater when the attractiveness of the alternatives is close than when the attractiveness of the alternatives is disparate, thus confirming the theoretical assumption. In addition, successful experiments based on choice certainty theory further indicate that this assumption has validity (Mills, 1965; Mills & Jellison, 1968; O'Neal & Mills, 1969).

The assumption that uncertainty is a function of the ratio of contradictory data provides a method for determining the degree of uncertainty that accompanies a given data distribution. Later in the chapter we will use the level of uncertainty to make certain predictions about behavior in a group situation where there are differences of opinion.

Chapter 5

CONFORMITY: CONSEQUENCES OF ATTRIBUTION OF ERROR TO SELF AND OTHER

CONSEQUENCES OF ATTRIBUTION OF ERROR TO SELF AND TO OTHER

Applying objective self awareness theory to a situation in which there are differences of opinion, we have concluded that the error of the contradiction will be attributed either to the self or the other, depending on the configuration of the social field. To complete the application of objective self awareness to conformity behavior it remains to understand what effects stem from the individual's attribution of error to his own opinion (the minority condition). In addition, our analysis has indicated that in a group situation where there are individuals who attribute the error of the contradiction to themselves, there will also be individuals who attribute the error to the other (the majority condition). Since this event occurs in the context of the original concern of Chapters 4 and 5, explaining why one person alters his opinion in the direction of the other, we will devote a separate section to the effects that stem from attributing error to the other. First we will deal with the consequences of attributing error to the self.

According to the present theory, any change in actual behavior or attitude is motivated by the person's attempt to avoid the negative affect generated by his awareness of a discrepancy between a standard of correctness and the actual attitude or behavior. If objective self awareness theory is to explain conformity behavior, then it must do so within this basic motivational framework. At the present juncture we know, by previous analysis, that the person who is in a minority subgroup within the group field will attribute error to his opinion. It is reasonable to believe that an errorful opinion would be discrepant from some personal standard. But to understand why the person will conform to others, we must first understand the precise content of the standard that applies to an incorrect opinion. Knowing the precise nature of the standard, we can predict that the person will adjust his behavior in the direction of that standard and in no other direction.

It appears reasonable to posit within each person the existence of a standard of correctness that prescribes that opinions about the world should be correct. In fact Festinger makes just such an assumption by suggesting that it is important to the organism's survival that his opinions be correct (1954). This is an acceptable formulation except that it considers only the opinion and fails to look at the relationship between an opinion and the person who holds that opinion. Consequently, the fact that opinions are a manifestation of the causal agent self's interaction with the world is overlooked. For example, when a person believes that something is good or bad, or that such and such state of affairs exists, the opinion itself is merely a reflection of the causal agent self's perceptual and mediational operations upon the world. Given this relationship, treating an opinion as if it were a separate entity that could be right or wrong apart from the source of the opinion is not permissible. When an opinion is judged by a person as correct or incorrect, he is actually passing judgment on the perceptual and mediational components of his causal agent self. Therefore we must look for a standard of correctness that applies to the causal agent self and not to a notion of correctness abstracted from the self.

An appropriate standard of correctness can be easily identified. Following the general direction of Festinger's original idea, it is justifiable to assume that any organism that seeks to interact successfully with its environment must do so on the strength of its ability to correctly understand that environment. Thus, implicit within any organism is an imperative stating that the organism's perceptual and mediational components should yield beliefs and attitudes that are veridical with reality. Using this implicit imperative as a standard of correctness, we can now specify the nature of the discrepancy between an opinion that a person believes is incorrect and this categorical standard of correctness. When the person attributes error to his opinion, he is attributing error to the perceptual and mediational components of the causal agent self. Any error within these components is discrepant from the person's implicit standard of correctness that prescribes that the causal agent self should reflect a veridical or correct view of the world.

REDUCTION OF THE DISCREPANCY: PERCEPTUAL REORGANIZATION

Given that the person who attributes error to his opinion is aware that his causal agent self is discrepant from the ideal, he can reduce the negative affect attendant upon such a discrepancy by altering his actual behavior so that it agrees with the standard. The question is, can he alter his perception and thinking that produced the opinion that he considers incorrect so that his causal agent self produces a correct opinion? If this behavior is possible, the discrepancy will be reduced and the negative affect eliminated. Alternately stated, the theory of objective self awareness predicts that the person will seek to change, reorganize, or otherwise alter his perception of the original object toward a perception the person can consider correct. Let us apply this process to a concrete situation.

Imagine a situation in which 10 people are discussing the virtues of the war in Vietnam and suppose that nine persons hold the opinion that the war is wrong while the other believes that it is correct. According to the previous reasoning, the organization of the field into two distinct areas, pro-war and con-war, should result in the pro-war individual attributing the error of the contradictory opinions to his own opinion. From the argument concerning the relationship between the opinion and the causal agent self, we can conclude that he has actually attributed error to the perceptual and mediational components of the self in the sense that he believes his causal agent self to be functioning improperly. Following this attributional decision, the person becomes aware of the discrepancy between the actual performance of those components of the self and that standard of correctness. This awareness produces negative affect which the person must reduce. According to our model, this attempt to reduce negative affect will first take the form of the person's attempt to change the performance of the self so that it will yield a correct opinion. How will this attempt to change the perception manifest itself?

There are several examples pertinent to this question. First, there is a general observation that can be made about people who learn that they have misperceived a situation. If a person attempts to solve a riddle or puzzle and then is informed that his solution, which is nothing more than an opinion, is incorrect, there usually follows a period in which the person will ask for more information, ask if he has understood the problem correctly, will look at the puzzle or riddle again, etc. A second example entails the Asch experimental records of the deviate's behavior immediately following the crucial trials in which the person learns that the majority perception differs from his own. This recorded behavior bears out the general observation well. Summing up his observations Asch (1952) writes,

> . . . the subjects now look with greater care and become more attentive and scrupulous in observing and comparing. They act to increase the clearness of their perceptions and judgments . . . . A particularly interesting example of this tendency is the desire expressed by a few of the more spontaneous subjects to see the lines again and to measure them. Some suddenly jump up and approach the cards [p. 463].

These examples indicate that the person's attempt to alter his performance of the self manifests itself in a reexamination of the object of perception; if the object of the opinion is a real object, as in the Asch experiment, he would want to examine the object from different angles and perhaps through different sensory modalities. In our hypothetical case of the disagreement over war, the person would want to reexamine the facts about the war in Vietnam, or perhaps seek new information from the other members of the group.

Even as the person in our example attempts to alter his ideas about war by reexamination of the object of perception, he faces a serious difficulty. By the previous analysis of the effects of a difference of opinion within a group, an opinion cannot be considered correct unless it agrees with the majority. The mere fact that a person holds an opinion which differs from that of the majority eventually leads the person to attribute error to that opinion and his causal agent self. Whether or not the opinion is true or factually correct in objective reality is immaterial in the face of the psychological forces at work. The inevitability of this psychological process means that the person's success in changing his initial perception of the object of opinion to another and different perception of the object may be to no avail. He will be forced continually to attribute error to his own opinion as long as that opinion is different from the majority opinion. We can imagine our hypothetical person attempting to force a change in his perception of war by reexamination, reflection, etc., and eventually coming to a second and different opinion about war. Then, to his consternation, he is again forced to attribute error to his position by virtue of the new contradiction between his revised opinion and the still differing opinion of the majority of the group. This new attribution of error begins the motivational process suggested by objective self awareness anew.

Is there any solution for the person? Obviously there is. If the man in the group should happen to arrive at an opinion that was in agreement with the other members of the group, he would cease attributing error to his opinion because there would no longer be any contradiction between the two opinions. Thus, if upon reexamination of war, the individual were to reach the conclusion that war was bad and so stand in agreement with the others in the group, all motivational forces to alter his opinion generated by his awareness of the discrepancy between the actual self and the ideal self would end. The discrepancy would no longer exist. Since no motivation (due to objective self awareness) is present within the person, his opinion would become stable and the conformity-behavioral sequence would be completed.

Thus the motivational component within objective self awareness theory predicts that the person's awareness of a discrepancy between the performance of his causal agent self and his standard of correctness for that self can be reduced if the person reorganizes his perception of the object so that his new opinion coincides with the dominant opinion. Unfortunately this notion is impaired by the absence of a direct causal link between the person's awareness of the discrepancy between self and standard and the resolution of that discrepancy. Without question, the person's opinion will be unstable as long as he believes the causal agent self has misperceived the situation. But there is no direct connection between this instability and the possibility that he may come to perceive the object in the same way the others in the group perceive the object. For example, a person may be convinced that his initial opinion about an object is incorrect. He initially thought it was a shade of blue but now believes that seeing the object as blue is incorrect, that his causal agent self has made a mistake, by virtue of the fact that six other people see it as red. So, in accordance with our hypothesis, he attempts to alter the performance of the self. But as we imagine this hypothetical person reexamining the object, we must keep in mind that the theory cannot predict whether or not the person can (1) bring about a change in the perception of this object at all or (2) if there is a change that it will always be in the direction of the majority opinion. About these intermediary events, the theory can say nothing. Since the causal link between the fact of a self-standard discrepancy and the change of opinion is not direct, we must be satisfied with a general statement about the person's reduction of discrepancy.

1. The minority person's opinion will be unstable because the person believes his causal agent self is in error.

2. The person will attempt to alter his perception of the object of the opinion. If the attempt to alter the perception is successful, the resulting opinion may or may not agree with the other members of the group.

3. The person's opinion, changed or original, will continue to be unstable until he hits upon a perception that is congruent with the group.

Although the person may be able to reduce the discrepancy by changing his perception of the target object, he might also find himself in the predicament where he is unable to alter his original opinion so that it agrees with the dominant point of view. What can the person do if this contingency arises? The theory predicts that the person will at some point shift from attempting to decrease the discrepancy to attempting to avoid the stimuli which generate objective self awareness. The shift will occur at the point at which negative affect can no longer be tolerated, which in fact is always reached when the person decides that the discrepant behavior is unchangeable. We can postulate that if a person reaches a stage in which his perception of the object appears intractable, he will begin seeking to avoid the stimuli that are producing objective self awareness.

Before discussing the specific behavior involved in avoidance it would be helpful to recall exactly what source generates objective self awareness in this situation. From the previous reasoning we know that it is the presence of a difference of opinion within the group that creates objective self awareness by initiating the awareness of self as an object in the world and by forcing the deviate's consciousness to remain fixed upon himself through segregation of the group field into weaker and stronger units. Thus it is the difference of opinion that the person must avoid if he is to successfully avoid objective self awareness.

Illustrated by the experiment on avoidance of objective self awareness (Chapter 2), the person's first option is clear; he can simply leave the group. By leaving the group, the person avoids the difference of opinion, thereby avoiding the awareness of the discrepancy between the performance of self and the standard of correctness for that performance.

In many cases, actual avoidance behavior will no doubt relieve the negative affect that the person suffers from while leaving his original opinion intact. But avoiding a group both physically and psychologically may not be easy to do under certain conditions. There can be physical and sociological barriers which prevent the person from leaving the group. There can be other forces operating in the situation such as liking for members of the group which push the person toward the group, and, finally, there can be the difficulty of leaving the group psychologically even though an actual physical distance has been achieved. Let us look more closely at these possible constraints which work against the person's tendency to leave the group.

Physical and sociological barriers fall within the boundaries of Lewin's (1935) conflict situation in which the person is faced with a field having two distinct and negatively valenced regions. There is the original situation or object toward which the person is negatively disposed, and there is a negatively valenced ring or area surrounding the person. In effect, the individual in this circumstance is caught between two areas he would like to avoid. Because he is encircled by a physical or sociological barrier which is more negative than the object, he is forced to remain in the original situation. Lewin indicates that the most primitive type of barrier that can prevent the person from leaving the field is the physical. The person may be obliged to stay in the group because he and the members of the group are locked up. Such would be the case when the members of a jury are physically forced to stay together until a decision is reached. However, he continues with the following:

> In general, however, the barriers are "sociological." The barriers surrounding the child are the instruments of power possessed by the adult in virtue of his social position and the inner relationship existing between him and the child [p. 126].

Although Lewin is speaking about the relationship between children and adults, this type of conflict holds for relationships between adults. Thus a person can be prevented from leaving the group by the implicit or explicit threat of punishment from a powerful other.

A situation in which the person wishes to avoid the group but is also attracted to the group falls into a second category of conflict Lewin has described:

> There exists finally the possibility that one of the two oppositely directed field vectors derives from a positive, the other from a negative valence [p. 123].

This type of constraint may occur whenever the group offers rewards to the person on dimensions other than similarity of opinions. Back (1951) has employed the term "cohesiveness" to describe the force which pushes the person toward the group. He specifically defines cohesiveness as the "resultant forces which are acting on the members to stay in a group." He lists three general attributes a group may possess that attract members to the group: similarity to other members (other than on the dimension in question), intrinsic reward value of a group such as prestige or status, and the ability of the group to mediate goals which the person seeks to attain. Thus, a person may not be able to avoid the group situation that causes negative affect because he must stay in the group to attain certain desired ends.

A third type of barrier that may prevent the person from avoiding the difference of opinion is the person's inability to avoid the group psychologically. A person may leave the group physically but be unable to put the difference of opinion out of his mind. Lewin describes this situation in the following way:

> The power of the adult . . . (has) so penetrated the whole life-sphere of the child that areas in which he (the child) can move freely and independently are as good as nonexistent. It is unnecessary to hinder the child's going-out-of-the-field by the erection of an outer barrier because the function of this barrier has spread out over the entire field [p. 131].

Lewin's description indicates that the presence of the adult, or in our case, the group, permeates the person's life space eliminating physical proximity as a prerequisite for impact upon the individual. Unfortunately, no research has been done that might elucidate what characteristics cause a group to spread throughout a person's life space or under what conditions it might or might not do so. At least for now, full understanding of this type of barrier is not possible.

Any of these three types of barriers can frustrate the person's attempt to avoid objective self awareness by avoiding the situation in which there are differences of opinion. Under these circumstances of constraint the person is forced to remain in the group, at least psychologically, and must reduce the negative affect generated by his awareness of the discrepancy between the causal agent self and his standard of correctness in some manner other than perceptual reorganization (which has already proven to be an impossibility) or avoidance of the difference of opinion. His only remaining alternative is to replace his incorrect perception of the object with a conception of the object that does not stem from his own organismic reaction.

REDUCTION OF THE DISCREPANCY: ADOPTING A CONCEPTION

It will be recalled that the standard of correctness that applies in a difference of opinion situation can be stated in the following way: the causal agent self ought to produce opinions about the world that are correct. We saw that when this standard was applied to a person's initial organismic perception that he believed to be incorrect, he attempted to alter his organismic response to the object by reexamination and reflection. But should this method fail to produce a satisfactory change in the person's perception, it should be clear that the possibilities for achieving a correct opinion are not exhausted. There remains the perhaps uniquely human ability to hold a conception about an object that is not founded upon the individual's organismic perception of that object. A completely naive layman who has never been in a laboratory, who has never even seen the evidence upon which a scientist bases his perception of the universe, can nonetheless hold the conception that a table which he perceives to be solid, firm, and continuous, is actually composed of tiny particles bounded together through space by energy. Many Americans can believe that there is an international Communist conspiracy oriented toward taking over the world, even though they may never have met a Communist or have any direct information on the nature of Communism. The examples could continue indefinitely, but the point is that an individual can hold a conception about an object, and believe that conception to be true even though the content of his beliefs is in no way based upon his actual perceptual experience of that object.

In summary, we have the following situation: the causal agent self is operating under the dictate of the standard of correctness which states that the causal agent self should operate to reflect a correct picture of the world. There are no specific guidelines implied by this standard that specify how the causal agent self is to arrive at a ''correct'' view of the world. Assuming that perception and conception can equally satisfy the need to know about the world, the person can reduce any discrepancy between the self and the standard of correctness by replacing his perception with a conception of which he is not the original source. Since the person forgoes or overrides his own perceptual process, this conception must come from somewhere outside him. We suggest that the group's opinion will most likely be the source from which the person will borrow a conception.

Given that the person could be described as in a state of intentional acquiescence, the next problem is to determine which opinion he will adopt. Since the essence of the categorical standard of correctness is that all opinions should be veridical, the person would attempt to seek out an opinion that is demonstrably correct. But within the context of the situation in which a difference of opinion is present, the "correct" opinion is one that does not result in a prolonged state of objective self awareness. This condition determines the outcome of the person's discrepancy-reducing behavior. The person will eventually adopt the opinion that reduces the contradiction and includes him with the larger part of the field. He will adopt the opinion of the dominant group.

As with the first method of discrepancy reduction, perceptual reorganization, adopting a conception results in what could be described as conformity. The person who is initially discrepant from the majority of the group comes to alter his opinion in the direction of the majority opinion.

Having introduced three possible courses of action for the minority person, a question arises as to the sequence in which these various options will occur. The order of occurrence that has been suggested is that first there will be an attempt at perceptual reorganization, then avoidance of the situation upon failure to successfully reorganize, and, finally, adoption of a conceptual point of view if avoidance is blocked. The first and second stage of the full sequence follow directly from previous motivational considerations. That adoption of a conception should occur only as a last resort needs further explanation.

Since an appropriate conception of an object satisfies the categorical standard of correctness as well as an organismic perception, why doesn't the person move directly from an unsuccessful attempt to reorganize his incorrect perception to the adoption of the group's point of view? Why would there be an intermediary avoidance tendency? The answer to this question lies in the resistance of the direct sensory impression to being replaced. If a person actually sees two lines as equal in length, the fact that he believes the perception to be incorrect does not make the visual impression disappear. Since a conception of an object is as real as the perception, adopting the group's perception comes into direct conflict with the residual organismic perception. We are of the opinion that this conflict must of itself be unpleasant. Thus, the prospect of adopting a conception to relieve the negative affect caused by the incorrect opinion is itself negatively valenced. In a situation where the remedy to an ailment is itself unpleasant, the person will simply try to leave the field altogether. Consider the person with a mild tooth ache who hates the pain involved in a filling. Rather than suffer the cure, the person tries to avoid thinking about the tooth ache. If this maneuver is successful, the person avoids both sources of pain. The deviating person in the group tries the same tactic of evasion. To further pursue the analogy, the person with a tooth ache will endure the momentary pain the dentist causes him only if he can't avoid the larger pain of the tooth ache. The minority person will likewise suffer the momentary unpleasantness of adopting a conception that is in conflict with his perception only when he can't avoid the conditions that precipitated the original negative affect. Thus the order of behavior will be: (1) the attempt to reorganize, (2) the attempt to avoid, and (3) adoption of a conceptual point of view.

The analysis of the sequence of behavioral options completes the attempt to understand what happens to a person who attributes the error of the contradiction to himself. Next we will consider the behavior of the individuals who attribute error to the other, that is, those in the position of being a majority.

CONSEQUENCES OF ATTRIBUTING ERROR TO THE OTHER

In order to understand the behavior of the majority member, we must keep in mind two postulates: (1) the majority has decided that the locus of the error belongs in the deviating minority, and (2) the majority spends some amount of time in objective self awareness. Let us explore the behavioral consequences of these two factors. We should recall that depending upon the relative size of the minority and majority, the majority will spend varying lengths of time in objective self awareness. As the size of the minority increases, the length of time in objective self awareness increases for the members of the majority. We will eventually have to deal with all of the cases from a negligible minority to a sizable minority, but for the present we will use an example in which the minority makes up about 25 percent of the group.

In concluding the first part of our discussion on attribution of error we noted that in a group divided 75 percent to 25 percent on an issue, the majority would spend some amount of time in objective self awareness, although the larger portion would be spent in subjective self awareness. We noted that the majority would attribute error both to itself and to the deviating individual in a proportion equal to the ratio of the size of the two opinion positions but would decide, when the majority was fairly large, that the minority was in error. We also indicated that the summation process did not result in the obliteration of the weaker data. This principle would imply that the majority person totally locates the error in the other, but remains aware that 25 percent of his information indicates the opposite decision.

The continued awareness of the negative data has an important ramification. To the extent that the majority member finds the error attributed to himself, he, like the minority person, will be aware of a discrepancy between his opinion and the standard of correctness that demands that the causal agent self be correct. This discrepancy in turn produces negative affect which the majority will attempt to avoid.

AVOIDANCE OF NEGATIVE AFFECT BY THE MAJORITY

In any group situation where there are differences of opinion, the negative affect contingent upon the presence of differences can be reduced by eliminating the contradictory opinions. The minority member can bring about group uniformity by changing his opinion toward the majority. The majority members can bring about uniformity by persuading the minority to conform to them. That the majority does in fact attempt to persuade the minority that its opinion is wrong has been empirically demonstrated numerous times. Objective self awareness offers a theoretical understanding of this behavior.

The motive that pushes the majority to take action is the negative affect experienced through awareness of discrepancy. But from the majority point of view, the discrepancy exists because of the presence of the minority's opinion. Just as the deviate locates the source of negative affect in his opinion, the majority members also locate the source of negative affect in the minority's opinion, because they locate the error of the contradiction in the minority. Since the majority members already consider the minority to be in error, they will move to eliminate the cause of the negative affect by altering the minority's opinon—hence the persuasive communication directed to the minority.

Not only can the persuasive attempts of the majority be predicted and explained, but the characteristics of the majority communication are also implied by the theory. Since the majority sees the minority as being in error, its communications to the minority will essentially be in the form of attacks upon the minority's position. The members of the larger group will spend little time articulating their own beliefs. The main thrust of their persuasive attempts will be to demonstrate to the minority that its position is untenable.

A second characteristic feature of group communication will be the tendency for the majority to initiate conversation, note writing, or whatever. This almost aggressive impulse is a consequence of the majority's belief that the minority is the source of the negative affect and is, at the same time, in error. The admonition, "Let he who is without sin cast the first stone" is intended to deter hasty retribution. It would fall on deaf ears were it addressed to the members of a large majority confronting a deviate. They know where the fault lies and will move quickly toward a remedy.

Depending upon the circumstances, the minority may or may not change its opinion to agree with the majority. If the minority changes and opinion uniformity is achieved, all self awareness-produced motivation in the majority ceases. If uniformity is not achieved, the majority must take other measures to eliminate its own negative affect.

Just as the minority can avoid negative affect by avoiding the situation, the majority members can also avoid the discrepancy by absenting themselves from a situation where there are differences of opinion. However, in the case where the error is attributed to the other, reducing negative affect by avoidance means rejecting the offending opinion from the group. Thus, if the minority does not alter its opinion, the majority will attempt to force minority members out of the group.

COMPARISON OF MINORITY AND MAJORITY BEHAVIOR

Thus far we have discussed the behavioral consequences of attributing error to self, the minority situation, and of attributing error to the other, the majority situation. Comparing the behavior of the two groups we see that the minority will tend to change its opinion toward the majority and the majority will tend not to change its opinion at all. In terms of intragroup communication, the majority will tend to initiate verbal or written intercourse with the minority and the communication will typically be an attack upon the minority's position. The minority will tend not to initiate communication. If minority members communicate to the majority at all, it will be from a defensive posture. Rather than attack the majority opinion, they will attempt to marshal support for the correctness of their own opinions, and only then in response to the verbal offensive from the larger group.

Both subgroups will enter into the avoidance stage of conflict resolution when the minority cannot or will not change its opinion. The minority will attempt to escape the differences of opinion; the majority will attempt to reject or otherwise remove the source of the difference of opinion. In a room containing a group with a sizable majority deployed against a small but unyielding minority, the larger group will tend to stand its ground, trying to force the other to leave. This attempt should meet with fair success because the deviate will be trying to escape from the group at the same time the majority is trying to get rid of him. Since the psychological forces in a split group operate to locate the error in the deviate, the majority will always tend to make the other go from them and the minority will always tend to escape from the other.

As we have seen, holding either one of two opinion positions in a divided group results in a measure of negative affect. This negative affect is a general state of unpleasant tension which the person tries to reduce by eliminating its sources. Thus group behavior is determined by where the individual decides the source of negative affect is located, which is in turn determined by the locus of error decision. Locating the error in the self implies opinion change, escape, or defensive communication depending on circumstances. Locating the error in the other implies offensive communication or ejection, depending on what conditions prevail in the situation.

Only those behaviors implied by the two possible locus of error decisions are psychologically possible for the individual in either the majority or minority. However, since the various behaviors are shaped by the locus of error decision, the strength of the individual's tendency to carry out these actions must vary as a function of the degree of uncertainty with which the decision is held. With respect to the majority: if uncertainty that the other is in error is high, the tendency to persuade or reject is low. With regard to the minority: if uncertainty that the self is in error is high, the tendency to change one's opinion or escape is correspondingly low. Since the level of uncertainty attached to the locus of error decision is a function of the relative subgroup size, the strength of any individual's tendency to change his opinion, communicate, or avoid will be determined by the ratio of the minority and majority group sizes.

The following subsection will delineate the predictions of the objective self awareness model with regard to the three typical modes of behavior as the ratio of the divided group field is varied between $x/y = 1/\infty$ and $x/y = 1/1$ where y represents the size of the majority and x the minority.

The relationship between subgroup ratio and uncertainty can be stated as a theorem: As the sizes of the minority and majority approach equality, the degree of uncertainty attached to the locus-of-error decision increases for both the majority and minority. The converse of this proposition is also true. As the size of the majority diverges from that of the minority, the degree of uncertainty which is attached to the majority and minority locus-of-error decision is decreased. The theorem and its converse are based on previous reasoning which we will briefly recapitulate.

As the size ratio of the minority and majority approach one, the amount of time that both groups spend in subjective and objective self awareness approaches equality. As the time spent in objective and subjective self awareness approaches equality, attribution of error to self and other approaches equality. At a size ratio of one, individuals in both the majority and minority are attributing error to themselves and the other equally. The uncertainty factor of the locus of error decision is based upon a weighting process. When the amount of attribution of error to self and attribution to other approaches equality, the uncertainty factor will approach its maximum intensity.

The opposite also holds true. As the size of the minority and majority diverge, the time the majority spends in objective self awareness decreases, and the time the minority spends in objective self awareness increases. As a result, each subgroup's uncertainty about the locus-of-error decision decreases.

An example can illustrate this relationship. Let us suppose that a group is divided into two opinions and that we can add and subtract from the sizes of the two positions, while maintaining a constant group size of twenty. Let us begin with 19 for one opinion position and 1 for the other opinion position. This configuration would produce a relative weighting of one part error to self to 19 parts error to other for the majority, and one part error to other to 19 parts error to self for the minority. Thus the locus of error decision would be in the direction of the one minority person with an uncertainty factor of .05 for both the minority and majority. As we increase the size of the minority and decrease the size of the majority to a ratio of 5/15, the locus of error decision will still be in the direction of the minority, but the uncertainty factor has increased to .33. This means that the individuals in both the majority and minority locate the error in the minority, but the decision is made with some hesitancy in view of the relatively large amount of negative data of which all members are aware. As we further increase the size of the minority to nine, thereby decreasing the size of the majority to 11, it becomes (1) more difficult to say where the locus of error may be placed, and (2) more likely that any such impression, once made, will carry almost a maximum amount of uncertainty.

Now that we have extended the model to encompass all values of the independent variable of ratio of subgroup size, we want to link the theorem and its converse to the major dependent variables: opinion change, communication, and avoidance of the other.

OPINION CHANGE

Opinion change is a function of both the locus of error and the uncertainty factor. Only when an individual finds the locus of error in himself will opinion change occur. Thus any majority, almost regardless of its size, will tend not to change its opinion. For the minority members, the tendency to change opinion is increased by any decrease in the uncertainty factor, and decreased by any increase in uncertainty. Thus we have the following relationship: As the size of the minority converges toward equality with the majority, the minority tendency toward opinion change decreases; as the size of the minority and majority diverge, the minority's tendency toward opinion change increases.

COMMUNICATION

The tendency toward intragroup communication can be broken down into two measures. First, there is the tendency to initiate communication. Second, there is the amount the two subgroups communicate to each other following initiation of communication. As we know, the tendency to initiate communication is controlled by the locus-of-error decision. If the self is seen as incorrect, there will be no tendency to initiate conversation. If the other is seen as incorrect, there will be a tendency to start verbal or written exchange with the other.

Further, the tendency to begin communication is a function of the degree of uncertainty of the belief that the other is incorrect. Thus we have the following relationship: As the sizes of majority and minority diverge, the majority tendency to initiate conversation increases. The converse also holds true.

Once the majority initiates communication, the amount of intragroup exchange will be determined by the degree of uncertainty within the situation. As uncertainty decreases for majority members they will become increasingly sure that the minority is in error, and their attempts to persuade the minority will increase. As uncertainty decreases for the minority members, they will become increasing aware of the error of their position. Consequently, the tendency to defend their position will decrease. Thus we have the following relationship between the ratio of the subgroup sizes and the tendency to communicate: As the sizes of the minority and majority diverge, the majority will tend to increase communication while the minority will tend to decrease communication. The converse also holds true.

AVOIDANCE OF THE SITUATION

If the minority members cannot reorganize their perceptions, both subgroups will enter into the avoidance phase of the group process. The majority will attempt to eject the minority and the minority will try to escape. The degree to which this tendency manifests itself is again a function of uncertainty. As the majority becomes more certain that the minority is in error, the latency and intensity of their tendency to eject the minority will increase. As the minority people become more certain of the error of their position, which they cannot alter, their tendency to escape decreases in latency and increases in intensity. Thus we have the following relationship between ratio of subgroup size and avoidance: As the size of the two subgroups diverges, the majority members will tend to decrease the latency of ejection and increase the intensity of their efforts to eject the others, while the minority will decrease the latency of escape and increase the intensity of the efforts to do so. The converse also holds true.

ADOPTING A CONCEPTION

If barriers prevent unyielding minority members from leaving the group, they will begin the attempt to replace their own organismic perceptions with a conceptual attitude borrowed from the dominant opinion position. As uncertainty decreases for the minority people, their tendency to alter their opinions by conceptual substitution increases. Thus we have the following relationship: As the size of the two subgroups diverges, the minority tendency toward opinion change will increase. The converse also holds true.

To retrace our steps to this point, we have attempted to show how the basic independent variable, ratio of size of two groups, is related to the main dependent variables: opinion change, communication (attack and defense), and avoidance of objective self awareness (escape and rejection). These relationships were developed by first showing the relationship between size ratio and uncertainty. Level of uncertainty was then linked to the three independent variables.

For reasons of clarity and simplicity, the model has so far applied to groups divided into only two opinions. The model is not, however, limited to this special case. The present extension of objective self awareness theory is applicable to groups in which any number of divergent positions is represented. Unfortunately, specification of the behavior of all individuals or subgroups although it can be done, is tedious and would not to our mind produce any theoretical insights or clarification of the basic points of the model. Still, it is not appropriate to simply ignore the problem, so we have elected to apply the model to multiple opinion groups, but in a way which does not create tiresome analytical problems.

What we propose to do is begin with several specific opinion configurations and then predict the resultant configurations that the group will exhibit following the interplay of the forces set in motion by objective self awareness mechanisms in the presence of differences of opinion.

The most important thing to remember about the objective self awareness model of groups is that the forces which govern the focus of attention flow away from any area that is defined as ground or "weak" by its relationship with surrounding areas and toward any area that is defined as figure or "strong" by its relationship to the surrounding area. Thus, all we need to do is recall what defines something as strong or weak to predict where consciousness will focus in any given group.

According to Gestalt principles of organization, any given field will be organized on the basis of similarities and differences. The areas that are similar will form units. The units of a field will be segregated by the differences between the units. Applying this law to any group we have the following rules of thumb: (1) there will be as many separate units or areas as there are differences of opinion within the group; (2) the size of these areas will depend upon the number of people (elements) who hold any one opinion. For example, in a group where there are six separate opinions, there would be six separate units of organization varying in size according to the number of people who hold a particular position. Let us take the case where there are 20 people divided into six groups in the following way. Opinion A, 13 people; B, two people; C, two people; D, one person; E, one person; and F, one person. From Gestalt principles we see that the group-field will be organized into six separate areas, with the following weights ranked from greatest to least: D, E, and F are all strongly figured areas, followed by C, B, and A, in that order.

If we apply the general rule that the forces which control the focus of attention flow toward any area with an intensity proportional to the figuredness of that area, we have the following result for the six subgroups: the members of groups D, E, and F spend the most time in objective self awareness, then Groups B and C, then Group A. From our previous analysis we know that the longer the duration of objective self awareness, the more likely it is that opinion change will occur. Thus the size of group A relative to the other five groups taken individually would suggest that the individuals within that group would not change their opinions. The size of Groups B and C suggests that their opinions will be unstable and will exhibit a tendency to change, although less so than the smallest groups, the members of which will exhibit the greatest tendency to alter their opinions. The direction of the opinion change is also under the control of the mechanism of objective self awareness. Group D, E, and F's opinions are in error with respect to all other groups. They can reduce some discrepancy if they change toward either Group B or C, and a great deal of discrepancy if they change toward group A. Groups B and C are in error only with respect to Group A, since, in relative terms, they have located the error of the contradiction between themselves and the opinion of D, E, and F in the latter groups. Thus Groups B and C will change only in the direction of Group A.

If we could take an overview of what is occurring within the group, the following would be observed. Groups D, E, and F have the greatest tendency to alter their opinions. They may change toward the opinions of B, C, or A. If they change toward Groups B or C, they reduce B's and C's tendency to alter their opinions somewhat. If they change to the opinion of Group A, they cause an increase in the pressure upon Groups B and C. In the former case, however, the increase in Groups B's and C's size does not substantially alter the relationship between themselves and Group A. Thus they are still in error because of their difference of opinion with Group A, an error that can only be reduced by moving toward Group A. In general, the direction of opinion change will be toward the dominant subgroup within the group. Given a subgroup of substantial size, within any multiple opinion group we would predict that, over time, the opinions of the group would tend to converge toward the dominant group's opinion. If there are two dominant and equal subgroups, then we can only predict that opinion will tend to converge toward both subgroups, and in an approximately equal proportion. If there are three dominant groups we would predict tripartite convergence.

The application of the objective self awareness model to multiple opinion groups concludes the theoretical portion of this chapter. We must now attempt to muster some empirical support for our various hypotheses. This effort will occupy the next section.

EVIDENCE

The primary independent variable we have related to conformity behavior has been the ratio of the minority and majority group sizes. A proper test of the theory presented in this chapter would entail an empirical test of the predictions generated by the postulated relationship between the subgroup ratios and the behavior of the members of the group. To provide evidence for this proposition, Duval (1972) tested the following hypothesis: in a situation where differences of opinion are occurring, the size of the segregated area of the total field associated with any individual will be inversely related to that individual's tendency to conform to the differing opinions; the smaller the area, the greater the conformity. Furthermore, the effects of area size should be accentuated by the presence of a stimulus to objective self awareness in addition to the stimulus represented by the differing opinions themselves. To test this hypothesis, subjects were given differential feedback concerning the proportion of a sample of 10,000 students who agreed with their ten most important attitudes. Since the size of the area associated with a person's attitudes, opinions, or whatever is a property of the self as stimulus object and should carry over into all situations, the proportion of others who agree with an individual on one dimension should theoretically affect that individual's tendency to conform on separate and unrelated dimensions. Thus, after the differential feedback as to the extent of others' agreement, all subjects were placed in an unrelated situation where they confronted two others who disagreed with their estimate of the number of objects presented on the screen. One half of the subjects were also exposed to a live t.v. image of themselves while remaining subjects were exposed to a blank t.v. screen.

Subjects were 82 female undergraduates and were run separately. Each subject was ushered into the experimental cubicle and was told that she was to participate in a visual perception study. Before beginning the "visual perception" experiment proper, the experimenter gave the subject a packet of cards. He indicated that the information on the cards represented the results of a questionnaire she had filled out earlier in the year. The subject then opened the package and found 11 cards with circles drawn on them. Part of each circle was darkened and part left white. The subject was led to believe that the darkened area of the circle represented the proportion of a sample of 10,000 students who agreed with her ten most important attitudes. In fact, subjects received cards that on the average were either 5%, 50%, or 95% dark, indicating that either 5%,

50%, or 95% of the sample of ten thousand agreed with her ten most important attitudes.

After the agreement manipulation subjects were asked to estimate the number of dots on ten sets, each set containing two slides, which were projected onto a screen one at a time. Subjects were told that two other people in separate cubicles were also participating in the experiment. In fact, there were no other subjects participating in the experiment. On the first slide of each of the ten sets of slides, subjects were asked to make estimates without knowing the responses of the bogus others. On the second slide of each set, which was identical to the first slide of each set, the subjects were asked to respond after seeing how the two bogus others supposedly responded. The different procedures for the first and second slides of each set were rationalized by telling the subject that the experimenter was interested in the process of visual estimation under both an "alone" and "knowing other responses" condition. In fact, the experimenter set the bogus others' estimates for the second slide so that one person was 200 and the other person 150 points over the subject's estimate on the first slide. In addition, one half of the subjects were exposed to their image on a t.v. set during the visual estimation portion of the experiment. The remaining half were exposed to a blank t.v. screen. The dependent measures were frequency and intensity of the subject's change in estimate toward the bogus others on the second slide of each set.

If the present theory is correct, the level of the subjects' conformity should be inversely related to the proportion of the sample of 10,000 students who they believed agreed with their ten attitudes. An analysis of the frequency of conformity (i.e., number of trials on which the subject conformed) and intensity of conformity data indicates that this is the case. The smaller the proportion of others who agreed on the attitude dimensions, the greater the conformity on the perceptual task. This appeared as a main effect for Level of Agreement ($p < .001$). Thus we have confirmation for the general notion that the ratio of subgroup size is inversely related to conformity. However, it must be remembered that the ratio of group size is important only as it affects the focus of attention. While group size is the observable portion of the model and one way to manipulate objective self awareness, the direction of focused attention is the underlying variable supposedly affected by group size. It follows that the presence of any additional stimulus which reminds the person that he is an object would increase the salience of properties of the self. In the present study, the person is defined as a small or large area of the field by the agreement manipulation. The presence of the person's image on the t.v. screen should, if the present theory is correct, increase effect of that property of the self on the direction of attention and, hence, the incidence of conformity behavior.

An analysis of variance indicated a t.v.-no t.v. × Level of Agreement

× blocks (first five versus second five trials) interaction. This interaction indicated that subjects in the t.v. conditions conformed less over the second five trials than over the first five trials. This decline in conformity can be interpreted as a decline in the ability of the camera to remind the person of his object status (cf. Ickes and Wicklund, Chapter 2). Since the effects of the camera appear to have weakened over trials, the first five trials represent a better test of the interaction hypothesis. An analysis of conformity over the first five trials reveals the presence of an interaction for both intensity ($p < .10$) and frequency ($p < .05$) of conforming responses. The form of this interaction is presented in Table 2.

TABLE 2

Mean Estimate Change Toward Bogus Others[a]

	Low agreement	Medium agreement	High agreement
Camera	470[b]	350	225
	3.10[c]	2.63	1.50
No camera	268	285	215
	2.09	1.90	2.00

[a] Means represent first five trials.
[b] Intensity of conformity (amount of change toward bogus others).
[c] Frequency of conformity (number of conforming responses on first five trials).

The present theory indicates that conformity is inversely related to the size of the area of the field associated with an individual, and that the relationship between conformity and subgroup size is mediated by the focus of attention. The t.v.-no t.v. × level of agreement interaction found in the above experiment tends to support this latter postulate. The presence of a strong stimulus which reminded the person of her object status increased the effects of subgroup size on level of conformity. Theoretically, this result obtained because t.v. image made properties of self more salient to that person's attention.

To add additional credence to the notion that the focus of attention mediates the relationship between subgroup size and conformity, the authors carried out a second experiment. This experiment manipulated the person's focus of attention while keeping the size of the subgroup constant. The hypothesis this experiment tests is the following: To the extent that a person is objectively self aware in a situation where there are differences of opinion, he will alter his opinion in the direction of the other.

The subjects were female undergraduates, and were run individually. The subject was seated at a desk that contained a tape recorder, a pile of questionnaires, and instructions for filling out the questionnaires. The experimenter proceeded to say that the purpose of the experiment was to investigate whether or not people project their attitudes in their voice inflexion, tone, and modulation. He told her that because of the purpose it was necessary that some people make a tape recording of their own voices. At this stage the two conditions diverged. In the Own Voice condition the subject read a dry passage from a grammar book while the experimenter recorded the reading, but in the Other's Voice condition the subject was told instead that she would hear someone else's voice. Then the manipulation of objective self awareness was introduced.

In the Own Voice condition the experimenter played back 15 seconds of the subject's voice so that she could listen, with the excuse that he wanted to be sure the recording was all right. On the basis of the theory, the subject's hearing her own voice should have caused her to focus attention upon the self. In an analogous manner the experimenter played back the Other's Voice condition, with the excuse that he wanted to be sure he had the right tape. Then the dependent measure was collected, as follows.

Several weeks prior to the experiment a premeasure had been administered to potential subjects in their introductory psychology classes. Nine political and social issues were selected for the experiment, and for the dependent measure, the questionnaire was altered slightly in order to allow an evaluation of conformity tendencies. A dot was marked on each of the nine scales with a marker pen. Each dot in fact represented the pretest mean from the introductory psychology sections sampled. The presence of the dots was justified by telling the subject that each question had been coded for computer analysis by means of dots that represented the most frequent choice of University of Texas undergraduates. Thus, the dots represented a differing point of view. In addition, she was told not to pay any attention to the dots while she responded to the nine scales.

Opinion change for each subject was computed by comparing the pretest with the responses given during the experimental session, and, as expected, opinion change in the direction of the mode (dot marked on scales) was greater among Own Voice subjects than among Other's Voice subjects ($p < .05$).

As the results show, the objectively self aware subjects conformed to the attitudes of the majority more than did subjects who were less objectively self aware. These results conform to predictions derived from the objective self awareness model of conformity and lend credence to the idea that the focus of attention is indeed one of the important underlying variables which determines conformity.

The two studies were specifically designed to test the relationship between self focus of attention and conformity. However, there have been numerous

studies whose experimental operations actually manipulated objective self awareness under another name. Specifically, numerous experiments have varied the
public-private dimension.

Public-Private

Studies by Argyle (1957), Asch (1951), Deutsch and Gerard (1955), Mouton,
Blake, and Olmstead (1956), and Raven (1959) have all found that an individual
is much more likely to conform to a bogus consensus when the interaction
or decision-making is done in public rather than in private circumstances. From
our viewpoint, the experimental conditions that were labeled public were in
fact conditions where objective self awareness was increased. The private conditions were comparable to the subjective self awareness conditions in our research.
For example, Deutsch and Gerard created a public condition by having subjects
seated in the visual presence of a bogus majority. In the private condition each
subject was placed in a separate, enclosed cubicle. The results showed that
on the line matching task subjects in the public condition conformed more
to the bogus majority than did the subjects in the private condition. Since the
theoretical effect of placing a person in public view is to increase objective
self awareness, we would argue that the experimental increase in conformity
was brought about by enhanced objective self awareness.

Another manipulation of the public-private dimension entailed asking the
subject in one case to reveal his name and in the other case to allow the subject
to remain anonymous (Mouton et al.). Again it is easy to interpret the manipulation
as one of objective self awareness. To the extent that a person can be identified
through either a name or through some other item uniquely associated with
himself as an individual, he will be reminded of his status as an object. Being
reminded of himself as an object, he will be more objectively self aware than
a person who cannot be identified. This being the case, we are inclined to
argue that identifiability leads to more conformity because it makes a person
objectively self aware.

In general, we would argue that any manipulation such as exposure to
the attention of others or increased identifiability varies the amount of objective
self awareness. From this point of view the studies which show a difference
in amount of conformity between the public and the private conditions are,
in fact, studies which have achieved differences through the manipulation of
objective self awareness.

Another interesting point that the public and private studies bring out is
that conformity can result under private conditions. One study with this finding
is the one mentioned earlier, by Deutsch and Gerard. From their data it is
apparent that the level of opinion change in the private condition was higher

than the level of change in a control condition in which there was no exposure to difference of opinion. This finding is consistent with the objective self awareness model, for the source of the forces that bring about conformity can be traced partially to the presence of a difference of opinion. Any time differences of opinion appear in a group, some amount of objective self awareness will be generated; consequently there is reason to expect conformity.

Attribution to Self and Conformity

Thus far we have marshalled some support for the idea that objective self awareness is related to conformity. But according to the model, the relationship between objective self awareness and conformity is postulated to be indirect. Being objectively self aware causes attribution of error to the self which, in turn, causes conformity behavior. Duval (1971) showed that the degree of objective self awareness is indeed related to the amount of attribution of causality to self regardless of the favorability of the event. Approximately one half of the subjects in the experiment were seated in front of a mirror; the remaining half were seated in front of the nonreflecting back side of the mirror. Positioned in this manner each subject was asked to imagine herself in a series of hypothetical situations. The subject was told that each situation would consist of another person and herself behaving within a situation where a specific event would take place. The subject was further instructed that the experimenter would ask her to determine the extent to which her behavior in the situations had caused the events to occur and the extent to which the other person's behavior had caused the events to occur. The subject was asked to make this estimate in terms of percentage of causality to self and other.

In addition to the mirror-no mirror manipulation, one half of the subjects in each of the mirror and no-mirror conditions were given five situations which involved a negative outcome such as a bad grade, loss of a book, hitting a child with a car, etc. The other subjects were given situations which involved a positive outcome such as getting a good grade or meeting an attractive person of the opposite sex. The dependent measure was the degree to which the subject attributed causality for the events to herself.

The results of the study indicated that persons who were caused to focus more upon themselves by the presence of the mirror showed a greater tendency to attribute causality to themselves than did persons who were not in the presence of a mirror ($p < .001$). This rather strong result obtained regardless of the favorability of the outcome. The mean percentage of attribution of causality to self in the negative outcome-mirror condition and positive outcome-mirror condition was essentially the same. This similarity between means is also observed in the negative and positive outcome-no mirror conditions (see Table 3).

TABLE 3

Mean Attribution to Self

Mirror—Positive	(N = 11)	60.00[a]
Mirror—Negative	(N = 10)	60.20
No Mirror—Positive	(N = 11)	49.91
No Mirror—Negative	(N = 11)	51.09

[a] Mean percentage responsibility attributed by the subject to herself.

Considering the strong main effect for the presence of the mirror and the failure to find any interaction between negative-positive outcome and mirror-no mirror (also see Feather, 1969), we have some confidence in the postulated first step of the chain of events leading from objective self awareness to conformity. Unfortunately the above study was not designed to demonstrate the postulated relationship between the tendency to attribute to self in a situation involving differences of opinion and conformity behavior. There are two studies, however, which make this point quite nicely.

Both Costanzo (1970) and Costanzo and Shaw (1966) have demonstrated that a person's tendency to attribute internally, that is, to attribute the responsibility for an event to the self, was highly related to conformity. In the Costanzo and Shaw study, subjects of varying age groups were asked to make judgments in an Asch type line matching situation and were exposed to the erroneous judgments of a bogus majority. After measuring each subject's level of conformity to the incorrect judgments, each subject was asked if he had noted any discrepancy between his own judgments and the group's judgments. He was also asked to attribute a cause for this discrepancy. The first question was answered affirmatively by all subjects, and the answers to the second question were scored on the basis of whether the subjects gave internal (self attribution) or external (other attribution) reasons. A high positive correlation (.87) was obtained between tendency to attribute internally and conformity.

The second study, by Costanzo, followed the same procedure as the first except that each subject's tendency toward self blame or other blame was measured before he participated in an Asch type conformity test. The self blame measurement consisted of 12 incidents involving the subject's hypothetical interaction with a peer. All incidents ended with a negative consequence for the peer. Each subject was asked to indicate how much blame he would attribute to himself for the incident on a 20-point scale. After administering this measure, 12 persons from each of the high, middle, and low self-blame groups were selected for participation in the conformity part of the experiment. The conformity measure was taken by measuring each subject's rate of conformity to a bogus majority simulated by an apparatus similar to the Crutchfield (1955) machine.

The results of the experiment again showed a strong positive relationship between the individual's tendency to attribute the situational responsibility to himself and his subsequent level of conformity.

Although both of the experiments use a theoretical rationale that is quite different from our own, we see the results as supportive of the notion that the tendency to attribute causality to the self in a situation involving differences of opinion is a major factor in noncoercive conformity. Our interpretation of the experiments is as follows.

The experimental measures of the individual's tendency to blame himself over others was actually a measure of the person's chronic tendency to attribute the cause for any event to himself rather than to something external. If the hypothetical situations in the second experiment cited had used positive instead of negative consequences, the same individual differences in the tendency to attribute the cause of those events to the self should have obtained. Both experiments were measuring a tendency which the Duval (1971) and Wicklund and Duval (Chapter 9) experiments manipulated, namely, the tendency to attribute causality either internally or externally. If the hypothesized tendency to attribute the error of the contradiction to the self in a difference of opinion situation is what leads to conformity, then any chronic differences in this tendency should be positively correlated with the magnitude of conformity. The greater the tendency to attribute to self, the greater the attribution of error to self and, thus, the greater the conformity. This is the precise result obtained in both of the above cited experiments.

To briefly recapitulate development to this point: the Duval (1972) conformity experiment, the authors' experiment on conformity, and the public-private studies demonstrate that level of objective self awareness is related to level of conformity. Costanzo, and Costanzo and Shaw show that the attribution of causality to self is related to level of conformity. So we have gained some confidence in the particulars of the theory. To sum up, the evidence presented thus far indicates that objective self awareness causes conformity via the intermediate mechanism of causal attribution.

Group Size and Confidence

Another aspect of the model centers on the relationship between the error of the contradiction and objective self awareness. In the introduction to this chapter we argued that a person who was aware of a difference between his own opinion and another opinion would also be aware of the error associated with that contradiction. Later we stated that to the extent the person is objectively self aware, he will attribute this error to himself. From this reasoning, we would expect to find that a measure of a person's feelings of confidence in his ability or opinion would be causally related to the amount of time he spends in objective self awareness in a situation where there are differences of opinion. Unfortunately we have no conformity experiment at the present time which directly varies the time spent in objective self awareness and then measures the person's confidence in his opinion. However, there is one experiment that first varied the size of the subgroups associated with two contradictory opinions and then measured the subject's level of confidence in his opinion. While this is not an ideal test of the relationship between objective self awareness and confidence, it is defensible as a test. Since the ratio of the subgroups is thought to be causally related to the focus of attention which is then causally related to attribution of error, we can expect the ratio of subgroup size to be related to the subject's level of confidence in his opinion. A specific prediction can be derived from this reasoning. As the percentage of the total aggregate of individuals associated with the subject's opinion declines, he will show decreasing confidence in his ability. The study we will use to substantiate this notion is by Julian, Regula, and Hollander (1968).

The experiment was specifically designed to test the effect of prior levels of agreement upon a person's performance on a second similar task and is, in that regard, not directly related to the present formulation. However, immediately after the first set of trials, there was a measure of the confidence with which subjects had made their first set of estimates. Given that level of agreement was manipulated during the first set of trials and that the measurement of confidence was taken immediately after the first session, we would argue that the results of the confidence measurement adequately test the postulated relationship between ratio of subgroup size and confidence.

The experimental design simulated a five person group whose members supposedly were to make perceptual estimates of unambiguous stimuli. By using an apparatus similar to the Crutchfield design, each subject was led to believe that he was seeing the actual responses of other individuals in the group. In fact, the responses the subjects observed were controlled by the experimenter. The purpose of this deception was to vary the subject's perception of the percentage of the five person group that agreed with his perception of the target object. In the initial phase of the experiment the subject was led to believe that he occupied the first response position. For a few warm-up trials a display panel indicated that the group showed unanimous opinions. After the warm-up period, the subjects were divided into six conditions. The conditions were differentiated on the basis of the percentage of the four other members of the group who were to show responses similar to those of the subjects. For instance, in the 100 percent agreement condition the subject believed that the four others in the group held the same estimate as he did. In the 75 percent condition, the subject believed that three agreed and one disagreed. In the 50 percent condition the subjects believed that two agreed and two disagreed. The 25

TABLE 4

Confidence in Estimates of Nonambiguous Stimuli

Experimental condition:	100%	75%	50%	25%	0%
	4.5	4.3	4.1	3.5	3.4

percent and 0 percent conditions followed the same pattern. In the control (no feedback) condition the subjects were not exposed to anyone else's opinion. Immediately after the first 20 trials, subjects were given a questionnaire that included a question designed to measure subjective feelings of confidence in the first 20 estimates. After filling out the confidence questionnaire the subjects were given the second set of trials, which are not relevant for our discussion.

As predicted from our model, the level of the subject's confidence in his ability declines as the proportion of the group constituted by the subject's position declines from 100 percent to 0 percent. Theoretically, each ratio should have produced different levels of objective self awareness, which in turn should have generated different levels of attribution of error to self. Any differences in attribution of error to self should be reflected in the confidence measure. At 100 percent agreement, the subject should have been maximally confident. At 75/25, the ratio of attribution of error to self to the attribution of error to other should have been about three to one, at 50/50, one to one, etc. If the postulated relationship between subgroup ratio and confidence is correct, the measured level of confidence should have shown an appropriate decrease at each ratio. As Table 4 shows, the confidence levels decreased as the ratio of the subgroups decreased, as expected.

A second interesting feature of the confidence level data is the sharp decline between the 50 percent level and the 25 percent level. Earlier we argued that the information indicating that the other was in error (time spent in subjective self awareness) would be averaged with the data that indicated the self was in error (time spent in objective self awareness). The averaging process would result in a decision about the locus of error. We also suggested that as the amount of time spent in objective self awareness rises above 50 percent, the person will tend to locate the error in himself (although with varying degrees of uncertainty depending on the exact ratio). Any ratio below 50 percent self to 50 percent other should cause the individual to locate the error in the other. If the 50/50 ratio is the pivot point, then the confidence level should show a sharp break between the 50/50 level and the 75/25 level. This is, in fact, what the data indicate. Starting from 100 percent agreement and moving downward, we see small shifts in confidence which reflect the uncertainty factor. Then a large difference occurs as the size of the subject's subgroup moves from 50 percent of the total to 25 percent of the total.

The Julian *et al.* experiment offers support for a section of the hypothetical chain of events which begins with difference of opinion and eventually leads to conformity. This segment of this chain was the postulated relationship between the ratio of two opinion groups and attribution of error to self as measured by a person's confidence in his performance. This evidence, however, says nothing about the supposed relationship between the person's belief that his opinion was in error and conformity.

Feeling of Error and Conformity

In the introduction we argued that a person would have to believe that his opinion was in error before he would alter that opinion. If this notion is correct, any manipulation, whether through objective self awareness or not, of the person's confidence in his opinion or ability should produce conformity. This relationship can be transformed into a secondary hypothesis: to the extent that a person believes his opinion or ability to be wrong, in error, or inadequate, he will attempt to alter that opinion. As a corollary to this hypothesis it would be predicted that the individual who believes his opinion to be in error would seek an opinion that is not in error. In the absence of any objective and nonsocial definition of correctness he will eventually move toward the dominant group's opinion. If a definition of correctness is apparent within the situational context, the person will move in that direction.

The evidence for the main proposition is convincing. When the subject believes he has failed on a task (objective indication of incorrectness) he later conforms much more to a stooge; if the subject believes he has succeeded on a task (objective indication of correctness) he conforms less (Asch, 1956; Goldberg & Lubin, 1958; Hochbaum, 1954; Kelman, 1950; Samelson, 1957). As far as data supporting the corollary are concerned, we have a study by Willis and Hollander (1964).

Each subject received information about the level of correctness of his performance and the level of correctness of his partner. As expected from the direction of change corollary, the subject conformed more to a partner who was supposedly correct 80 percent of the time than to a partner who was supposedly correct only 20 percent of the time. This experiment illustrates that the motivation of the conforming subject is based upon reducing the discrepancy between his own behavior and the correct behavior. Otherwise the subject's level of conformity when exposed to the 80 percent correct partner would be the same as with the 20 percent correct partner. However, it must be kept in mind that the usual difference of opinion situation has no objective definition of correctness. There is no experimenter or authority to say what is right and wrong. Without an objective marker for the correct opinion or ability, correctness is always defined by the position held by the dominant subgroup.

THREE VARIABLES AS FUNCTIONS
OF SUBGROUP SIZE: EVIDENCE

The next topic for discussion will be the relationship between the size ratio of the subgroups and opinion change, avoidance, and communication. In this area the objective self awareness model makes specific predictions about the behavior of the individual members of the groups based on the relationship between the size of the ratio of the subgroups and the various intermediary mechanisms we have discussed. For each specific prediction we will briefly recount the conceptual linkage between the ratio of the sizes and the several dependent measures.

Opinion Change

PREDICTION 1

The ratio of the subgroup sizes affects the amount of time members spend in objective and subjective self awareness. The locus of error decision is a function of the self-focused/other-focused ratio. From the theoretical reasoning, the minority and majority both will locate the error of the contradiction in the minority subgroup. Since opinion change is solely a function of the locus of error, the members of a minority will show the greatest tendency to alter their opinions.

This prediction has strong empirical support. In fact, out of the following studies which used a fairly high ratio of majority to minority size, Asch (1956), Festinger, Gerard, Hymovitch, Kelley, and Raven (1952), Gerard (1954), and Hochbaum (1954), all showed considerable yielding by the minority in contrast to the majority. The only study known to the authors which has demonstrated substantial opinion change in the majority obtained the results by leading members of the majority to believe that their ability to do the task was low (Hochbaum).

PREDICTION 2

As the size of the majority increases relative to the minority, the uncertainty factor associated with the locus of error impression decreases for both the majority and minority. As uncertainty decreases for the minority members, their tendency toward opinion change will increase. From this reasoning, we have the following prediction: As the size of the majority increases relative to the size of the minority, opinion change in the minority will increase.

Evidence on the above prediction was gathered by Asch (1951). By varying the size of the bogus majority from 0 to 16 in the experimental context of a line matching task, he obtained the data shown in Table 5.

As predicted by our model, there is a steady increase in the rate of the

TABLE 5

Level of Conformity (Mean Number of Errors) in Asch Experiment

Size of Majority:	0	1	2	3	4	8	16
	0.08	0.33	1.52	4.00	4.20	3.84	3.75

subject's conformity from size 0 to size 4, with the largest increase occurring in the shift between 2 and 3. However, there appears to be a slight decrease in conformity at levels 8 and 16 which, if reliable, would sharply contradict the theory. However, the reliability of the 8 person and 16 person data is brought into question by Gerard, Wilhelmy, and Conolley (1968). This study steadily increased bogus group sizes from 2 to 8 while the naive subject attempted to estimate ambiguous lines. The study shows a significant linear relationship between majority size and conformity, supporting the general contention of a linear relationship between the two variables. However, the tendency toward a curvilinear relationship in Asch's data should not be ignored, and we would like to offer one possible reason for the apparent failure of group size above 4 to significantly increase the conformity effect. Earlier we argued that degree of opinion change in the minority was strictly a function of the intensity of the uncertainty factor. As uncertainty decreases the minority should show more conformity. In Figure 4 the intensity of this uncertainty is shown as a function of the ratio of subgroup sizes ($y = 1/x$, with y representing level of uncertainty; x, the size of the majority; and the size of the minority held constant at a value of 1). As the figure indicates, the sizable decreases in uncertainty occur between ratios 1/1 and 1/4. This decrease amounts to 75 percent of the total possible range from complete uncertainty to complete certainty. By contrast, the proportion of decrease in uncertainty from ratio 1/4 to 1/8 amounts only to about 13 percent, and the decrease from 1/8 to 1/16 amounts to only 6 percent of the total possible. Since opinion change is seen as a function of this uncertainty, it would follow that the largest increases in magnitude of opinion change would correspond to the larger decreases in uncertainty. In groups where the size of the majority is varied from 1 to 16, the rate of conformity would increase rapidly between majority sizes of 1 and approximately 4, then slowly level out as uncertainty approaches asymptote.

Figure 4 describes Asch's data reasonably well, assuming that the apparent decreases in conformity for majority sizes above five were not statistically reliable. Other findings in the research area of majority size have also shown that conformity effects increase up to a majority of approximately 3, with group sizes above 3 having little additional impact (Blake & Mouton, 1961).

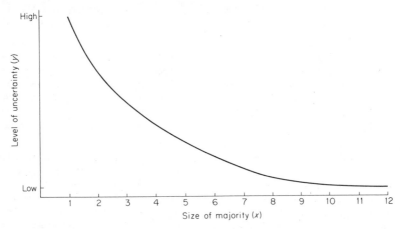

Fig. 4. The relationship between majority size and level of uncertainty. Note: $y = 1/x$.

PREDICTION 3

As the sizes of the minority and majority converge, uncertainty for both the majority and minority increases toward the maximum. Therefore, as minority size increases relative to the majority, opinion change in the minority will decrease. The available evidence clearly shows that an increase in the size of the minority will decrease the minority's tendency to conform. For example Hardy (1957) compared the subjects' level of conformity when they were supported or not supported by others. In one case, subjects in a six person group had no support, that is, no one agreed with them. In the other condition subjects in a six person group were supported by one other person. The results of the study show that the no-support condition yielded an attitude change score of 6.97 while subjects in the support condition averaged only 2.0 points of attitude change. Additional and rather persuasive evidence for this proposition was found by Asch (1951). By decreasing the size of the majority opposition to one, he found that yielding was almost eliminated. Results similar to both of the above studies were also obtained by Allen and Levine (1969).

PREDICTION 4

As the sizes of the majority and minority converge toward equality, individuals in the majority will hold their decision that the minority is in error with decreasing confidence.

The only evidence we have for this proposition comes from Asch's comparison of two groups divided 15 to 1 and 11 to 9, respectively. These groups differed from those in his earlier experiments in that the majority was naive.

The minority members were instructed helpers of the experimenter. Asch (1952) compared the interaction between the naive majority and bogus minority in the following way:

> As might be expected, this condition (a naive majority of 15) did not alter the estimates of the majority. However, the responses of the majority members were in clear contrast to those of the critical subjects of the first experiment (those involving a single naive subject confronted by a unanimous majority). At the outset they greeted the estimates of the dissenter with incredulity. On the later trials there were smiles and impromptu comments [p. 479].

In tabulating the subjects' responses to the question "What was your reaction to the disagreements in the estimates?" Asch says,

> The written reactions confirm that the majority has not the slightest doubts of their own accuracy: (for example one subject wrote) "I was distinctly surprised to hear a person disagree with something I thought was an obvious fact easily seen. I felt the person was attempting a stupid joke, at which I was annoyed. Then I felt a pitying contempt for a person who could so misinterpret directions as to be comparing the wrong lines. Then I felt sorry for a person with such poor eyesight." And another: "The differences in size were quite obvious and the disagreement seemed either deliberate (dishonest) or else a manifestation of an abnormality in perception. . . . I felt annoyed at the constant disagreement with my judgment [p. 480]."

In contrast to the naive majority of 15, Asch formed a group which included 11 naive persons and 9 instructed confederates. He says,

> The naive subgroup maintained confidence in their responses, and the main problem was why the others disagreed. The tenor of the reactions to the opposition was now quite different (in comparison to the naive majority of 15). The note of ridicule and derision, which previously was quite insistent, now occurred only rarely . . . . The reactions of the naive group changed from outright repudiation to a more respectful attitude as the ranks of the opposition increased [p. 480].

As far as the evidence can be trusted, it does appear that the majority manifests signs of an increasing uncertainty that the minority is in error as the two groups become equal in size.

Avoidance of the Difference of Opinion

Opinion change is not the only variable related to the ratio of the subgroups. According to our model, the tendency to avoid the differences of opinion is also a function of the relative size of two opinion groups. Since evidence is not available for all predictions, the points substantiated below represent only a sampling of the total number of possible theoretical derivations.

PREDICTION 1

Since the majority locates the error of the contradiction in the minority, they will attempt to eject the unyielding minority from the group.

The desire of the majority to eject the minority can be measured either by behavioral indicators, that is, actions taken by the majority, or by the majority's liking for the minority. An early experiment by Schachter (1951) used both types of measures in demonstrating the majority's attitude toward a deviate.

The experiment was designed to compare a naive majority's attitude toward three categories of group members; an unchanging deviate, a changing deviate, and a person who had agreed from the beginning. This design was achieved by placing three confederates of the experimenter in the discussion group and having two of them begin with deviant opinions. Once the discussion of the chosen topic had begun, one confederate (the slider) slowly altered his intially discrepant position until he agreed with the naive majority. The second confederate (the deviate) maintained his discrepant position throughout the discussion. The third confederate (the mode) started off agreeing with the group and maintained this position throughout the encounter. At the end of the discussion, two measures were taken. One measure asked each subject how much he wanted other members of the group to stay in the club. The second asked each individual to nominate other group members for three possible committees. These committees were to aid the group in its future operation and were assigned different levels of importance. An executive committee was most important, with the steering and correspondence committees following in that order. The results of the study show that on both measures, the deviate was rejected far more than either the slider or the mode. The subjects wanted the deviate to stay in the group far less than they wanted nondeviating members to stay, and overnominated the deviate to the lowest ranking committee. Thus our prediction that the majority would attempt to reject an unyielding deviate is supported by the experimental comparison between agreeing and disagreeing group members. Streufert (1965) found a similar difference in the majority's attitude toward dissimilar as opposed to similar others.

PREDICTION 2

As the majority size increases relative to the minority, uncertainty decreases for both subgroups. As uncertainty decreases for the majority, its desire to eject the unchanging minority from the group will increase.

Evidence for this prediction comes from a study by Strickland, Jones, and Smith (1960) which found that a subject who believed he was in agreement with two other subjects showed a stronger negative evaluation of a disagreeing other than subjects who did not have the support of two others. While this effect was limited to subjects who had an initially favorable impression of the target person, the experiment does provide evidence on the variation of the majority's attitude toward the minority as a function of majority group size.

Communication

PREDICTION 1

As uncertainty decreases in the minority, minority members will show a decreasing tendency to communicate to the majority.

The available evidence for this proposition is indirect. To get to it we must develop a roundabout line of thought such as the following. Since opinion change is a function of uncertainty, deviates who change their positions should have little uncertainty about the error of their opinion. If opinion changers have a low amount of uncertainty it would follow from the uncertainty postulate above that they should communicate to others less than minority members who do not change their opinions. This relationship was in fact found by Festinger *et al.* The experiment divided groups of seven into conformers and deviates. Conformers were led to believe that their opinions on the group's discussion topic agreed with four others in the group, disagreed with one other by 1 point on the opinion scale, and disagreed with the other member by 3 points. The subjects who were randomly chosen to be deviates found the situation reversed. They were led to believe that all others disagreed with them, one person by one point and 5 persons by 3 points on the opinion scale. After receiving this information, all subjects were instructed to engage in a note writing session. This part of the experiment was designed to measure the rate and direction of communication. Later a second opinion questionnaire was given.

The finding we are interested in was that the deviates who altered their positions during the course of the experiments showed significantly less communication to the rest of the group than did the deviates who did not change. If uncertainty is linked to opinion change, as we have argued, then it was to be expected that deviating subjects who had low uncertainty as shown by their change of opinion would also communicate less than deviating subjects who had a higher degree of uncertainty about their own incorrectness. While the evidence is indirect, it still substantiates predictions that stem from this model of conformity.

Thus far, we have tried to marshal the available empirical support for various aspects of the objective self awareness model of conformity. At this point we can say with a fair amount of confidence that noncoercive conformity and the behavior of the nonconforming majority are the result of the interplay of forces that control the direction of attention interacting with the presence of the error of the contradiction. Now we would like to consider the effects of two variables on conformity (stimulus ambiguity and attraction to the group), neither of which is a direct variation in objective self awareness. We will attempt to show how the effects of these variables are implied by the objective self awareness model.

Stimulus Ambiguity

After the person in the minority has attributed the error of the contradiction to himself, his causal agent self is discrepant from a standard of correctness and he suffers from negative affect. In order to reduce this negative effect, the person will attempt to reorganize his perception so that it will not be incorrect. By reorganization we mean that the person will attempt to adjust his internal perceptual schema. An example of this perceptual adjustment is given by Fisher and Lubin (1958). In this experiment subjects were asked to estimate the number of parachutes in two separate pictures, A and B. The subjects were first asked to estimate the number in picture A. After this initial estimate, the subject received a bogus estimate of the number of paratroopers in the picture. He then made four additional estimates without the presence of the actual picture. A bogus estimate accompanied each trial. After these four estimates, the subject was reexposed to the initial picture and was asked to make a final judgment. The subject was then asked to estimate the number of paratroopers in a second picture, B. The findings show that when picture A was shown to the subject again after four interim estimate trials, any error in the estimate induced by the presence of a bogus estimate supposedly coming from a disagreeing other persisted into the final trial on picture A. Furthermore, the error, whether over or under the true estimate of picture A, transferred to the second picture B. In our opinion, this transfer of the error from one task to a different but similar task represents a genuine cognitive reorganization on the part of the individual. If the subject's revised estimate had been an adopted conception, there would have been no transfer. An adopted conception should remain specific to the stimuli it originally concerns. A genuine cognitive reorganization transfers to all similar situations. In other words, the subjects were saying something like,

> Given that my number estimate of that cluster of points is too low, I will alter my number response upward to correspond to a set of stimuli of that density.

In fact, a substantial number of subjects made numerical errors even when they were allowed to count the actual number of dots in the picture.

The relevance of this discussion of cognitive reorganization is this: Experimental evidence by Asch, Deutsch and Gerard, Kelley and Lamb (1957), Rappoport (1965), and Sherif (1935) indicates that the greater the ambiguity of the stimulus, the more the subject will conform in the presence of different opinions. If the self awareness model is viable, then it should provide an explanation for this frequently replicated finding in the area of conformity research. The objective self awareness explanation is as follows. If the person is attempting to reorganize his perception of a given stimulus configuration, the less the initial judgment is based upon specifiable characteristics of the stimulus field, the more easily the person can reorganize the perception. If the stimulus is two straight lines of different length, it may be impossible for the person to alter the perceptual basis of his estimate so that the lines actually look equal. But as we interpret Fisher and Lubin, an ambiguous stimulus can support a wide range of objectively incorrect estimates, even when the actual stimulus object is present. Thus, if an ambiguous stimulus facilitates quick cognitive reorganization, the person facing an ambiguous picture will show much greater initial opinion change than a person faced with unambiguous stimuli.

The following are two experiments supporting the idea that stimulus ambiguity facilitates opinion change.

Deutsch and Gerard found that conformity was higher when the stimulus object was briefly exposed and then taken away, as opposed to being permanently displayed. In one condition the Asch comparison lines were fully exposed while the subjects were making their decisions. Other subjects were given only a brief look at the cards and then asked to make their decisions in the absence of the actual stimulus. Conformity was greater in the "memory" condition than in the "visual" condition. A study by Rappoport found similar results. The experimenter instructed subjects to use either an analytical set or an intuitive set in judging the stimulus. In the analytical-set instructions, the subject was told to pay close attention to the particulars of the object. In the intuitive set instructions, the subjects were told not to pay attention to specifics but to make their judgments intuitively. The study showed that subjects given the intuitive set conformed to their partners more than subjects given an analytical set.

The conclusion we draw is that the more easily a person can reorganize his perception of an object, the more he will conform in the early stages of group dissention. Thus, an environment whose features are unclear will produce greater initial conformity than an environment whose features are nonambiguous.

The conclusions we draw about the relationship between ambiguity and magnitude of opinion change apply only to the early period of the opinion conflict. In the long run, we would predict that the levels of opinion change in the presence of an ambiguous or nonambiguous stimulus will be equal if the individual is prevented from leaving the field. The reason for this prediction lies in the fact that a person who holds a minority opinion about an unambiguous stimulus is as discrepant from his standard of correctness as the person who holds a minority opinion about an ambiguous stimulus. A minority opinion about the length of two lines is just as wrong as a minority opinion about the number of dots on a card. In each case the person must find a way to eliminate the negative affect contingent on his discrepancy from the standard. Therefore, if the person cannot alter his perception and is prevented from leaving the group, his initial opinion should eventually be replaced by a conceptual opinion borrowed from the dominant opinon of the group.

Stimulus ambiguity can be considered a separate variable tangentially related to our explanation of conformity. The attraction of any individual to the group also falls into this category.

After an extensive review of the field, Hare (1962) concludes that one of the most reliable findings in the area of group research is that attraction to the group increases conformity within the group. How is this explained in terms of objective self awareness theory? In the theoretical portion of this chapter, we alluded to the role of barriers in the conformity process. According to that statement, barriers prevent an individual who cannot reorganize his perception from leaving the field. Being prevented from leaving the group, the individual must either endure the negative affect generated by the violation of his standard of correctness or he must resolve the discrepancy. Therefore, he should alter his opinion by holding his organismic perception in abeyance and adopting the opinion of the dominant subgroup.

From the point of view of objective self awareness, attraction to the group is nothing more than a special kind of barrier. Any kind of barrier that prevents the person from avoiding the group would accomplish the same result. Without going into a great amount of detail on the various experiments which demonstrate this point, we would like to mention one study that supports the barrier interpretation of attraction.

In a conformity type situation involving the task of ranking ten pieces of modern art, Kiesler and Corbin (1965) divided subjects into six conditions. There were three levels of attraction to the group: high, below average, and low; and two levels of commitment: either high or low. Attraction was manipulated by giving the subjects different feedback about how much the other members of the group liked them. For the high attraction condition, subjects believed they were liked very much by the group, for the below average a middle range of liking, and so forth. Commitment to the group was varied by telling the subjects that they had either a 5 percent or 95 percent chance of changing groups if they were dissatisfied with the group to which they had been assigned. Since the subjects believed that they would have to continue the experiment over several group interaction sessions, the 5 percent condition presumably forced the subjects to commit themselves to future interaction with the original group. The 95 percent condition should have had little if any enforced commitment to the group since these subjects had an excellent chance of leaving if they so desired. The dependent measure was how much subjects conformed to the opinions of the experimental confederates.

The results of the study show several interesting relationships. The two commitment conditions show a similar effect in that both show a decreased conformity as group attractiveness declines from high to below average. But the commitment conditions diverge as group attractiveness declines to the low level: the low commitment subjects show a further decline in conformity, while the high commitment subjects manifest a slight increase.

In general, the results of the study support the idea that attraction increases conformity by acting as a barrier which prevents the reduction of negative affect through avoidance of differences of opinion. Attraction to the group functions much like commitment to future interaction with the group. The crucial finding is the relatively high amount of opinion change in the low-attraction-committed condition. Even though subjects in this condition were unattracted to the group, their commitment to stay in the group for several sessions produced a good deal of attitude change compared with the unattracted uncommitted group. Thus we would argue that attraction to a group is essentially a commitment to future interaction with that group and produces conformity by preventing the person from avoiding the differences of opinion either psychologically or physically.

The objective self awareness interpretation of attraction concludes the evidential portion of this chapter. The evidence that has been presented in support of the objective self awareness model of conformity is of course incomplete. Hopefully, however, the calibre of experimental studies we have discussed will produce enough confidence in the basic model to stimulate further research.

IMPLICATIONS AND EXTENSIONS

The examples that have been used to illustrate the workings of the objective self awareness model of conformity have been restricted to the case in which the actual members of the group constituted the total social field. However, time should be taken to discuss how the principles, abstract in themselves, apply to other situations. In many cases, the application is fairly complex and deserves to be explicitly delimited to avoid confusion. As examples, we will use situations where the individual's opinions have anchorage in reference groups that lie outside the immediate group situation.

It has been suggested that the forces that bring about conformity are a function of the group opinion configuration. In the event that a particular opinion calls to mind individuals who lie outside the immediate group, calculation of the locus of error decision and the uncertainty accompanying it on the basis of the actual group could result in error. If a person holds an opinion that is anchored in the membership of another group, the individuals of that group must be taken into consideration when specifying the configuration of the group field. If an individual were to know the opinions of all people in the world, then, in fact, the entire population would be relevant for him in the determination of the correctness (or incorrectness) of his own opinions. Sampling the whole world of course is not the ordinary case, though such advances as accurate estimates of population opinion parameters and world wide communications systems make it seem increasingly probable. But the individual ordinarily has knowledge of the opinions of a small portion of the population. Thus we must add rules to the general theory which determine the parameters of the social field.

The first of these rules can be stated in the following way: To the extent that a person has knowledge of the opinions of individuals, any differences between his opinion and that of the others will result in a discrepancy between his opinion and the ideal opinion. However, an individual may have knowledge of the opinions of a number of persons in the sense that he could, if asked, recall what their positions were, but he may not be presently thinking of all those individuals for which he has a memory trace. For whatever reason, he may at any one time be thinking of only a small proportion of the total aggregate of individuals whose opinions he knows, such as the people he associates with at work or his club. Clearly only those individuals who he is considering at any one moment can have any bearing upon the correctness of his opinion. Thus in addition to the rule that the opinions of individuals must be known to the person, we must add a second rule of saliency or emphasis. To figure in the determination of the correctness of an opinion, any individual or aggregate of individuals must be present in the individual's consciousness at the moment that the opinion is being considered.

An example may be helpful. In Newcomb's Bennington study (1943) it was discovered that after a period of time in college a substantial difference in political opinions existed between girls who maintained close contact with parents and those who did not, even though all of the girls originally came from similar ideological backgrounds. This difference can be interpreted as the effects of differential emphasis. The girls who maintained close contact with parents were thinking about their conservative parents and home town associates more than their liberal peers were thinking about their conservative parents. This emphasis on the parents through continued contact could mean that old acquaintances were made more salient than new acquaintances in deter mining the correctness of opinions, which would in turn imply that the old political attitudes would be preserved. Conversely, the girls who had more contact with liberal upperclass peers and faculty than with family should have been thinking more about the faculty and their peers as reference points for the correctness of opinions. For these girls, faculty and peers were more salient and opinions shifted toward the liberal side of the spectrum, in accordance with the principles we have set down.

As qualifying factors, knowledge and saliency can be condensed into the idea of presence: individuals and aggregates of individuals must be present in the awareness of the person before they can figure in the determination of the correctness of the person's opinions, values, and abilities. Further, any individual or aggregate present to a person's awareness will necessarily affect the configuration of the social field and, thus the correctness of an opinion. If an aggregate of individuals whose opinions are known to the person becomes present to his awareness, the opinions of these individuals will in part determine the correctness of his opinion, even though he seldom thinks about their opinions at other times.

In any situation, experimental or otherwise, the necessity of determining or manipulating what groups or individuals are present to the subject's mind is paramount. If the opinions of Group A and not Group B are present in a person's awareness, then obviously it is Group A one must consider in attempting a prediction about the person's attitude change. Although we have suggested one fairly obvious varible, contact, there are undoubtedly many other conditions that affect whether or not and the extent to which an individual or group is present to the mind of a given individual. However, the task of fully ascertaining which variables have influence upon presence will be left to future writings.

Just as the theory is meant to apply to numerous common situations, it also applies to all types of behavior, opinion change and conformity being just one application. In fact, the theory applies to any dimension of the self where there are differences between two individuals. For example, the three other types of self attributes—abilities, traits, and goals—are covered by the theory. If a person stutters in the presence of fluent speakers, he will come to attribute the error of the contradiction to himself. The model operates in the same way for abilities and goals. If a person has an ability or goal which differs from those around him, he is likely to attribute the error of the contradiction either to himself or to the other depending upon the form of the total social field.

The examples which have been used in the chapter were mainly groups discussing a common issue. The theoretical implications extend beyond this limited situation. For example, it is conceivable to interpret the credibility effect often mentioned in the   persuasive communication literature as the result of the operation of the same mechanism that produces conformity in groups.

Although we have argued that a social field equally divided would produce maximum uncertainty but little attitude change, attempting to apply the theory to two-person interactions is not inconsistent with the theory. Attention will not favor one or the other of two apparently equal regions of a field only as long as the immediate social field has complete control over attention. If one person's opinon is linked to another group, and that group is present in the consciousness of both participants, it is possible that attention will direct itself to one person or the other. This reasoning permits us to analyze credibility effects. For example, take the situation where an expert is addressing a layman. It is conceivable that the layman associates large numbers of people with the expert's opinion, that is, the social field is expanded to include more individuals than are actually present. If the layman imagines that a large number of other people would hold opinions similar to that of the expert (which he might very well do since expertise is linked to objectivity), the field would be organized into two disproportionate regions with the layman being the area that attracted attention. Since the layman would be focusing upon himself most of the time, any contradiction between his and the expert's points of view would result in the attribution of error to the layman's opinion and attitude change toward the expert.

Applying the model to the phenomenon of credibility brings up an important point. Relative size is not the only variable affecting the directionality of attention. While no complete understanding has been achieved along these lines, it is a fertile ground for exploration. There could be any number of variables which could bring about the same effects that relative size does. Thus the theory is not limited to groups divided into unequal subgroups, but extends to any situation containing stimuli that effect the direction of attention and which has within itself two real or imagined points of view.

In conclusion, let us reiterate our position with regard to the model here presented. We believe that it represents a general approach to conformity which is correct, but we hold no reverential attitude toward any particular proposition. Hopefully, the theory is organic and can grow and adapt within the boundaries of reality.

Chapter 6

ATTITUDE-BEHAVIOR DISCREPANCY

In the present chapter we will focus on one specific application of the theory. The area of interest normally might be called "cognitive dissonance," but because we neither want to limit our discussion to the specific variables said to arouse dissonance nor to the usual dissonance effects, we have chosen to discuss the concept of "attitude-behavior discrepancy." The purpose of the chapter is to examine research that has typically focused on the relationship between attitudes and behavior. For the most part, the theoretical basis for this research has assumed that the behavior is causal in altering and forming attitudes, hence the labeling of this chapter as "attitude-behavior discrepancy." This label, however, is not meant to imply that the theory of objective self awareness requires that the individual's behavior plays a causal role in attitude change. The impetus of this chapter is toward an understanding of the "attitude-behavior" paradigms in such a way that the person's behavior plays no part in the attitude change. Obviously such an approach entails a considerable deviation from the theoretical thinking of the balance theorists, hence our immediate purpose is to attempt to show how the theory operates in this context.

THE APPLICATION OF THE THEORY
TO ATTITUDE-BEHAVIOR DISCREPANCY

Although our statement of the theory may imply that we have concocted just another balance theory that is roughly equivalent to the statements of Abelson and Rosenberg (1958), Festinger (1957), Heider (1958), Newcomb (1953), and Osgood and Tannenbaum (1955), it is important to note that the "balance restoration" aspect of the theory comes into play only when the central motivational mechanism—objective self awareness—is created. With this in mind we should examine more carefully what is meant by the theoretical notion of discrepancy and discrepancy reduction.

The balance theories all appear to agree on the definition of imbalance. Very generally, imbalance is characterized by a logical inconsistency between at least two cognitions. Some "imbalanced" situations are not obviously illogical, but that is only to say that the elements underlying the imbalance have not been adequately explicated. We will not take exception to this definition of imbalance, but we have built on it through the theoretical notion of correctness, making our notion of discrepancy slightly different from the usual conception of cognitive imbalance. From the viewpoint of objective self awareness, a case of discrepancy will not always have motivational consequences, for two theoretical conditions must first be fulfilled; first, the person must be objectively self aware and, second, the discrepancy must entail deviation from a personal standard of correctness or else a contradiction within the self. The first stipulation need not be elaborated upon, for we have already examined the conditions leading to objective self awareness, and it should be clear that the person will neither be aware of the discrepancy nor will he attempt to resolve it until the situation leads him to become objectively self aware. Once the objective state is engaged he will focus on the contradiction to the extent that the elements of the contradiction are salient for him. The second condition has to do with our notion of the personal standard of correctness. Many instances of personal discrepancy are similar to failure to reach aspiration levels, in the sense that the individual has an ideal state which has not been attained, and this disparity is necessarily a case of cognitive imbalance. More important, in this kind of cognitive imbalance the elements of the imbalance are generated from the causal agent self, and for this reason we refer to the cases of imbalance dealt with by theory as within-self discrepancies. It has been noted in earlier chapters that the individual will not evaluate himself according to the standards of others, and this point is particularly germane here. Objective self awareness will have no motivational consequences due to discrepancies between the individual's present state and the standard of correctness imposed by others, unless, of course, the person adopts those standards as his own.

Not all cases of imbalance dealt with by the theory entail the person's falling short of a personal criterion of excellence. In many instances the person carries out a self contradictory behavior where neither pole of the contradiction constitutes a personal standard of correctness, even though both elements of the contradiction emanate from the causal agent self. When the person engages in two contradictory behaviors but neither of them corresponds to a preexisting personal standard, the motivational consequences of objective self awareness will result in his altering at least one of the conflicting elements such that the contradiction is eliminated. The direction of discrepancy resolution in these instances will, unfortunately, not always be predictable, for the theory specifies only that discrepancies will be resolved in the direction of the personal standard. If this standard is lacking, all that can be predicted, except with extra-theoretical help, is movement toward consistency. It should be noted that we can find no research examples of this "case of no standards." Therefore, we will not discuss the problem further in this section.

There will also be cases in which each aspect of the contradiction coincides with a personal standard of correctness, and where the two standards are opposite but nonetheless respected by the person. Presumably such a state of affairs could persist only if the two standards were seldom brought into juxtaposition. In such an event there is no clear theoretical basis for ascertaining the direction that will be taken in the person's efforts to redress the discrepancy. In the case of a within self discrepancy where some aspect of the person is disparate from one standard of correctness, the discrepancy can be reduced in only one direction—toward that of the standard. But where there is no good reason for supposing that the discrepancy reduction will be unidirectional, the clearest theoretical statement that can be made about the motivational effects of objective self awareness is that the individual will strive to reduce the discrepancy. When two counterpoised criteria of correctness are involved, discrepancy reduction should consist of a reconciliation among the disparate poles such that they are no longer contradictory. Alternatively there could be an eradication of one of them as a standard worth pursuing. Ideally, the direction taken by the resolution might be predicted by understanding the importance or relative dominance of the two disparate standards, although experimentally and practically this is not feasible.

An exhaustive list of the forms of within-self discrepancy would number at least four. Of the following, only the first is prominent in the present chapter, and the second is dwelled upon in numerous other chapters. The last two are likely possibilities when the theory is extended to practical situations, but neither of them receives much treatment in the present work. (1) An attitude is discrepant from the attitudes of others; (2) a behavior is disparate from an attitude or value; (3) two behaviors are discrepant, and a motivational state is created through the individual's value on consistent behaviors; and (4) two behaviors are discrepant, each of which is consistent with a preexisting attitude.

We might consider an example of the application of objective self awareness in the context of some typical cognitive balance research. Undoubtedly the most common form of research to date has taken the form we discussed first: a discrepancy between the individual's present state and one personal standard of correctness. An overwhelming number of experiments inspired by cognitive dissonance theory have taken this form and have involved the subject's commitment to a behavior that violates a personal norm or attitude that he has held as correct. Subjects have been asked to lie to others, misrepresenting what they have perceived earlier to be correct (e.g., Carlsmith, Collins, & Helmreich, 1966; Festinger & Carlsmith, 1959), they have written or otherwise recorded statements that contradict their personal convictions (e.g., Cohen, 1959; Helmreich & Collins, 1968; Sherman, 1970; Zimbardo, 1965), they have been induced to struggle or suffer for consequences that their own value systems would not lead them to pursue (e.g., Aronson, 1961; Brehm, 1959; Wicklund, Cooper, & Linder, 1967; Yaryan & Festinger, 1961), and undergone numerous other conceptually similar situations. In virtually every instance of these experiments it is a change in the attitude, the preexisting personal standard or moral ethic, that has changed toward balance restoration; the discrepant behavior was not the element to move. At face value it appears that the objective self awareness notion is contradicted by this often replicated finding, but before drawing this conclusion we should examine more closely whether or not it is possible that the personal standard could remain intact in these situations. We should also consider the possibility that behavioral change is either impossible or simply not measured.

An individual is requested by an experimenter to perform an overt behavior that is contrary to one of his personal values. According to any cognitive balance theory, the subject will experience imbalance and will attempt to mitigate that state. Cognitive dissonance theory says even more. Festinger (1957) has argued that the elements that will change when dissonance is aroused are those least resistant to change, and almost without exception (the clearest exception being Cohen, 1962) researchers have taken this statement to mean that the subject's attitude, not his behavior, is the least resistant element. Consequently, it is the attitude change that is measured, and typically, the individual's attitude is modified somewhat to coincide more closely with the overt commitment. Thus the results have generally followed the theory, although in the situations that have been examined there is rarely an effort to measure balance restoration with respect to the opposite pole of the contradiction, for this would entail a change in the subject's behavior. In short, there is seldom an experimental attempt to validate the presumption that the behavioral component of the dissonance is the element more resistant to change. We will deal with the experimental treatment of behavior change later in the chapter. The behavior change effects hardly need any elaboration because they follow directly from objective self awareness theory. But because a preponderance of dissonance research has focused on attitude change, we have proposed the following analysis of that effect.

Social Influence in the Forced Compliance Context

This analysis of forced compliance effects is a direct application of the thinking in the earlier chapters on conformity. When a subject complies with the experimenter's request to perform a behavior that runs contrary to his attitudes, there is little reason to think that the person's personal standards regarding the performance of that behavior will remain totally intact. In fact, it would seem reasonable that the mere request by an experimenter, in addition to the possible awareness that others are performing the same behavior, will alter the subject's own personal standards sufficiently to allow him to engage in the behavior. This follows from our comments on conformity. Thus, the behavior that is executed may still be somewhat discrepant from a standard, but the discrepancy between that behavior and the original standard would have been far greater. If a person values freedom of speech but is asked to denounce freedom of expression, the mere knowledge that others would ask him to perform the behavior and the knowledge that others have carried out the behavior should be sufficient to create a new standard of correctness—one that mollifies slightly his prior value of free speech.

In short, we are suggesting that most of the forced compliance studies entail substantial social influence that goes unobserved, and that this influence creates the impression that cognitive imbalance has brought about attitude change. In fact, the imbalance may be unnecessary for attitude change if our analysis of social influence in the forced compliance setting is valid.

The subject enters the situation with his values about the subject matter of the attitude dealt with in the experiment, and after finding that a considerable body of people, including experimenters and other subjects, have condoned either implicitly or explicitly an attitudinal position disparate from one he holds, he alters his standard of correctness (attitude) in the direction of the standard implied by the experimenter's comments and actions. This situation is not unlike that of the experiment reported by Wicklund and Duval on social influence (Chapter 5), in which subjects whose objective self awareness was increased altered their attitudes in the direction of the attitudes held by a positive reference group.

Given this analysis, several variables that would control the amount of attitude change in the direction of the contra-attitudinal behavior may be spelled out, especially variables that are relevant to the likelihood that the subject will adjust his attitude (standard of correctness) toward the position represented by the experimenter and other subjects. In addition, there are the variables that serve to increase the amount of objective self awareness. From the conformity chapters it should be clear that the social influence process can only occur to the degree that the person is objectively self aware. We will not discuss the latter class of variables at present, since they have already been considered in some detail.

First, whether or not the subject respects the opinions of those who appear to represent the opposite position will be a strong determinant of the amount of attitude change. If the experimenter or other authorities who recommend that the subject engage in the behavior appear to be expert with respect to the issue, and if the subject perceives that other subjects who have performed the same behavior are attractive and/or expert, conditions are maximal for his altering his personal standard of correctness in the direction of the behavioral commitment (e.g., Aronson & Golden, 1963). An individual should tend to accept a standard as his own to the extent that it is represented by people who know more than himself or are similar to himself.

Second, we would expect that he would alter his attitude to the extent that he engages in the behavior repeatedly, has to incur cost or effort to engage in the behavior, or, in general, as he finds that performance of the behavior is disagreeable given his values at the outset of the procedure. Again, the reason relates to the social context of the experiment. If the experimenter would ask the subject to struggle, suffer, gain inadequate rewards, and so forth to carry out the behavior, the experimenter must believe rather strongly that the value associated with that behavior has some merit. The evidence for this proposition is abundant. For example, see Arrowood and Ross, 1966; Brehm, 1962; Brehm, Back, and Bogdonoff, 1964; Carlsmith, Collins, and Helmreich, 1966; Cohen, 1959; Cohen, Brehm, and Fleming, 1958; Festinger and Carlsmith, 1959; Helmreich and Collins, 1968; Linder, Cooper, and Wicklund, 1968; Linder and Worchel, 1970; Mansson, 1969; Rabbie, Brehm, and Cohen, 1959; Sherman, 1970; Wicklund, Cooper, and Linder, 1967; Yaryan and Festinger, 1961; and Zimbardo, 1965. Even if the experimenter is not seen as representing the position implied by the behavior, the individual commonly can assume that others have been requested to perform the same inconvenient and uncomfortable behavior and have complied, which would imply again that the behavior reflects a value worth defending.

Our social influence analysis directly implies that a social setting is required in order for the "dissonance" effects to be realized. In terms of existing experimental research, the interpretation is successful, because in the forced compliance situation there is always an experimenter who goads the subject on. Our explanation should be extended to explain effects outside the laboratory also, and obviously the analysis applies whenever a person is coerced into performing a behavior disparate from his values, or whenever he encounters others with attitudes different from his own. However, there is a point at which the dissonance and social influence interpretations diverge, and, as might be expected, the source of this divergence is the absence of social influence. When a person undertakes a behavior that contradicts his values and there are no pressures in his social milieu associated with the onset of that behavior, dissonance theory would make approximately the same prediction as if the behavior were suggested by an experimenter. Very simply, the person will come to alter his attitude in the direction of the behavioral commitment. But our analysis offers no such prediction in the absence of social influence. Presently there is no experimental research of which we are aware that would distinguish between the dissonance and social influence explanations of the forced compliance effect, thus both theoretical arguments remain tenable.

Social Influence in the Free Decision Context

A common dissonance-arousing paradigm requires the subject to choose among two or more decision alternatives, and, subsequent to the decision, the attractiveness of the alternatives is measured. The crucial distinction between the free decision and forced compliance paradigms is with respect to explicit social influence: in the forced compliance case the experimenter openly presses the subject toward one of the alternatives. Normally this alternative consists of the counterattitudinal behavior, and the other alternative (which is usually rejected due to the experimenter's influence) is refusal to take part in that behavior. The predicted effect in the case of free decisions is identical to that in forced compliance. It is expected that the chosen course of action will increase in attractiveness, and, further, the unchosen is expected to decline.

But the two paradigms do differ in one vital respect, as we have noted: the presence or absence of social influence. But the absence of explicit influence in free decisions does not rule out a social influence interpretation of the free decision effects.

When a subject is asked to rate the attractiveness of decision alternatives, the experimenter's request can easily carry the implication that there are discriminable differences between the alternatives. From the subject's standpoint, why would there be a questionnaire at all unless the experimenter or interviewer were searching for differences in perception of the alternatives? If the subject thinks that the experimenter thinks there are meaningful differences between the alternatives, it would follow that subjects would generally exaggerate the difference between the preferred course of action and those he finds less preferable. This would lead to a spreading of the alternatives that would operate independently of the person's actual commitment to one or the other alternative.

At least one question has occurred to us in regard to this analysis. If social influence mediates what has been termed "postdecisional spreading," then why is the spreading phenomenon commonly observed only after decisions?

The answer to this is that there is virtually no evidence that decisions are necessary for the spreading effect. For example, Wicklund (1968) found a spreading effect among the decision alternatives prior to subjects' overt statement of decision. Further, Harris (1969) has reported an experiment that brings into serious question the importance of a decision in generating the spreading effect.

A second question is more important. As with the forced compliance paradigm, it is obvious that a social agent must mediate the attitude change according to our analysis, but it is true that many free decisions occur in the absence of interviewers, experimenters, or even passive onlookers. If the spreading effect occurs without the influence of others, then we can hardly make a case, but, to date, we are unaware of any research that clearly demonstrates postdecisional spreading of alternatives in the absence of a person to administer a measuring device. An unobtrusive measure is necessary in order to determine whether or not the presence of others is necessary.

Volition

Although our social influence interpretation of forced compliance and free decision paradigms appears to make some sense with respect to the variables we have discussed thus far, there remains the variable of volition that has received extended treatment by dissonance theorists, particularly within the forced compliance paradigm (see Brehm & Cohen, 1962). The role of volition in the social influence explanation should be discussed briefly. If an experimenter asks a subject to violate a personal value, will the experimenter be seen as more strongly against the subject's value if he demands the subject's obedience, or if he leaves the subject freedom to refuse? If the experimenter demands compliance, the subject then has reason to suspect the experimenter's judgment and intentions. Further, the experimenter's use of force will make apparent that he generally expects people to be opposed to the form of commitment required. In other words, the forceful experimenter will lose credibility, and at the same time he will communicate his expectation that everyone will be opposed to the commitment and to the attitude associated with the commitment. Thus attitude change will be most likely when the subject is given maximal volition, consistent with the usual experimental finding.

RESEARCH EVIDENCE

There is no advantage in our reviewing all dissonance literature that fits our analysis. We have already listed some examples of the forced compliance type of experiments. The research discussed below is given some elaboration because some of the manipulations performed within the context of cognitive dissonance research are simultaneously direct manipulations of objective self awareness. Our purpose in discussing these studies is that of emphasizing the role of objective self awareness in the experimental effects. When a researcher varies whether or not the discrepant behavior is performed in public or private, if anonymity is varied, if television cameras are introduced, or if the subject hears himself after recording a speech, it should be clear that "dissonance reduction" effects will depend on these objective self awareness-generating stimuli. Even though it is possible to find direct manipulations of the objective state in existing literature, most of these are not pure manipulations of just that factor; these variations are simultaneously manipulations of the amount of cognitive imbalance. Consequently, the experimental results generally follow from both the objective self awareness analysis and the dissonance analysis.

Previous Forced Compliance Research
That Has Varied Objective Self Awareness

CARLSMITH, COLLINS, AND HELMREICH (1966)

In the context of the present experiment it is possible to examine the effect of the presence of others on dissonance reduction. Subjects engaged in a behavior that was directly contradictory to their feelings about a certain matter, and they were either in the presence of others or alone. It was argued by the authors that the manipulation of whether or not the discrepant act was public would affect dissonance arousal and consequent dissonance reduction. Following a brief description of the procedure of their experiment we will attempt to demonstrate how that public-private variable, which received more detailed discussion in Chapter 5, is an ideal variation of objective self awareness.

The subject was brought into the laboratory, and borrowing from a well publicized experiment by Festinger and Carlsmith (1959), the authors confronted the subject with a seemingly trivial and dull task that consisted of crossing out random numbers printed in a booklet. After the subject had worked at this activity for an hour he was either asked to lie to a person who was said to be the next subject or else to write an essay that was also a lie. In both instances the lie took the form of some remarks praising the one-hour task; the major difference was that subjects in one condition had to lie in person to someone they believed was the next subject, while in the other condition subjects recorded the lies anonymously in an essay.

An additional variable was employed which consisted of various amounts of monetary incentive for the counterattitudinal performance. This variable was introduced into both the "face-to-face" condition and the "essay-writing" condition.

Given these two variables, the predictions from dissonance theory are straightforward. Subjects should reduce dissonance in direct proportion to the number of dissonant cognitions generated by the commitment and in inverse proportion to the amount of external justification provided for compliance. The results were entirely consistent with this analysis. When subjects were asked, after performance of the overt lying or essay writing, to indicate how interesting the task was, a relatively low monetary incentive effected higher ratings of interest provided the subject was in the face-to-face condition; but for subjects who merely wrote the essay, the same relationship did not hold. In fact, among the essay-writing subjects, more interest resulted when the incentive was high. This latter result was explained by Carlsmith *et al.* in terms alien to dissonance theory and we will not be concerned with that effect at present. For dissonance theory, and for the present analysis, the important result was that subjects justified their presence in a situation that did not offer ample reward only to the extent that they were in face-to-face contact with the person who was lied to while they carried out the dishonest behavior.

If we focus just on the face-to-face condition of this experiment, we find that the inverse relationship between amount of incentive and subsequent attitude change may be explained either through the dissonance argument or in terms of the social influence analysis we have proposed. With respect to dissonance theory, the individual should experience dissonance when he engages in a behavior he would otherwise avoid and he lacks sufficient reasons (cognitions consonant with the behavior) for doing so. From the social influence interpretation, the experimenter's offering only a pittance would indicate to the subject that the lie was not especially heinous and the task may be a desirable one from the experimenter's standpoint. It is the second variable, which we shall call the public-private dimension, that is critical for our analysis. According to the cognitive dissonance argument, the effectiveness of the public treatment in generating dissonance reduction can be attributed to the additional dissonant cognitions contributed by the public deceit. This analysis assumes that subjects generally would have preferred to remain anonymous and write an essay rather than role-play in front of another subject. Alternatively, one could conceptualize the essay-writing and overt lying as quantitatively similar in that each is the basis of a dissonant cognition. Then the added assumption that one of these cognitions is more important than the other is necessary for the analysis. Festinger's 1957 theory would allow either of these solutions, thus the theory does appear to predict that dissonance arousal will be maximized by the combination of the public dissonant act and a minimal incentive.

The theory of objective self awareness would offer a different view of the public-private dimension. The theory clearly implies an increase in objective self awareness when the individual is confronted with the attention of another person. As a consequence of felt evaluation, he will come to evaluate himself, especially along dimensions that are salient in his current situation, and in the present experiment that would mean an evaluation of his current attitude relative to the attitude conveyed by the experimenter and experimental situation. We need only assume that the subject sees the experimenter as attracted to the experimental task, and from this assumption it follows that liking for the task will be a positive function of the amount of objective self awareness.

HELMREICH AND COLLINS (1968)

As in the prior experiment, subjects were induced to carry out a behavior that contradicted an attitude. In this case the attitude held by subjects was a strong bias against government control over family size, and all subjects were asked to record a statement arguing that the size of families should be governmentally controlled. They were requested to record the statement under one of three conditions: an anonymous audio recording, an identified video recording with an opportunity for subsequent explanation by the subject that the communication did not represent his own viewpoint, and an identified video recording with no such opportunity. It was argued that dissonance would be maximal in the condition where there was no possibility of recanting the counterattitudinal statement because the subject would be obligated to leave the lasting impression on his audience that his stated views reflected his personal opinions. In contrast, dissonance should have been less in the "take-back" condition simply because the commitment had few permanent implications. The authors contended that dissonance arousal would be minimal in the third condition (anonymous audio tape) because subjects did not identify themselves and would never be personally identified with the message. These three conditions were each divided in half according to the amount of monetary incentive (small or large) offered for compliance.

On a dependent measure of agreement with the counterattitudinal statement, a negative relationship between amount of incentive and subsequent agreement was found within both of the conditions in which a video tape was employed, in contrast to a positive relationship within the audio tape condition. In part, these results were consistent with the expectations, and in part they were discrepant. We should examine the hypotheses closely to understand the implications of the results for dissonance theory.

It was originally expected that the subjects in the video tape condition, all of whom were asked to announce their names while recording the tape, would experience the most dissonance. After all, they were told that they would be held responsible for their progovernment regulation speeches when the tapes were played to the audience. Surely, under these conditions we would expect a considerable monetary incentive to attenuate the dissonance reduction processes. This is, of course, exactly what happened. The second video tape condition was identical in procedure to the first except that the subjects were allowed to recant, in the sense that they were allowed to follow the video recorded speech by recording a full explanation of the circumstances that led them to record the speech. In short, the audiences that were to see the tapes made by these subjects would be aware that the subjects had not expressed their true beliefs. The authors expected less dissonance arousal in this take-back condition, which was an entirely reasonable expectation in light of dissonance theory. Very simply, the number of dissonant cognitions is greater in the first condition than in the second, for in one case the subject is represented to the public as believing the counterattitudinal statement, while in the second it is made clear to the audience that he believes otherwise.

The authors expected less dissonance arousal in the take-back condition, thus the negative relationship between monetary incentive and attitude change should have been less than in the other video condition. In fact, the relationship in the take-back condition was negative, and virtually as strong as in the first condition. The result was unexpected, and the authors suggest that the similarity between the two conditions may be attributable to the general ineffectiveness of "undoing." In short, they consider the possibility that the disavowal did not reduce dissonance. But this is difficult to comprehend theoretically. From dissonance theory the take-back should have been effective in reducing dissonance, since the subject's explanation to the future audience essentially reduced the number of dissonant cognitions in that condition to a level approximating the control (audio) condition. Of course, it is possible that the subjects felt awkward and silly when presenting the recantation, and the resulting dissonance may have been reduced by coming to agree more with the communication. In any event, an explanation consistent with dissonance theory is not easy to contrive.

The case can be made that the theory of objective self awareness corresponds more closely to the Helmreich and Collins findings than does dissonance theory. Again, an experimenter was present; thus there was ample opportunity for unintended social influence. But for influence to occur, the subject must first become objectively self aware. We would suggest that facing a television camera is a strong means of arousing objective self awareness because the person can easily anticipate attention by numerous others once a video tape is made, and further, a television camera should be especially effective because very few people are accustomed to being evaluated via the television screen. In contrast, the audio tape recorder should lead to fewer evaluations from the potential audience, for they can never see the subject nor even know his name. It follows that attitude change would be more prevalent in the video conditions. The absence of a difference between the take-back and no-take-back condition is not surprising because objective self awareness should have been aroused equally in the two conditions. The fact of being able to recant following the initial recording session does not nullify the initial effect of the camera, thus the results of those two conditions should have been similar, as they were, if the experimental effects were mediated by objective self awareness. The effect of the monetary incentive will not be discussed in the present context, because the analysis is identical to that for the preceding experiment.

WICKLUND, COOPER, AND LINDER (1967)

The purpose of the second experiment reported by these authors was to demonstrate that anticipated effort can create dissonance and eventually increase the dissonance reduction that is due to anticipation of hearing a counterattitudinal communication. Male subjects were led to expect to hear a tape-recorded communication advocating that draft deferments be abolished for college students, and under a plausible pretext they were told that they would have to engage in an additional activity for a few minutes prior to hearing the tape. Some of the subjects expected only to sit and relax during that period, while others were told that they would have to run in place for seven minutes. From dissonance theory it was argued that the anticipation of running in place for seven minutes in an uncomfortably small cubicle would constitute a cognition dissonant with what subjects would choose to do given a choice of whether or not to exercise, and, as a consequence, dissonance reduction in the form of agreement with the forthcoming communication would be bolstered by the anticipated running. Very simply, by coming to agree with the communication the subject can convince himself that his effort is not totally in vain. The results were entirely consistent with this analysis, in that more attitude change toward the position of the antici-pated communication occurred when subjects expected to exercise than when they expected only to sit and relax. What does the experiment have to do with objective self awareness?

An individual who is asked to run in place for seven minutes in a cubicle barely big enough for two people should become objectively self aware through the anticipation of the experimenter watching him while he runs. The prospect of appearing slightly foolish in the eyes of someone else is entirely likely to bring forth self evaluation. Once the person is objectively self aware, he will evaluate himself along whatever dimensions are salient for him in the situation, and because he should become aware of the discrepancy between his private opinion of draft deferments and the anti-draft-deferment flavor of the experimental setting, attitude change should follow provided there is a source of social influ-ence.

We might note that the social influence explanation proposed earlier applies especially well in the present case. The subject could assume that an experimenter who plays a speech opposing draft deferments in an experimental context must be in favor of the speech for one reason or another, and if the experimenter is seen as credible and intelligent by the subject, the subject will alter his standard of correctness in the direction of the position taken in the speech, but only in proportion to his degree of objective self awareness. The standard of correctness, of course, is the attitude toward draft deferment.

SUMMARY

In general, it should be found that any research using the forced compliance paradigm has the potential to put the subject on the spot, render him incompetent, foolish, and otherwise cause him to perform unusual behaviors. If the extent of the person's involvement in unusual circumstances is correlated with the variation of dissonance arousal, and if an experimenter or anyone else is present to observe the person engage in the behavior, the case can be made that objective self awareness is bolstered by the experimental manipulation. As a result, discrepancy reduction should be greater whenever the subject is asked to engage in unusual behavior.

By pointing to elements in the preceding experiments that might have created objective self awareness, we do not intend a refutation of the cognitive dissonance analysis. The introduction of the objective self awareness notion does help appreciably in the Helmreich and Collins experiment, but in the other two cases the dissonance formulation explains the data as well. The purpose of employing these experiments as examples is to demonstrate the application of the social-influence extension of objective self awareness, so it is not surprising that other theories are applicable.

Research on the Effect
of Direct Awareness of Discrepancies

In three experiments conceived within the context of dissonance theory there was an experimental attempt to force the subject's attention onto the elements basic to the imbalance. In all three cases the conclusion was the same: dissonance reduction is bolstered if the person's attention is focused directly on the discrepant elements. The first two studies fall into the category of forced compliance, and the third is an example of the free decision paradigm.

CARLSMITH, EBBESEN, LEPPER,
ZANNA, JONCAS, AND ABELSON (1969)

The paradigm for these two studies was taken from an experiment by Aronson and Carlsmith (1963) in which dissonance was aroused in small children. The procedure involved tempting a child to engage in a deviant behavior, and the child was given either a strong or weak reason for not performing the behavior. It was crucial for the design of the experiment that the subjects not actually execute the deviant behavior, and only those children who abstained were kept as subjects.

Each child was shown several toys and was led to expect that he could play with them. The experimenter obtained rankings of the toys, then he prepared to leave the room. Prior to leaving, the subject was instructed not to play with a certain toy, the instruction being accompanied by either a mild or severe threat. The threat was not physical, but simply a promise of a mild or severe admonishment should the child disregard the instruction and play with the toy. At that point the experimenter left the room, and during the interim the subject was observed to insure that he did not play with the toy.

The purpose of the experiment was to ascertain the effect on dissonance reduction processes of forcing the child's attention onto the elements in the situation creating dissonance. This was accomplished in either of two ways: in the first experiment a pseudojanitor entered the room, pretended to sweep the floor, and in the process pointed to the forbidden toy, asking the child why he was not playing with it. In the second experiment the janitor did not enter. Instead, a light directly over the toy repeatedly flashed during the play period, presumably calling the subject's attention to the toy.

After several minutes of play the experimenter reentered the room and again asked the child to rank order the toys. The dependent measure consisted of changes in rankings, and it was expected that forcing the subject's attention onto the dissonant cognitions would boost dissonance reduction. The dissonance, of course, was conceptually between the decision to abstain from playing with the toy and the absence of reasons for doing so; thus dissonance should have been maximal when the threat was small, and should have been reduced by derogating the critical toy.

The authors expected dissonance reduction processes to be bolstered by the janitor's remark and flashing light only to the extent that dissonance was originally aroused at all, which means that the focusing stimuli should have had a small effect, if any, in the strong threat condition. In fact, the data did not follow this pattern. Instead, dissonance reduction was facilitated by the focusing stimuli no matter whether the threat was weak or strong.

BREHM AND WICKLUND (1970)

This experiment was designed initially to test a proposition set forth about postdecision regret by Festinger in 1964. The notion of regret will be examined below, and we need not pursue it further at present.

The design of the experiment involved a free decision between two alternatives, and, similar to the experiments reported above, some of the subjects were forced to examine the "dissonance-arousing" components of the experimental situation. Only two of the conditions need to be discussed. Subjects were led to believe they were taking a type of personality test and that they would be evaluated on the basis of whether or not they could ascertain which of two men was better qualified for a certain type of position. A list of several traits was furnished to aid the subject in making her choice, and in addition to the list a picture of each man was supplied. In each case the picture reflected the sole negative aspect of the man: One person appeared shifty, a trait that could only hinder his job performance, and the second man's drawback was his extreme age. After the subject chose one of the two men she was given ten minutes to reconsider each man while the experimenter asked for an additional rating of the two men at one-minute intervals. In one condition the subject was confronted with the picture of the chosen man during the interval; in the second condition the picture was absent.

Because ten postdecisional measurements were taken for each subject it was possible to examine for each subject the maximum amount of regret and dissonance reduction. Regret was defined as a tendency for the decisional alternatives to reverse in attractiveness, whereas dissonance reduction was defined as a spreading of the alternatives in attractiveness. The difference between conditions in mean amount of regret was significantly different, and it might be noted that the most regret resulted in the condition with no focused attention, contrary to Festinger's 1964 suggestion. More important for the objective self awareness analysis were the dissonance reduction results. The obtained difference indicated that the forced focusing of subjects' attention on the negative characteristic of the chosen alternative resulted in increased dissonance reduction. The latter result was consistent with the finding of Carlsmith et al.; thus it would appear that the general idea is well supported.

The research by Carlsmith et al. and Brehm and Wicklund was not drawn directly from dissonance theory, but from an extratheoretical assumption that forcing the person's attention on an inconsistency will enhance the inconsistency-reduction process. The results of the Carlsmith et al. experiments could be explained especially well by the objective self awareness notion because the salience manipulation should have created the objective state and because the forced-compliance nature of the study should have created the results through social influence. The social influence was an obvious one: the experimenter told the subject not to play with the toy, and he either threatened the subject mildly or strongly. From the standpoint of social influence, the experimenter's derogation should have been most influential when the threat was mild, for a severe threat would reduce his credibility in addition to suggesting that the toy possessed hidden virtues. The other variable in the Carlsmith et al. study is essentially a manipulation of objective self awareness. The subject's attention is drawn to that aspect of himself that is in discord with the experimenter's wishes. It would follow that social influence (derogation of the critical toy) would be maximal when attention is focused on that aspect of the self. The results bear a strong conceptual resemblance to the first experiment reported by Wicklund and Duval that involved the subject hearing his tape-recorded voice.

The results of the Brehm and Wicklund experiment are interpretable in terms of social influence if we recall the previous remarks on free decisions. By asking for ratings of the decision alternatives, the experimenter is suggesting that there are meaningful differences between the alternatives, and his power to influence the subject toward exaggerating the differences in ratings increases as the subject is objectively self aware with respect to his evaluation of the alternatives.

An Experiment on Objective Self Awareness
and Discrepancy Reduction

A somewhat stronger case could be made for our objective self awareness analysis of attitude-behavior discrepancies if the objective state were created in a fashion that did not focus the person's attention directly on the disparate elements, and in a way that did not simultaneously vary the amount of discrepancy between attitude and behavior. This was accomplished in the second study reported by Wicklund and Duval (1971), using an experimental paradigm similar to many of the forced compliance experiments.

The subjects, undergraduate females, were run individually in a small cubicle. Half of them were assigned to a "Camera" condition, and half to "No camera" condition. The purpose of employing a camera was to arouse objective self awareness in some of the subjects during the session, and it was expected that subjects would show more attitude change in the presence of the camera. The camera was in fact a television camera, described to the subject as operating for the purpose of testing the equipment. Since the subject had good reason to think that the video tape of her session would be viewed later by someone in the department of psychology, the theory of objective self awareness allows us to argue that she would become objectively self aware through the anticipation of being viewed. The camera was aimed directly at the subject, and the experimenter announced that it would run throughout the session.

The subject was then told that some handwritten essays were needed for future research, and at this point the experimenter directed her to copy five strongly worded essays in her own handwriting. The essays all took unpopular positions on five issues related to the college life of the subjects. Finally the subject was asked to fill out an attitude questionnaire that included the five critical issues, and because a premeasure had been given previously, change scores could be computed for all five issues.

Consistent with the theoretical expectation there was more attitude change toward the positions taken in the speeches when subjects were in the presence of the camera ($p < .02$), and this relationship held for all five issues. Given these results, the experiment suggests that objective self awareness can mediate dissonance reduction, and, more important, it appears that the method used to induce objective self awareness need not point directly at the dissonance. In the present example, the attention of the subject was focused on her face, if anything, and the operation of the effect relied upon the subject's switching from an objective self awareness with respect to her face into a critical examination of her attitude-behavior discrepancy. We think the underlying principle is a general state of self awareness, instigated whenever the person is forced to examine any aspect of himself. Once his face, his attitude on some issue, his tone of voice, or any other single aspect becomes the focus of attention, the resulting general objective state will predispose him to be self critical toward any salient aspect of the self.

An important aspect of this experiment that favors our theoretical interpretation is the apparent independence of the manipulation of objective self awareness from dissonance arousal. Only the face of the subject was to be represented on video tape, not her counterattitudinal behavior. In experiments derived from cognitive dissonance theory the television camera typically would have been employed to make the performance more public or to impart greater personalism to the tape (e.g., Helmreich & Collins), but in this experiment the counterattitudinal performance was identical in both conditions. Consequently, unless the subject was unusually paranoid and supposed that her essays would be read together with the showing of her video tape, there was no theoretical reason for believing there to be more dissonance in the presence of the camera.

Obviously the social influence interpretation applies as well here as in the previous research, but we need not spell it out in the present instance.

A Choice of Strategy in Examining the Evidence

Before proceeding, we would like to point out an optional strategy. Throughout the chapter the research evidence can be examined from either of two perspectives. The social influence analysis can be adopted where appropriate, and experimental results can then be seen as a product of influence and objective self awareness. Alternatively, the cognitive dissonance interpretations can be left intact, but qualified in the sense that objective self awareness is a necessary precondition for dissonance arousal and reduction. In looking back at the evidence just reviewed, it seems clear that either of these viewpoints applies. The one we have adopted assumes only the tenets of the theory of objective self awareness, while the other uses the theory as a supplement to existing balance theories. For reasons of parsimony we prefer the former approach, but the reader is left to decide for himself which alternative makes most sense.

FURTHER EXTENSIONS AND QUESTIONS

We have seen in Chapters 4 and 5 that an objective self awareness analysis of social influence and conformity phenomena can provide insight into the conditions mediating the influence process. Similarly, it would appear that an extension of the theory to attitude-behavior discrepancy research performed in the context of dissonance theory can facilitate understanding of the individual's efforts to reduce dissonance. Specifically, there is theoretical reason to suppose that dissonance reduction will occur only when the individual is objectively self aware, and we have seen several examples of the role of stimuli leading to the objective state in enhancing dissonance reduction. In this sense the theory is used as a supplement to balance theories in order to point to the circumstances under which balance restoration phenomena might be observed, but not as an explanatory device for the balance restoration process itself. There is also a more powerful way to use the theory. If the social influence extension of the theory is combined with the arousal of objective self awareness in the dissonance paradigms, much of the existing research can be explained adequately through the objective self awareness notion without reference to balance principles.

Selective Exposure to Information

We have already discussed the social influence interpretations of forced compliance and free decision phenomena, and the remaining significant area of cognitive dissonance research—selective exposure to information—can be analyzed through the theory as well.

When an individual engages in a decision he can be expected to abide by the personal value that he desires to make correct decisions. This has been assumed implicitly in the dissonance research on selective exposure and free decisions. Any information he encounters following the decision that implies a failure to follow the standard will arouse objective self awareness, for such information will emphasize his uniqueness. From our postulate concerning the negative affect associated with the objective state, we would expect the person to avoid the information provided that it implies an incorrect decision. We will return to our discussion of avoidance below.

Not only should we expect avoidance, but there are good reasons to expect approach, or exposure to certain types of information as well. From the assumption that people value correct decisions it would follow from the theory of objective self awareness that a person will engage in activities to reduce any discrepancies between his present state and that standard, and if there is information available which tells him that his behavior is not discrepant from the standard, he would be expected to absorb himself in such information, but only to the degree that there was self doubt about the correctness of his decision in the first place. This proposition was supported by Mills (1965b), who allowed subjects to choose among alternatives that were either rated closely or else a considerable distance apart. He found that interest in advertisements for the chosen alternatives was positively related to the degree of uncertainty. His research was cast in terms of dissonance theory, but it is also possible to interpret the exposure effect in terms of objective self awareness. Presumably the subjects had a standard of correctness consisting of the desire to be correct in their decisions, and following the decision there should have been a substantial degree of self doubt among subjects who chose between closely rated alternatives. In order to reduce this self doubt, that is, reduce the discrepancy between behavior and standard, the subject could easily expose himself to information that told him his behavior was not discrepant from his standard.

In another experiment Mills (1965a) demonstrated the same phenomenon, with one major difference: subjects had not yet decided, and instead of exposing themselves to information favoring the chosen alternative, they were given the possibility of seeing information favorable to the preferred alternative. The results of this study were interpreted in terms of Mills' notion of choice certainty, which proposes a general tendency for people to attempt to become certain that they will choose the correct alternative. An objective self awareness analysis of this experiment is not different from that in the preceding paragraph. When objectively self aware, the person will entertain possible discrepancies between the standard of choosing correctly and his actual behavior, whether the behavior consists of a current preference (tentative commitment) or an accomplished decision. The more self doubt about the correctness of the preference, the greater the exposure to information that tells him he will choose correctly.

There is a considerable body of literature on selective exposure, but we will not discuss it for two reasons: much of it fails to support the proposition of selective exposure because of insufficient experimental controls, as McGuire (1968) has noted, and some of it simply demonstrates the phenomenon without investigating variables relevant to the theory of objective self awareness. From our standpoint the advantages of dwelling on Mills' research are at least two: the experimental controls offer considerable improvement over other research, and his investigation of the role of certainty brings the research closer to a clear objective self awareness interpretation.

Wicklund and Ickes (1972)

If we may assume that arriving at a correct decision constitutes a standard of correctness, it is a simple step to propose that the objectively self aware person will be increasingly concerned about making a correct decision. In short, he will desire to minimize any discrepancy between the outcome of his decision and his aspiration of arriving at the best possible decision. It follows that a person will expose himself to certainty-increasing information to the degree that he is objectively self aware, and this derivation is the focus of the experiment to be reported below.

In addition to exploring the effects of objective self awareness on exposure, one additional variable will be examined. In Mills' (1965a) study, the subjects' certainty was varied prior to the choice point and, as noted previously, the relatively uncertain subjects evidenced greater exposure to certainty-bolstering material. A priori certainty will also be manipulated in the present experiment in a manner similar to Mills, although the precise nature of the relationship between this variable and the self awareness variable is unclear. Obviously there should generally be an overall effect for certainty, such that exposure to certainty-increasing information is greater with low certainty, but there is no firm basis for predicting whether or not objective self awareness and prior certainty will interact. Conceivably the objective self awareness variable will only make a difference for subjects who are highly uncertain, but, on the other hand, it is also possible that heightened objective self awareness will cause all subjects to devote their efforts to making the correct decision, independent of the difficulty of the decision.

In summary, the following hypothesis is proposed: exposure to certainty-increasing information will increase directly with objective self awareness and with difficulty of decision.

The subject (all subjects were female undergraduates) was greeted by the experimenter and ushered into an experimental cubicle where she was invited to sit down. She was then given the cover story for what was described as a two-part study. For the first part of the study the subject was told that she would be asked to read some material into a tape recorder. The experimenter indicated that her recording would be used in later research. The second part of the study was described as a survey involving new courses.

Once the preliminary instructions had been given, the subject was asked to make a three-to four-minute audio tape recording in which she read the introductory pages of a social psychology textbook. This recording was supposedly to be used as part of the experimenter's control data in a future study he was planning to run for his master's thesis. The instructions given to the subject for her tape recording were as follows:

> While making the recording please speak about as rapidly as you would in a telephone conversation with a friend. Once we start recording I won't be able to stop and erase, so if you make a mistake just correct yourself and finish reading the material through to the end. Wait until I introduce you on the tape and then begin reading.

When the taping was completed, the experimenter proceeded to explain the second part of the study, an ostensible survey on proposed courses relating to sex. The survey was described as being unrelated to the tape recording the subject had just made, and the following rationale was given:

> Last spring the curriculum committee asked a random sample of students to suggest some courses they would like to have offered. One of the categories the students chose most often dealt with sex and sexual behavior. The curriculum committee has developed a list of prospective courses dealing specifically with sex, and two of these courses will be offered next fall on a trial basis. The committee has asked us to get a sample of students' opinions about these courses and pass the reactions along to them. I'm now going to read you short descriptions of the two courses, and in a few minutes I will ask you which of the courses you would most like to take.

For subjects in the Easy Choice conditions the experimenter read descriptions of an anthropology course entitled "The Sexual Behavior of Primitive Man," and a zoology course entitled "The Physiology of Sex." The anthropology course supposedly dealt with such topics as incest taboos and fertility rites in preliterate societies, while the zoology course primarily concerned the neurophysiological correlates of sexual behavior in the rat brain. These course descriptions had been written to deliberately enhance the attractiveness of the anthropology course over the zoology course in order to make the choice between these alternatives an "easy" one.

For subjects in the Difficult Choice conditions the description of the anthropology course was followed by the description of an English course entitled "Eroticism and Modern Literature." This course promised Lawrence's *Lady Chatterley's Lover* (1932) and Miller's *Tropic of Cancer* (1961) as samples of the course titles. According to pretest data, the choice between these two alternatives could be considered a "difficult" one.

After reading the course descriptions aloud to the subject, the experimenter stated that although the two courses would not be offered until the fall semester of the next school year, it would be possible for her to preregister early for one of the courses since she had participated in the survey. To help her decide whether or not to preregister and which course to register for, the experimenter said that he had several sources of information she could see before making her choice. He then gave the subject the "survey" questionnaire.

The questionnaire contained the measure of desire for exposure. It simply listed 12 different types of course-related information, such as reading assignments and sample test questions, and asked the subject to check whichever items she would like the experimenter to furnish her before deciding.

The subject was instructed to complete the survey, indicating all the sources of information she would like to see before making her decision. While delivering these instructions, the experimenter simultaneously rewound the tape, so that just as the subject was about to begin filling out the survey, he suddenly "remembered" to give her these additional instructions:

> Oh, by the way, I just remembered that I wanted to get your opinion on the quality of the tapes I've been making. Specifically, I would like to know how natural the recording sounds to you—whether the reproduction is good or whether it sounds artificial and unnatural. I'm going to play back (your own tape/the tape I made earlier today of another girl), and, to save time, why don't you just give half an ear to it while you fill out the survey questionnaire? I've got to go downstairs to get the folders with the information about the courses, so I'll ask you for your opinion of the tape when I get back.

Thus, subjects in the High Objective Self Awareness (High OSA) condition were asked to listen to a playback of their own recorded voices, while subjects in the Low Objective Self Awareness (Low OSA) condition heard the same selection recorded by another girl. The control tape was randomly selected from the tapes of subjects used to pretest the experimental procedures. The experimenter left the room and waited outside the door until the tape ended. He returned to collect the dependent measure, then the subject was tested for suspicion and given a thorough debriefing.

In accordance with the predictions, the amount of information requested prior to making the choice was greater for the High OSA condition than for the Low OSA condition ($p < .005$) (see Table 6). Likewise, subjects who made a difficult choice requested more information than those who made an easy choice ($p < .05$). There was no hint of an interaction.

The theoretical basis of the present experiment assumed that objective self awareness causes the person to become increasingly concerned about making a correct decision, this concern or doubt being reflected in exposure to relevant information. The data indicated that the desire for information conducive to arriving at a correct decision was higher among subjects who heard their own voices than among those who heard another's voice. This result is consistent with the hypothesis, similar to the first experiment reported by Wicklund and Duval, and suggests that a tape-recorded voice is an effective means of raising objective self awareness. The second finding in the experiment replicated earlier results of Mills: exposure to relevant information was a positive function of the difficulty of the decision. However, there was no indication that objective self awareness interacts with difficulty of decision. It should be noted that subjects given an easy decision did not reject the possibility of exposure to information. The typical easy decision subject wanted to see approximately three or four items of information. In short, even in the easy choice condition there was room for doubt, and it remains for future research to ascertain whether or not objective self awareness has any effect on the decision-making process when the choice is completely obvious and free of ambiguity.

The experiment indicates that predecisional exposure to information may be affected considerably by the individual's self awareness, and in order to place the experiment in proper perspective we should note that the present research is not the first to indicate that variations in focused attention play a part in the decision-making process. Three experiments cited earlier in this chapter (one by Brehm and Wicklund, 1970, and two by Carlsmith *et al.*)

TABLE 6

Desire for Exposure to Information

	Easy decision	Difficult decision
High OSA	5.00[a] (10)[b]	6.00 (10)
Low OSA	2.43 (7)	4.30 (10)

[a]Mean number of items of information requested out of a possible twelve.
[b]N.

found that dissonance-reduction processes are facilitated when attention is forced directly on the elements of the decision that are basic to dissonance arousal. These experimental procedures made the subject objectively self aware, and did so specifically on the self-related dimension of whether or not the dissonance-arousing decision was correct. In the experiment by Brehm and Wicklund the subject's attention was focused on the negative attributes of the chosen alternative. The study showed that dissonance reduction in the form of spreading of the attractiveness of two alternatives was enhanced under conditions of focused attention. Similarly, Carlsmith *et al.* demonstrated in two experiments that children justify their deciding not to play with a toy to the degree that their attention is focused directly on the critical toy. We may view these studies as having focused the individual's attention upon a salient aspect of himself as decision-maker. In essence, the procedures forced the subject to examine the wisdom of his decision and, in that sense, were powerful instigators of objective self awareness with respect to choice of certain alternatives.

The Brehm and Wicklund study and Carlsmith *et al.* study are closely related to two experiments accomplished with the framework of objective self awareness theory, the major difference being that the experiments designed from the theory did not focus the subject's attention directly on the elements in his decision. First, an experiment on the forced-compliance effect reported earlier in this chapter showed that subjects increased their agreement with positions they were committed to defend, but only under conditions where a television camera was focused on them throughout the procedure. Second, the present experiment showed that the attempt to increase certainty about a decision was bolstered by the sound of one's own voice. These latter two experiments strongly imply that objective self awareness can alter the person's cognitive handling of the decision-making process, even when he is made self aware on dimensions seemingly unrelated to the decision. This is entirely consistent with the theory, for it has been postulated that attention will shift toward whatever aspect of the individual is salient once he becomes objectively self aware. Thus the present experiment could have begun with forcing the subject's attention onto any dimension of himself such as his personality traits or face, and attention should have then shifted to that aspect of himself most salient, which presumably was the decision process.

Selective Avoidance of Information

Turning to the selective avoidance of information, the best evidence for this phenomenon comes from two experiments by Mills (1965c). Subjects chose among two alternatives, then rated their interest in exposure to advertisements for the chosen and unchosen alternatives. It was found that interest in information supportive of the chosen alternative was greater than would be expected from the desirability of the product; and conversely, interest in information supportive of the rejected alternative was less than would be expected from the desirability of the product.

Mills' experiments on avoidance are vaguely similar to the study by Duval, Wicklund, and Fine (1970) on avoidance of the objective state (Chapter 2). In that study, subjects were confronted with either positive or negative information about themselves; then objective self awareness was created for some subjects by means of a mirror and television camera. Subjects showed avoidance of conditions leading to the objective state only when they carried into the situation a prior failure experience. Presumably Mills' subjects were objectively self aware at the time they indicated whether or not they wanted exposure to certain information, for they were confronted by the experimenter and were forced to contemplate the possibility of discovering that they made an erroneous decision. Had Mills' experiments been run in such a way that the subject's ratings of interest in exposure could be made while the person was subjectively self aware, the avoidance effect should have decreased markedly.

Regret and Awareness of Discrepancy

Until 1964 cognitive dissonance theory appeared to postulate that the arousal of dissonance led directly to dissonance reduction, but in his 1964 revision of the theory Festinger suggested that the onset of dissonance reduction can be preceded by a phase of "regret" which amounts to an admission by the person that his decision carries certain undesirable elements. The regret notion was applied only to the case of the free decision in experiments by Festinger and Walster (1964) and Walster (1964), where regret was measured in terms of whether or not the individual tended toward decreasing his evaluation of the chosen alternative relative to the unchosen. The conception need not be so limited, however, and it obviously applies to any dissonance arousal generated by a decision. In the forced compliance research, regret should be manifested in a change of attitude away from the attitude implied by the behavioral commitment.

Festinger's explanation of regret assumes that regret is instrumental in dissonance reduction. Shortly after the decision, the person is said to focus on the dissonance (presumably this means on the elements creating the dissonance) in an effort to deal with the dissonant cognitions—to rationalize, deny, derogate, or otherwise alter the cognitions in the interest of consistency. The more the individual focuses on these cognitions, the more dissonance reduction should result. This implies that regret will be positively related to the amount of dissonance, and, further, when dissonance is high there should be a considerable regret effect followed by a dissonance reduction effect of some consequence. Given this two-process theoretical statement it is always tempting to look for parameters, but it would generally be poor theoretical thinking to imagine that the relative lengths of the regret and dissonance reduction phases can be specified, just as it would be pointless to quantify dissonance itself. We need not pursue the issue of parameters at present, for we are only interested in Festinger's basic statement that the processes described by dissonance theory are three-fold: first the decision, then regret, and, finally, dissonance reduction.

One problem with Festinger's interpretation of regret is that it simply does not correspond to regret as observed in experiments. In the experiment by Walster, subjects chose freely, and evaluative changes in the alternatives were measured subsequently at four different time intervals after the decision. A substantial regret effect resulted four minutes after the decision, which was followed by dissonance reduction eleven minutes later. This much of the data seems to coincide with the theoretical statement, but the interpretation is dealt a blow by measurements taken immediately after the decision. At that point there was a strong tendency toward dissonance reduction which was significantly different from the regret that occurred slightly later at four minutes. This result clearly contradicts the prediction that dissonance reduction will be followed by regret.

A second difficulty with Festinger's proposition arises from the experiment by Brehm and Wicklund, in which the artificially imposed salience of dissonant cognitions decreased postdecisional regret. If it is correct that regret has its basis in the individual's awareness of dissonant cognitions, that result should have been the opposite. In summary, Festinger's explanation of regret is weak, certainly in need of modification, and might better be usurped by other explanations. At present, a more accurate analysis of regret is available in reactance theory (Brehm, 1966; Brehm & Wicklund, 1970; Walster & Berscheid, 1968; Wicklund, 1970), although we will not examine that theoretical statement at present.

The purpose of our discussing regret is that the phenomenon could be as important to the objective self awareness formulation as it is to dissonance theory. When the person first becomes objectively self aware, it is postulated that he will realize various intra-self discrepancies that went unnoticed in the state of subjective self awareness, and upon this realization that he will attempt to reduce the uncomfortable state of objective self awareness either by avoiding the stimuli provoking the state or through attempts at reduction in the discrepancy. It is the realization of discrepancy—the self criticism that necessarily precedes the discrepancy reduction—that concerns us because of its evasiveness. There is indirect evidence for the realization of discrepancy in the attribution research reported in Chapter 9, and one piece of direct evidence for admission of discrepancies in Chapter 2 (Ickles and Wicklund). But aside from this evidence, the self-critical phase seems more difficult to tap into than the discrepancy-reduction phase. This could mean any of the following: First, the theory may be incorrect and the experiments spurious confirmation, a possibility which we think unlikely in light of the consistent positive results. Second, the self critical period might consist of processes that cannot be verbalized. The individual might be vaguely uneasy, unable to point directly to the source of his discomfort, but nonetheless proceed to reduce discrepancies or avoid objective self awareness in any case. Third, our methods of measurement may be inappropriate to reflect the self criticism. We are inclined to entertain the last of these possibilities, in part because of the nature of the theory, which depends on cognitive mediation, and in part because the measurement problem applies to dissonance theory and regret as well.

The measurement problem is at least two-fold. There are questions of timing of measurements, and questions of appropriateness. With respect to timing of measurement we can revert to dissonance theory for examples, where the measurement of regret is relatively straightforward in that changes in attractiveness constitute what Festinger calls regret. The Walster experiment is quite informative, because the evaluative changes virtually oscillated from one moment to the next. Immediately after the decision there was a trend toward dissonance reduction, followed by regret, followed by dissonance reduction, followed by the absence of any effect. The implications of Walster's experiment are ominous. In nearly all dissonance research only one measurement is taken following the decision, and there is no *a priori* method of knowing whether the timing of the measurement is appropriate for tapping into the regret phase or the dissonance reduction phase. Further, the problem is not as simple as knowing when these phases occur for the average subject, for the onset and termination of the two phases would undoubtedly vary depending on who is being measured and other factors.

Irrespective of any individual differences in the sequence of these phases, it is theoretically sound to expect the period of self criticism to come shortly after the introduction of objective self awareness, for it is at this point that the person first becomes aware of his discrepancies and has neither had the opportunity to avoid the objective state nor to reduce the discrepancy. The only problem is in the definition of immediacy: this could mean nothing more than seconds in numerous situations, and, as a consequence, we could never be completely sure that the timing is appropriate. Probably the best assurance that the self critical phase is being tapped would be provided by forcing objective self awareness in a situation allowing no discrepancy reduction. This was accomplished in the experiment by Duval, Wicklund, and Fine, but no information on self criticism was obtained in that study.

Assuming that we know something about the conditions that would lead people to show self criticism, there still remains the question of an appropriate measure of self criticism. In the dissonance experiments the only strategy has been to employ the same measure for both regret and dissonance reduction, but there is no reason to believe that this is appropriate in the context of objective self awareness. In general, when one is interested in measuring a given effect, he designs his measure with the intent of uncovering the phenomenon—he does not use an identical measure for two effects simply because they occur in conjunction. There is no necessity that self criticism and discrepancy reduction are two opposite poles on a single continuum, and instead of measuring the individual's estimate of the discrepancy it may well be more enlightening to ask him whether or not he is satisfied with himself on the dimension in question (Ickes and Wicklund), obtain from him a list of his shortcomings on the dimension, or any other method of eliciting self criticism. Perhaps a more indirect route to measurement of self criticism would entail asking the person to embark on a task that requires competence on the dimension in question. We might expect the self critical person to show reluctance to proceed with the task, in contrast with a subjectively self aware person who should be at the other extreme with his self confidence and absence of reflection.

Behavior Change

It is obvious by now that dissonance research has focused on attitude change to the near exclusion of behavioral change. In the forced compliance research the dissonance is postulated to occur from inconsistency between attitudes and behavior, and the justification for measuring attitude change is that the dissonance is expected to be resolved primarily through attitude change, for attitudes are viewed by researchers as the least resistant to change of the two elements. When there is behavioral commitment, the cognition corresponding to that commitment is highly resistant to change simply because it is difficult to deny that one has behaved, and from this line of argument dissonance researchers have justified their consistent use of attitude change as the only measure.

We do not intend to imply that investigations of behavior change are nonexistent in the cognitive dissonance literature; however, most of the research on behavior change has substituted behavior change for attitude change, in that the person's attempt to behave consistently with an experimental commitment is measured. The problem of realigning behavior with the preexisting standard has seldom been attacked within the dissonance literature. The following experiments will give a representative idea of dissonance-reduction through behavior change as the problem has been approached.

THE GAMBLING EXPERIMENTS

Festinger (1957) reported an experiment on gambling that was replicated by Cohen, Brehm, and Latané (1959). Festinger's subjects were given a small amount of money to use in a card game and were allowed to play on either of two sides. At the outset it was fairly clear from the description of the game which side should win. Once the subject had chosen a side several hands were played, and unknown to the subject the deck was stacked such that after twelve hands a few subjects were winning slightly while the remainder of the subjects were losing, and their losses were anywhere from a slight amount to a substantial loss.

After the twelfth hand the subject was allowed to examine freely a graph that ostensibly showed the true probability of winning throughout the remainder of the game. It was found that the subjects who were winning or losing slightly studied the graph for a long time, whereas those who were losing moderately or quite badly spent less time in examination of the graph. According to Festinger, the results follow from the theory because the dissonance created by losing would only be increased by exposure telling the loser that he is going to lose. But the result was more complicated, and here is where behavior change enters. Subjects were allowed to switch sides at the twelve-trial juncture, and those who were losing extremely badly spent more time examining the graph than those who were losing moderately. Festinger's argument for this effect is as follows:

> If the dissonance becomes greater than the resistance to change of behavior, the behavior should change. In this manner the dissonance is eliminated and what was dissonant with knowledge about the old behavior is, of course, consonant with knowledge about the new behavior. If the dissonance is so large that it is *almost* sufficient to overcome the resistance to changing the behavior, one may expect that the easiest way to eliminate the dissonance is temporarily to increase it sufficiently so as to change the behavior. Under these circumstances one would expect persons to expose themselves to dissonance-increasing information. However, this would occur only in instances of extremely large, near maximum, dissonance [1957, p. 163].

Perhaps this effect is not surprising, but whether unexpected or not, this research is one of the few instances of a behavior change in the direction of an existing value (the value of winning) that has been described as dissonance reduction.

BREHM AND CROCKER (1962)

Subjects were required to fast through breakfast and lunch, then, when they arrived for the experiment, the experimenter asked them to continue fasting through the dinner hour. Some subjects were promised five dollars for this continued fasting while no monetary justification was provided for the other subjects. Subsequent to the commitment to fasting, a subjective measure of hunger was taken, and, as would be expected from dissonance theory, the subjects who were not paid indicated the least hunger. The behavioral measure consisted of the subject's ordering food to eat later. They were told that some food would be furnished at the end of the evening following the fast, and they were simply asked how many of various items they would like to eat at the end of the evening. The results for this measure paralleled those of the subjective hunger measure: subjects who were not paid ordered less food.

It might be noted that the behavioral index of dissonance reduction took a much different form in the present experiment from that in the study by

Festinger. Subjects in the earlier experiment exposed themselves to information in preparation for changing to a behavior that was coincident with a preexisting value of performing well, and the new behavior was opposite to the behavioral commitment that aroused dissonance. But in the present case there was no reversion to a preexisting value. Instead, the behavioral measure was an indication of the subject's tendency to act contrary to the value that was basic to the dissonance—this value, being one against personal fasting. As such, this behavioral index corresponds with the change in attitude toward one's hunger.

There is no advantage in our dwelling on other studies conceptually similar, but we might note that the following are additional examples of forced compliance experiments in which there was a behavioral measure of the person's tendency to align his cognitions with an experimental behavioral commitment. In 1962 Aronson and Carlsmith found that subjects who had an expectancy for a certain performance that was based on several previous successes or failures tended to adjust subsequent performance in accordance with the expectations. Brock, Edelman, Edwards, and Schuck (1965), Cottrell (1965), and Ward and Sandvold (1963) replicated, at least in part, the finding of Aronson and Carlsmith. In a different context Harris (1969) found a behavioral manifestation of the "spreading" of attractiveness of alternatives following a decision. A rather dramatic finding was produced by Zimbardo et al. (1969), who gave subjects varying amounts of justification for undergoing electric shock during a learning procedure. It was argued that subjects given insufficient justification would come to minimize the pain, and, accordingly, the shock should therefore interfere less with their performance. The results unequivocally supported this contention. Additional experiments with behavioral measures are reported by Zimbardo (1969a) in his treatise on the cognitive control of motivation, and although they are extremely interesting studies, we have already given sufficient examples. Dissonance reduction can be manifested by a behavior that is consonant with a prior behavioral commitment, just as dissonance reduction is manifested by attitude change in the direction of behavioral commitment in the studies we examined earlier.

As we have seen from the research examples above, behavioral change in the sense of reversal of the original commitment is seldom the focus of dissonance research. The closely related experiments of Festinger and Cohen et al. are the only exceptions, and even in those experiments there is no hint that the change from the original commitment was the primary focus of the research. Why is change in the original commitment never studied? Perhaps because revocation of the commitment is an obvious effect. In the forced compliance studies, the subject who agrees to perform an unpleasant action that is dissonant with an attitude could be given the option of not continuing with his action. Certainly many of the subjects would opt out, and presumably this would be dissonance-reduction. In more conceptual terms, this effect involves the person's behaving so that he fulfills a preexisting value, but from the standpoint of those who study dissonance processes, the interesting effects are the cases of the value changing to fit the behavior.

We should examine more thoroughly the assumption about the behavioral cognition. Apparently the resistance to change of a cognitive element has been assumed to lie in the recency of behaviors performed that underlie the element, but this assumption leads to some questionable implications. For example, if someone has always loved his mother, has behaved in a manner consistent with his feelings throughout his life, then is asked by a social psychologist to tape record an anti-mother statement, does the anti-mother cognition thereby acquire the status of least resistant to change? Certainly, recency of commitment cannot be such a powerful determinant of cognitive work. "Resistance to change" in this example only means that the subject has no opportunity to change the commitment in the experimental setting. In the dissonance research there are no allowances for the possibility that the original attitude might be the most resistant element, and if such allowances were made we might be surprised at the strength of certain balance effects. What does the objective self awareness formulation have to say about the question of the least resistant element to change?

The theory is clear about the form that discrepancy reduction will take: the person will move his behaviors or attitudes toward the direction of his personal standard of correctness provided that one pole of the discrepancy constitutes a correct standard. We would equate resistance to change with personal correctness, and we would expect the person to attempt to bring the behavior into line with the standard if he were given free rein. In an experimental situation there are constraints against this behavior change. The person cannot reverse his behavior back toward the standard until he leaves the experimental setting. If attitude change occurs, that is, a shift in the personal standard, such change can usually be attributed to the social influence interpretation described earlier.

Were behavior change allowed in an experiment, it would seem that discrepancy reduction would be served by a change of behavior in the direction of the preexisting standard of correctness. More important, behavior change in the direction of the standard should result to the degree that the person is objectively self aware. If the person is given a certain amount of freedom in the forced compliance situation, such as control over the length, persuasiveness, or future implications of his behavior, we would expect his attempted discrepancy reduction to be manifested in an effort to minimize his involvement in the behavior. Moreover, were the subject given an opportunity to recant or otherwise undo his behavior in the experimental situation, we should expect the objectively self aware person to show little hesitancy in doing so.

Finally, it should be noted that counterattitudinal behavior as conceived by dissonance researchers might best be obtained from someone who is subjectively self aware, for the reluctance to engage in such behavior constitutes an avoidance of discrepancy in itself. The exploration of the conditions that lead to engagement in behaviors deviating from personal standards of correctness is an untapped area for research. Perhaps one answer to obtaining compliant behavior that would normally be deemed undesirable by those complying is through the creation of subjective self awareness, but this is a topic reserved for Chapters 9 and 10.

Chapter 7

SOCIAL FACILITATION

We have stated the theory in as general a manner as possible, with the consequence that it potentially applies to any behavior that might be controllable by the individual, whether the behavior be performance on routine tasks, walking to school, or checking opinion questionnaires. With the exception of reflex behavior we have assumed that the theory can be applied universally. One implication of drawing a general statement is the possibility of reinterpretation of phenomena that until now have been explained within more molecular systems. We would like to think that the theory of objective self awareness can offer a valid alternative to many of these phenomena-specific theories, in many cases without the addition of ambiguity and lack of precision. For the present we shall examine a phenomenon called ''social facilitation,'' some of the theoretical treatments addressed to it, an interpretation in terms of objective self awareness, and some research consistent with our analysis.

Zajonc (1968) suggests that social facilitation, a ''positive'' change in behavior as the result of the presence of another organism, was by a historical accident the first topic of study for social psychology. In a comprehensive article he traces the history of social facilitation research on humans. The history need not concern us here, although we will trace briefly the theoretical developments within the area.

154

THEORETICAL POSITIONS

A Brief History

The earliest relevant theory seems to have been devised by Triplett (1897), although the labeling of his explanations as theory must be severely qualified. His thinking was bound up primarily in interpretation of various effects that were due to the presence of others at bicycle races, and, as such, contributes little to our understanding of social facilitation in general. For example, his "shelter theory" would hold that a pacer has a facilitating effect on the bicyclist's rate of travel because he shields the racer from the wind. Apparently Triplett's favorite theory was the notion of "dynamogenesis," according to which the presence of another individual releases in a person nervous energy he cannot unleash of his own accord; and, further, the presence of the other was said to arouse the competitive instinct. The dynamogenesis notion was elaborated by Allport (1924), who proposed that individuals in groups are likely to perform at higher rates than when alone because of two factors. The first of these Allport called "social facilitation." He defined the concept as the increase in behavior that results from the sight or sound of others making the same movements, and it will become obvious that his definition is considerably more narrow than that usually accepted by current theorists. The second concept Allport labeled "rivalry," and defined it as an "emotional reinforcement of movement occurring together with a desire to win." Allport's thinking may apply handily to situations involving competition, but since his time it has been well demonstrated that the presence of others, whether competitors or not, can enhance performance. Consequently, his definition and explanation of social facilitation are inadequate except insofar as the phenomenon is constrained within the limits of individuals performing similar tasks.

Zajonc

In 1965 Zajonc broadened the area of social facilitation with an intriguing theoretical integration that employs the concept of "non-specific drive." First, the theory assumes that the responses of an individual in any particular situation can be categorized into "dominant" and "subordinate." The distinction is not always easy to follow, but, generally, a dominant response may be defined as one that occurs with greater frequency, probability, and intensity. The difficulty in applying this conception occurs when the different measures of response strength do not coincide. The observer must single out one potential response that should dominate over all others, and it alone should benefit from the presence of others. Perhaps it is possible to examine a person's behavior in a situation and to evaluate the relative strengths of alternative behaviors, but what criterion is to be used if the criteria of response strength are conflicting? For example, if a man is constrained to hit a punching bag for several minutes, and he alternates between left-handed and right-handed punches, which response (left or right) is dominant if he spends most of his time hitting with his left hand but the right hand packs more wallop? Should the criterion be frequency, or magnitude of response? More difficult to evaluate is the relative dominance of responses in different modes. If a man punches a bag and performs push-ups in an experimental setting, how is the relative dominance of the responses to be assessed? Certainly not in terms of which response is dominant when other people are present, for that would be a circular use of Zajonc's treatment of social facilitation.

The theory also assumes a connection between the presence of others —"mere" presence being sufficient theoretically—and increased general drive. Zajonc does not delve into the developmental antecedents of this assumed connection, and we will not attempt to understand the connection at present. Cottrell (1968) deals with the issue, as will be discussed below. The idea that "mere" presence can create social facilitation effects, and that competition or evaluation from others is unnecessary, is interesting, but not particularly testable. The "mere" presence of other humans inevitably has several meanings to the actor, even if the others present are asleep, dead, or otherwise inactive. If the others present are awake, the individual can easily feel evaluated by them. If he does not experience evaluation, he undoubtedly carries out some form of nonverbal communication with them. When the others present are incapable of communicating or evaluating, it is still questionable to speak of "mere" presence. To talk only about their mere presence is to ignore potentially crucial variables such as physical distance, size, social status, activity being pursued, and so on, ad infinitum. Of course neglect of potentially influential variables is not a severe indictment of the theory, provided that the theory leads to adequate understanding of facilitation phenomena, but as some of the research to be discussed below will indicate, a consideration of additional variables seems vital in prediction of facilitation effects.

The virtue of Zajonc's theoretical treatment is its ability to explain some diverse findings in the area of social facilitation. The presence of others does not always cause increased response strength, for the opposite has been observed frequently in animals and humans alike. The meaning of these "decrements" in response is rather simple when viewed from Zajonc's formulation: The "decrements" are decrements only with respect to certain responses in the situation. Those responses, according to Zajonc, would be the subordinate responses in the situation, and if the alternative or opposing dominant behavior could be specified it should be observed to increase in strength. In his research (e.g., Zajonc & Sales, 1966) Zajonc has arranged a situation in which the relative strengths of dominant and subordinate responses could be ascertained, which was accomplished by training a verbal habit at relatively strong or weak levels prior to the introduction of observers. Quite clearly, the probability with which someone emits a verbal response when confronted with a certain pattern of stimuli is a suitable definition of the relative dominance of the verbal behavior. Consistent with the theoretical treatment Zajonc and Sales found that performance increased when others were present, provided the response was strong in training; but just the opposite resulted when the response had been trained to a weak level.

Cottrell

The next major refinement in social facilitation theory was proposed by Cottrell (1968) as the result of an experiment by Cottrell, Wack, Sekerak, and Rittle (1968). The experiment will be discussed more completely below and for the present we need only describe it briefly. The experiment involved three conditions: in one case the subject was alone, in a second condition an audience was present and blindfolded, and in a third condition the audience watched the subject and was not blindfolded. The results showed a social facilitation effect only for the nonblindfolded condition, with no differences between the "alone" and "mere presence" (blindfolded) conditions. Given these results Cottrell has formulated a variation of Zajonc's treatment, which runs as follows.

Early in life social facilitation effects presumably would not occur. After numerous experiences with situations that call for performance and which bring forth potential evaluation including physical punishment, the presence of others who appear to evaluate may come to evoke "conditioned fear" or "anticipatory frustration responses" through the process of classical conditioning. It is Cottrell's thesis that these conditioned responses nonselectively energize other responses in the task situation, including the dominant and subordinate responses related to the task. If we assume with Cottrell that the fear reactions are conditioned only to audiences that evaluate—that is, audiences that could potentially deal out punishment—then the results of his experiment appear to be explainable.

The connection between the arousal of a conditioned fear response and the energizing of the task response is a vague one. We find it difficult to understand how a fear response can nonselectively energize a task response when the drive corresponding to the fear would seem to be a specific one—not the "general arousal" state that is supposed to enhance the emission of dominant responses. If states of fear and anticipatory frustration are capable of acting as nonspecific sources of drive, then at least some specific drives other than avoidance of fear and avoidance of frustration should be equally effective, and, in that case,

Cottrell's theoretical statement could be broadened considerably. For example, his notion could be extended to say that the presence of any drive such as need for approval or affiliation will act as a general state of arousal and facilitate dominant responses, but, in that case, an audience could easily produce social facilitation effects independent of the potential for evaluation, contrary to the results of the Cottrell *et al.* experiment, and contrary to the theoretical statement.

An additional problem with Cottrell's notion is posed by his suggestion that social facilitation is not limited to the drive resulting from prior punishment and frustration. A concise summary of his revision of social facilitation theory is as follows:

> On a more general level, we must discover the process responsible for audience and coaction effects. It does not appear that the simple presence of others increases drive level. I believe the additional process involved is the anticipation of positive or negative outcomes; the presence of others has nondirective energizing effects upon performance only when their presence creates anticipations of positive or negative outcomes [p. 103].

We simply fail to understand how the anticipation of positive outcomes has the effect of facilitating responses through enhanced general drive level. Parenthetically, we should note that we are in complete agreement with the notion that social facilitation results from evaluative processes, but we agree for different reasons. In summary, Cottrell's modification or some other modification is necessary in the sense that Zajonc's assumption of "mere presence" appears inadequate; however, the analysis leaves several questions unanswered.

Henchy and Glass

A further modification of Zajonc's analysis was proposed by Henchy and Glass (1968), and is almost the same as Cottrell's. The authors suggest that the mediating mechanism for social facilitation effects is the apprehension created by anticipated evaluation, which in turn bolsters drive level or "behavioral arousal." The Henchy-Glass statement would appear to be a micro-theory implied by Cottrell's treeatment: Cottrell assumes that arousal is created by the anticipation of positive or negative outcomes from others present, whereas Henchy and Glass limit the arousal-generating conditions to the anticipation of a specific form of positive or negative outcome, which is the evaluation from others present. Although this variation from Cottrell's theory limits the generality of Cottrell's statement slightly, the Henchy-Glass formulation does appear to have a testable precision about it. One general difficulty with Cottrell's argument we did not discuss above lies in his use of "positive" and "negative" outcomes. Even when the activity, potential for evaluation, expertise, and other potent factors that can be associated with an audience are absent, there is still every reason to think that positive or negative outcomes will follow the individual's performance. If outcomes did not follow, the person would not perform. Unless

Cottrell's use of positive and negative reinforcement is clarified, it is difficult to imagine a reasonable test of his theory. In contrast, the Henchy and Glass treatment has some clear and testable implications when the idea of evaluation apprehension is expanded. For example, the expertise of the audience should be directly related to degree of arousal as they have suggested, and other factors tending to generate arousal and consequent facilitation (or debilitation) should be the possibility of direct evaluation of the person's performance, his incompetence at the task, and his uncertainty about the form that postperformance evaluation will take. The concept "evaluation apprehension" has not been totally explicated by Henchy and Glass, and we suppose that they intend, by the concept, something like the person's uncertainty with respect to the form of evaluation that will follow a certain performance in addition to the expected impact of the evaluation.

Objective Self Awareness

There are very good justifications in empirical research for the formulations by Cottrell and Henchy and Glass, as we will see below in summaries of some of the research. At present, we might note simply that the research suggests that social facilitation is obtained most readily when an audience is attuned to the individual's performance from an evaluative standpoint. Cottrell *et al.* have shown that the presence of others who cannot visually observe the subject and who have shown no direct interest in observing him fails to effect social facilitation. Henchy and Glass have found that the expertness, or status, of the others present has a marked effect on the amount of social facilitation, in that social facilitation is greatest when an expert audience is present. Apparently there is something about the prospect of being evaluated, critically compared, criticized, or praised that strengthens the dominant response. We are in agreement with the theoretical implications of this research and, to the extent that audience evaluation is an implication, we propose that the effects noted in that research can be explained easily in terms of our theory of self awareness. Our language will deviate considerably from that of Cottrell, Henchy and Glass, and Zajonc, because we do not employ the concept of general arousal, nor is the idea of dominant and subordinate responses of any theoretical value for the theory of objective self awareness. Our approach to social facilitation assumes only a relationship between self evaluation and performance change; general arousal, general drive, and related concepts are unnecessary.

One of the many alternative modes of creating objective self awareness is the presence of other people. We have argued previously that in the presence of others a person typically will suppose that others are attending to him, and that often he will have reason to think that their attention is toward certain specific dimensions of himself. When the situation is structured around a single task the person will be likely to assume that their attention is on his task performance. Once he becomes objectively self aware with respect to his task performance he will attempt to reduce the discrepancy between his aspirations and his current performance; that is, as objective self awareness increases, the individual will show increasing efforts to improve his task performance; thus it seems clear that when an audience is introduced he will bolster his efforts to attain high standards. If the audience is composed of experts, or of people evaluating the individual, objective self awareness is more likely because expertise and evaluation will generally be correlated with the amount of attention the person thinks others are paying to him.

Our analysis would appear to be congruent with the simple phenomenon of social facilitation: the presence of others in some circumstances bolsters task performance. The more complicated issue of debilitation of certain responses in the presence of others is not difficult to handle theoretically, provided that the correct response is also the dominant response in a situation. If a person can perform a task with either his right hand or his left, but the right one is dominant, the presence of others should increase his tendency to use the right hand on the basis of the arousal theories of Cottrell, Henchy and Glass, and Zajonc. From our framework, an identical result should be manifested, but not because of arousal: frequency of use of the right hand will result to the extent that the individual sees the use of the right hand as the correct response, relative to left-handedness. Since subordinate responses are defined in terms of their inverse relationship to dominant responses, in that the two are mutually exclusive, our theory predicts that incorrect responses which are necessarily incompatible with and inversely related to correct responses will appear with less frequency or intensity when others are present, simply because the incorrect and correct responses cannot occur simultaneously.

The analysis becomes more difficult when the dominant response is also the incorrect one. At first it looks as if our theory and the arousal theories predict opposite results—although the question becomes more complex. We do not know precisely what would happen in terms of our theory, although we think a tentative answer is as follows. The person who is in the presence of others will at least exert more effort to attempt to reach a standard of correctness, and if effort, persistence, or motivation to be correct were measured, the theory definitely predicts that objective self awareness will lead the person to try to narrow the gap between ideal (correct) performance and actual performance. Whether or not such attempts will lead to actual improved performance is an entirely different question. If the individual has rehearsed the correct response frequently, then the attempt to reproduce that response when objectively self aware is likely to meet with success; but, in contrast, he may never have learned to carry out the correct response with any proficiency, and perhaps when called upon to perform he behaves in some way that is adequate, but not completely correct or coincident with a level of aspiration. If the correct response is a poorly trained one (hence probably subordinate to a relatively incorrect but commonly performed one), the person will be likely to show a decrement in performance when confronted with an audience because he will attempt the most correct response possible and will be unable to carry it out effectively. An example is an amateur musician. When practicing alone he probably plays somewhat more slowly than is called for by the composer and he may engage in various kinds of slurs and shortcuts which result in acceptable sound but are not entirely correct. To the extent that the presence of an audience causes the individual to attempt to attain correctness, which means greater speed and precision, a number of blunders would seem inevitable. In short, we suggest that the correct (and subordinate) response may well suffer due to the presence of an audience, not because the dominant and incorrect response is energized, but, instead, because the objectively self aware person tries beyond his capabilities.

There has been a small amount of social facilitation research in which a correct response was also subordinate (e.g., Martens, 1969), and it is interesting to note that "subordinate" was defined in this research through the subject's lack of skill. When the appropriate response had not been well learned, the presence of an audience decreased the accuracy of performance, as would be expected from Zajonc's thesis. But in light of our preceding remarks we question whether or not this effect would hold given that the correct and subordinate response were at the same time a well rehearsed one. Under such conditions we suspect that the "subordinate" response would be facilitated by the presence of an audience.

Our comments about actual performance, given that the response is correct but subordinate, are conjecture, and certainly are not implied unequivocally by the theory. It is important to note that the theory does predict that the individual will exert greater effort in the direction of correctness when he is objectively self aware, but whether or not such effort will be reflected in performance is a question that cannot be answered without the aid of some research, for we would regard the actual performance rate in this situation as a matter to be determined empirically.

The distinction between striving, or effort, and actual performance is a crucial one, for it is difficult to make accurate predictions for performance outside a well-controlled experimental paradigm on the basis of the dominant-subordinate analysis of facilitation. As Cottrell (1972) has noted, the type of analysis first proposed by Zajonc and himself is difficult to apply unless there can be independent knowledge of which responses are dominant and which are subordinate. This precondition is difficult to invoke anywhere other than in the experimental laboratory. But if the investigator is interested in effort rather than output, the objective self awareness analysis can be employed readily as a tool of prediction, and, given such a dependent measure, the theory offers a clear prediction independent of the investigator's knowledge of dominant and subordinate responses.

SOME EXPERIMENTAL RESEARCH

It is unnecessary for us to trace the entire development of research in social facilitation: this has been accomplished in some detail by Cottrell (1968, 1972), Scott (1968), Tolman (1968), and Zajonc (1968), and our reason for discussing some of the more recent experiments is that only the research accomplished in the last few years brings out the importance of a formulation that deals with the degree of attention from the audience. The earlier research (e.g., Allport, 1924) is consistent with our formulation, but since the intensity of attention focused toward the subject was not varied in the earlier research, those experiments were not a direct test of our ideas. The first experiment we will consider is by Zajonc and Sales (1966). Potential for evaluation (hence amount of attention) was not manipulated directly, but the study is worth discussing because it establishes a paradigm that has been employed successfully in other research.

Zajonc and Sales (1966)

We have already examined Zajonc's formulation of social facilitation. The present experiment was designed to test the notion directly and to examine the possibility that the presence of others can have two opposing effects on response emission, depending on the relative dominance of the habit. All subjects were initially given training on a recognition task. A number of seven-letter nonsense words had been printed on some cards, and the training consisted of the experimenter showing the subject the visual stimulus, pronouncing the word, then asking the subject to pronounce the same word. There were ten stimulus words, which were presented to the subjects in varied frequencies in order to manipulate the strength of the relevant habit. Two of the ten stimulus words were included in each of five training frequency classes so that each subject had a given level of training on each pair of words. The training frequencies for the five pairs of words were as follows: 1, 2, 4, 8, and 16.

After the habit strength had been created differentially, the subjects were put through a "pseudorecognition" test which consisted of presentation of visual material to the subject by means of a shutter projector. For the pseudorecognition task the shutter was set to open for 1/100 of a second. The authors state that this is sufficiently quick not to allow recognition of any presented material.

Although the subjects were told that the stimulus words from the original cards were being shown to them through this device, the material actually flashed on the screen consisted of nothing except some irregular lines. There were 31 separate presentations of the irregular black lines, and on each presentation the subject was asked to respond with one of the 10 original words. Obviously it was impossible for subjects to respond correctly, but this method did enable an assessment of the strength of the original habit. Presumably, the higher the training frequency of a given word, the stronger the tendency to emit that word when the situation calls for emission of one of the 10 words.

The subjects were either run alone with the experimenter located in a separate room, or together with two people presented as students of the experimenter. During the pseudorecognition task the two others were seated a few feet away from the subject and remained silent.

Zajonc's analysis would suggest that the relatively dominant responses, those with a high training frequency, would benefit most from the presence of others in the sense that they would be emitted most frequently. Consistent with the hypothesis, the emission of well trained responses was bolstered by the presence of spectators while weak habits suffered in the presence of spectators.

The Zajonc and Sales experiment sets the paradigm for two experiments to follow. Before discussing them we might note briefly how our conception of objective self awareness applies to the experiment just discussed. We must presume that a standard of correctness exists, and it is reasonable to think that the subject considers a response correct to the extent that he has been trained to produce it. In terms of the specific experimental situation there could be two reasons for the subject's equating training frequency with correctness.

First, he might suppose that the experimenter favors some of the words for one reason or another and expects subjects to produce them in the situation more often than "unfavored" or low training frequency words. Second, the subject was operating totally from guesswork during the pseudorecognition trials, and one of the few cues available indicating a possible correct response would be the training frequency of that response. In short, since the well trained words were more frequent during training, why shouldn't the subject assume that they would be more frequent at a later point in the experiment? Assuming that correctness and training frequency can be treated as correlated, it is a short step to an explanation of the results.

The subjects who were together with spectators became objectively self aware, more so than those who were alone, and evaluated their performance against whatever standards of correctness prevailed—thus they bolstered emission of the responses they had come to consider as correct. To the extent that the frequently trained responses were emitted, the other responses had to suffer, which is to say that the presence of others had the effect of reducing emission of the relatively incorrect responses.

There is an additional way to arrive at the obtained results with the use of the self awareness notion. Although the authors did not discuss any pronunciation problems evidenced by the subjects, the words were of such a nature that subjects would feel much more comfortable in pronouncing them after considerable practice. If we may assume that subjects were apprehensive about correct pronunciation when the audience was present during the pseudorecognition task, then they should have felt more correct in responding with the words that had a high training frequency. There is no way of knowing how salient correct pronunciation was for the subjects, but we find it an intriguing possibility that they may have attended more to pronunciation than to guessing.

The experiments to be reported below, with one exception, employ the paradigm of Zajonc and Sales but utilize some additional variations. We will see that these variations create an atmosphere of potential evaluation, and for this reason they are quite germane for our theory.

Cottrell, Wack, Sekerak, and Rittle (1968)

The experiment differed from the Zajonc-Sales study in one important respect: to determine whether or not the "mere" presence of an audience is sufficient to create social facilitation effects, the spectator condition employed by Zajonc and Sales was broken into two parts, one of them devoid of visual contact. In the condition that was comparable to the Zajonc and Sales spectator condition the subject heard the two accomplices request to watch the subject while he performed, and, as before, they sat attentively but quietly. In a second condition the subject did not hear the accomplices ask to observe, the purpose being to create the impression that they were relatively uninterested. Furthermore, they wore blindfolds under the pretext that they were to take part in a perception experiment requiring subjects' eyes to be adapted to the dark. The subjects in a third control condition were alone as in the Zajonc-Sales study. If the condition involving blindfolds is disregarded, the experiment is essentially a replication of the Zajonc and Sales study, and as would be expected the results were replicated rather closely. The well-trained responses benefited at the expense of under-trained responses when the audience was present. It was the condition with blindfolded subjects that produced the result inconsistent with Zajonc's contention that "mere" presence is sufficient: the results in that condition closely paralleled those of the alone condition. On the basis of these data Cottrell has worked toward a modified drive explanation of social facilitation, discussed above.

The difference between the "mere presence" and "audience" conditions should be examined more closely. In essence there were two differences between them: (1) subjects in the audience condition appeared motivated to observe the subject, whereas those in the mere presence condition did not; and (2) the confederates were blindfolded in the mere presence condition. The purpose of the unusual characteristics of the mere presence condition was to make that condition one of "mere presence," and in the present experiment that seems to have meant that the audience was neither motivated to be present while the subject performed nor capable of watching the subject respond to the visual stimuli. Although the notion of "mere presence" is an elusive one, causing Zajonc's contention to be a hard one to test, it does happen that the differences between the mere presence and audience conditions in Cottrell's study are closely tied to the evaluation variable; consequently the study is quite amenable to an objective self awareness interpretation.

In considering an objective self awareness interpretation of the experiment we will first examine the "motivation to observe" differences between the mere presence and audience conditions. An individual's knowledge that others are motivated to watch him perform a task will narrow the range of objective self awareness generated by their presence. If he knows nothing about their reasons for observing he may come to assume that they are evluating his dress, posture, or other dimensions. But in the audience condition of Cottrell *et al.* the subjects could be sure that their performance was under examination; thus they should have come to focus attention on that specific dimension. Given this consideration, the remainder of the explanation is the same as that we gave for Zajonc-Sales experiment. The second difference between conditions was the "blindfolded" variable. Cottrell's argument seems to have been that the possibility of positive or negative outcomes is reduced by rendering visual monitoring impossible, since the observers would have considerably less information on which to base potential evaluations. The viewpoint of the objective self awareness interpretation is similar. The observer's power to effect self evaluation in the subject will be considerably attenuated by their blindfolds, just as a deaf audience would have difficulty producing objective self awareness in a singer. It would have been interesting to have varied the two elements (ostensible motivation to watch and possibilty of visual contact) independently, for we think it would be likely that the motivation-to-watch variable would suffice to create objective self awareness. It is the other variable, blindfolded or not, that we find provocative and deserving of additional discussion.

In the Cottrell *et al.* experimental situation it is clear that the visual contact would have a great impact, because vision is an important prerequisite for evaluation of accuracy. But suppose that the dimension to be evaluated did not require vision. We can conceive of an experimental situation analogous to that of the pseudorecognition task in which the subject's task is to listen to a tape recorded sound, and then to sing a note exactly two octaves above the sound. Should the eye contact of observers enhance objective self awareness? Obviously whether or not they are deaf will be of central importance, but it is conceivable that the sight of their attentive eyes will also make a difference—for the following reasons. First, a person's gaze is one of many possible indications of his interest in the subject's performance, and in this respect visual attention is a manifestation of the observer's interest in the subject's performance. Second, it is possible that the mere sight of another's eye is sufficient to create objective self awareness with respect to whatever dimension is salient at the moment, simply because visual contact is so intimately bound up with attention. We would not be surprised if the sight of a pair of eyeballs hung on a wall caused the individual to evaluate himself.

Henchy and Glass (1968)

When the evaluation apprehension interpretation of social facilitation was discussed above we noted that the authors implied that status of the evaluator mediates social facilitation effects. This is one of the variables treated in the present study. The experiment was similar in format to that of Zajonc and Sales, but included two notable innovations. First, since the arousal theories are clearly dependent on the notion of physiological arousal as a mediator of social facilitation effects it would make sense to examine some physiological measures; therefore, the authors took continuous recordings of skin-resistance and heart-rate throughout the experimental procedure. Second, a number of variations were introduced in regard to the audience. In one condition the subject was alone, in a second he was together with people who were described as experts in the area that subsumed the experimental task, in a third condition the audience was not described as expert, and in the fourth condition the subject was led to believe that his performance was being tape-recorded and filmed for a later evaluation by experts in the area relevant to recognition tasks. On the basis of their notion of evaluation apprehension, Henchy and Glass hypothesized that arousal, hence social facilitation, would be a direct function of the expertise of the audience present. Further, they supposed that the effects in the "alone recorded" condition would be intermediate between those of the "expert together" and "nonexpert together" conditions. The results were entirely consistent with their predictions: The expert audience created the greatest facilitation effect, followed by the anticipated evaluation condition, the non-expert condition, and the alone condition, in that order. The results fit the Henchy-Glass evaluation apprehension notion quite well. To the extent that a person expects to be evaluated or is currently being evaluated he will become physiologically aroused with the result that dominant responses will be directly energized. To complete the theoretical argument we should examine the physiological data. If the results for skin-conductance and heart-rate reactivity parallel the social facilitation results, their argument for the centrality of general arousal will be somewhat more cogent. (At the same time, it is true that any motivational phenomenon should have physiological components, no matter what theoretical terms are used to describe the phenomenon.) But contrary to expectation, the physiological data showed nothing. There were no significant differences between conditions; and to quote the authors,

The presence of others did not increase autonomic arousal, and there was no evidence to indicate that the ET [expert together] and AR [alone recorded] conditions produced greater arousal than the NET [nonexpert together] condition [p. 452].

These findings cast a slight doubt on the arousal interpretation of social facilitation, although Henchy and Glass offer a few suggestions in the way of a rationale for the failure to find physiological effects. Generally their suggestions take the form of postulating other types of arousal, thus allowing the possibility that their measurements were inappropriate. It is appropriate to note that Martens (1969) found a relationship between presence of an audience and arousal as measured by a palmar sweat technique.

Henchy and Glass quote Lacey's (1967) list of three different kinds of arousal: electrocortical, autonomic, and behavioral, and they suggest the following:

At present the precise conditions under which these different "arousals" occur together cannot be specified, hence one form of arousal cannot be used as a valid indicator of another [p. 453].

Implicit in their remarks is a hint that the arousal versions of social facilitation theory are in trouble, for the direction to take in measuring arousal is not at all clear. Of course, the psychological world would probably not be totally adverse to allowing the arousal concept to retain the status of an unmeasured intervening variable, but the difficulty is that "arousal" has been operationalized sufficiently in terms of autonomic arousal such that it would be a theoretical regression to relegate the concept to the status of an unmeasurable construct.

Paulus and Murdoch (1971)

Again the pseudorecognition task was used, and, as in the study by Cottrell *et al.*, a variable relevant to evaluation was introduced. Consistent with the previous research, some of the subjects were tested on the pseudorecognition task in the presence of two bystanders, other subjects were alone, and to explore further the effect of evaluation, each of these conditions was divided in half. Within the audience condition the audience took either of two forms in a manner similar to the Cottrell *et al.* manipulation. Within the alone condition, some subjects were led to expect their recorded performance to be evaluated later, while other subjects expected no evaluation. In short, the design was a factorial including the variables of audience-no audience and evaluation-no evaluation. Perhaps the most interesting finding of the study was the absence of an effect for the audience. The only significant result was a main effect for evaluation, and, as expected by the authors, anticipated evaluation enhanced the emission of dominant responses. It is not easy to understand why the audience failed to have an effect, for blindfolds were not used as in the Cottrell *et al.* experiment. We will not dwell on that failure to replicate at present—the important feature of the study is the effect for evaluation.

It has become clear from the research by Cottrell *et al.*, Henchy and Glass, and Paulus and Murdoch that an important variable in social facilitation effects is the possibility of evaluation from an audience, or if not evaluation, at least a variable correlated with the presence of an audience whose members could easily evaluate the subject. These researchers have altered Zajonc's notion of drive X habit by stipulating a precondition for the arousal of drive: unless the audience creates expectations of positive or negative outcomes (Cottrell) or evaluation apprehension (Henchy and Glass), facilitation effects are not likely to occur.

Given the difficulty of specifying the observable concomitants of arousal and the strong suggestion from recent research that evaluation is central in social facilitation, we would suggest that our notion of self evaluation is an entirely suitable analysis of social facilitation. The theory of objective self awareness is in no way dependent on the concept of physiological arousal, and it is obvious that the concept of evaluation, which is highly correlated with attention from others, is easily amenable to a theoretical interpretation. There is considerable advantage in a theory with wide scope, provided it does not lack precision, and in this regard the theory of objective self awareness would seem to have an advantage over other conceptions attempting to account for social facilitation. This is because our account of social facilitation is not at all a social facilitation theory per se, but instead, is a general analysis whose boundaries are the individual's conscious states. While it is true that Zajonc's 1965 formulation is a broad theoretical framework, the recent evidence indicates that a theory encompassing at least the cognitive variable of attention from others is urgently needed.

By way of a short review, the research summarized above has indicated quite strongly that evaluation from others, whether present or anticipated, increases the social facilitation effect. In all of this research there is good reason to think that attention and evaluation are closely related, in that the subject who is being evaluated or expects to be evaluated feels the considerable impact of others' attention upon his work. Because the directed attention of others is one of the prime factors leading to objective self awareness, the research of Cottrell *et al.*, Henchy and Glass, and Paulus and Murdoch is quite amenable to an objective self awareness interpretation. This interpretation applies especially well in that there is good reason to think that dominance was positively related to the subject's conception of what was a correct response.

Wicklund and Duval (1971)

Although it might be sufficient at present to criticize some of the inadequacies of the prior research in social facilitation, it is appropriate with the introduction of a new theory to conceive of situations in which the new conception fosters unique derivations about the effects of various stimuli on performance facilitation. One of the main respects in which our theory is unique is in the idea of self evaluation. Cottrell, and Henchy and Glass both discuss evaluation from others in the situation, but in their models the evaluation does not motivate the individual directly: it must first lead to arousal then to enhancement of dominant responses. From our conception it is assumed only that the knowledge of others' evaluations leads to evaluation of oneself according to personal standards. Because part of the uniqueness of our theory is in the idea of self evaluation, it would be appropriate to show that performance facilitation can result from self evalution without the presence of others. If "asocial" conditions leading to objective self awareness can generate performance facilitation, we will have more basis for our argument. Accordingly, the following experiment was conducted, and is reported in more detail by Wicklund and Duval.

It was assumed from the outset that the sight of oneself in a mirror generates objective self awareness, and that once the objective state is engaged, the individual will evaluate himself on dimensions salient in the situation. Thus he should come to evaluate his task performance and increase his efforts to perform at a high level. The prediction seems straightforward, but there is one special difficulty we should entertain. A stimulus such as a mirror or another person that results in increased objective self awareness may well have two opposing effects on an individual's performance. First, the person will evaluate himself a greater proportion of the time when the stimulus is present and, consequently, will attempt to remove any discrepancies between his performance and his aspiration level. But the presence of a mirror and the consequent increased frequency of self evaluation will have an additional effect opposite to that of the first: to the extent that the person examines his performance and evaluates himself he cannot concentrate on the task. It is assumed that when the task is straightforward and the subject is competent, the first effect (increased effort) will predominate over the second effect (distraction from the task). However, if a complex and unfamiliar task were used in the present research, the second effect would become increasingly important. The reason is as follows. When a person has difficulty on a task, the creation of conditions leading to objective self awareness and subsequent self evaluation will result in his spending a relatively great amount of time in self examinaton. The incompetent performer spends much of his "self evaluation" time considering alternative approaches to success (see Lazarus, Deese, & Osler, 1952), and, as a result, concentration on task performance is subject to extensive interference. In contrast, the competent performer simply notes the discrepancy and proceeds routinely to improve his performance.

With these remarks as a background, we can describe the experiment, which obviously used a simple task in order to avoid the difficulty discussed above. The subjects, 34 female undergraduates at the University of Texas, were run individually by a male experimenter. When the subject arrived for the experiment she was seated at a table that contained a large and unavoidable mirror. In every case the mirror had previously been turned backward, so that the subject could not see her image. The experimenter provided the subject with a suitable excuse for her presence in the experiment: it was said that the purpose of the experiment was to ask some people to copy a certain passage in English. The ostensible purpose of the research was an investigation of whether or not familiar material is easier to copy than unfamiliar material. The experimenter said that the experiment would consist of three parts: First, the subject would be given five minutes to copy as much as possible from the first German selection; second, she would be given five additional minutes to copy as much as possible from a second selection; and, finally, she would perform some mirror-writing. In fact, the mirror-writing was unnecessary in the procedure. The expectation of mirror-writing was introduced only to provide a justification for the presence of the mirror.

Once the subject understood what was supposed to transpire the experimenter instructed her to begin to copy the first passage as soon as he left the room and to work as rapidly as possible for five minutes, at which time he would return. When the experimenter returned after five minutes he left the mirror in its original position in the control condition and simply instructed the subject to begin to copy the second passage. Again the subject was given five minutes. In the condition where a mirror was employed he went through an identical sequence except that he turned the mirror over, causing the subject to see her reflection, and excusing this behavior by suggesting that turning it over at this point would save time later.

The dependent measure was simply the number of letters of prose copied by each subject. Of central importance was the difference between the first and second five-minute copying sessions, for it would be expected that quantity would increase when subjects were in the presence of a mirror. The results indicated that the increase in the presence of the mirror (43.33 letters) was significantly greater ($p < .05$) than the increase in the control condition (17.65 letters), thus the derivation from the theory was clearly confirmed.

There is a real sense in which our explanation of social facilitation has already been adequately tested by previous research with humans. The importance of the present experiment lies in the demonstration that the presence of others is unnecessary for performance facilitation effects, and that self evaluation would appear to be a central determining variable. In examining performance facilitation from our theoretical perspective we understand social facilitation to be one class of phenomena that fall within the scope of our treatment of behavior. Other people are one possible source of arousal of objective self awareness; we have seen that a mirror can have a similar effect, and so should numerous other impersonal events we have discussed earlier. Further, change in task performance is by no means the only type of "facilitation" dealt with by the theory. In another experiment reported by Wicklund and Duval (see Chapter 5) it was shown that opinions will change toward a standard of correctness given an increase in objective self awareness, and we have suggested that numerous other behaviors—especially matters such as social graces—are subject to correction by the objectively self aware individual.

CONCLUSION

The case of a response that is both subordinate and correct needs further elaboration, and measures of trying or effort expenditure obviously are important in further research that relates performance facilitation to the theory. In conclusion, we would suggest that social facilitation effects do not require a unique "social facilitation" theory, for a broader conception seems to predict social facilitation effects with some success. The interesting aspect of a comparison among the relevant theories is the finding that there are considerable differences between the theories in their implications, and eventually we would hope that these differences can be resolved through experimental research.

Chapter 8

COMMUNICATION SETS

The extension of objective self awareness to communication sets is just one of many possible areas of application of the theory. In general, if a situation entails the presence of any of a person's values, and if there is potential for variation in objective self awareness, the theory can be applied. In the case of communication sets, the prominent individual values have to do with internal consistency of transmitted messages, and, typically, the variations in the objective state are attributable to the anticipation of an audience.

A theoretically important distinction between the ways in which people deal with information is in terms of receiving versus transmitting. It is consistent with our analysis that an individual who is actively involved in a monologue will be subjectively self aware, and that when he pauses, or otherwise contemplates his remarks, objective self awareness is likely to ensue. The implication is that people frequently will be objectively self aware when preparing to send information, but subjectively self aware when engaged in the communication process. There is a second implication. When exposing himself to information, the person who expects to convey that information to others should be more objectively self aware than the person who simply expects to absorb the same information passively—the reason being that the communicator anticipates focused attention from his audience, and this anticipation will cause him to focus on the correctness and consistency of the material to be communicated. The distinction between the two modes of dealing with information—sending and receiving—and some psychological consequences of these modes, is attributable to Zajonc (1960), whose theory and research are summarized below. We shall also discuss some research by Brock and Fromkin (1968) and Cohen (1961) before returning to our theoretical analysis of communication sets.

ZAJONC

Zajonc's analysis of communication sets places the notion of "cognitive structure" in a central position. He defines it in the following manner:

> . . . an organized subset of the given cognitive universe in terms of which the individual identifies and discriminates a particular object or event. The morphological properties of cognitive structures describe various relationships among attributes [p. 159].

Some of the properties of the cognitive structure are "differentiation," "complexity," and "unity." By "differentiation" is meant the number of attributes a person uses in his cognitive structure corresponding to any given object. The second concept, "complexity," denotes the number of categories into which the attributes of the cognitive structure are placed. The more categories and subcategories the person employs in his cognitive structure, the more complex is the structure. Finally, "unity" refers to the degree to which the attributes depend on each other. Unity characterizes a cognitive structure if a change in one attribute is very likely to necessitate changes in other attributes. A fourth property, "organization," will not be discussed at present.

Given these basic properties of cognitive structures, Zajonc proceeds to explain how the relative dominance and strength of the properties are a function of the individual's set with regard to incoming information. To show how the analysis operates it is easiest to look at one of Zajonc's experiments, in which the variable of interest was whether or not the subject expected to receive passively, or to transmit, a certain body of information.

The subjects, male college students, were asked to read a description of a job applicant. They were instructed to form a general first impression of the applicant, and not to attempt to memorize the infomation. Two minutes later the subjects were stopped and the manipulation of cognitive tuning was carried out. Those in the "Transmitter" condition were told that they would have to communicate the information they had read to a group of people in the building whom they had not yet met. The "Receiver" condition subjects were also told of a group in the building, but in this case the role of the group was reversed: the group was purportedly to tell the subject about the job applicant with whom he was already familiar. Following these instructions the dependent measure was administered.

First, the subject was given a number of blank cards and told to write on each card a characteristic that described the applicant. The instructions were worded so that the subject would not feel constrained to limit himself to the precise language used in the original description of the applicant. No limit was set on the number of the cards used, thus it was possible to obtain a differentiation (definition above) measure for each subject simply by counting the number of attributes listed. Second, the subject was requested to spread the cards before him, then to place the attributes into groupings and subgroupings. The number of groupings and subgroupings provided the basis for computing a complexity score, as mentioned previously. Third, the subject was instructed to examine each attribute individually and to list all of the other attributes that would change if it were changed. This third measure constituted the index of unity of the subject's cognitive structure.

The results indicated a consistent pattern: on the three properties of differentiation, complexity, and unity, the Transmitter condition was in every case higher than the Receiver condition. To explain these results Zajonc invokes several characterizations of the difference between the cognitive structure of the person set to receive and the person set to transmit, and the explanation is broken into separate analyses of differentiation, complexity, unity, and organization, the first three of which we will discuss.

Differentiation

The account for the tendency of receivers to describe the object of the communication with a relatively low number of attributes assumes that the number of attributes will be positively correlated with their specificity, and, further, that the individual who receives requires a broader, more flexible cognitive structure than the transmitter. (Zajonc obtained independent evidence that the transmitters used a higher percentage of specific attributes.) The function of the attributes used by the receiver is to admit many types of information, and according to Zajonc these attributes must serve as "files" or "codes" into which new items of information are placed. The files have to be comprehensive enough for all possible information to be categorized.

Complexity

The account of more complexity among the transmitters is not a separate explanation from that for differentiation. To the extent that an individual's cognitive structure is highly differentiated and specific, it would follow that more categories (complexity) are necessary.

Unity

The explanation for the difference between conditions in unity assumes first that the person in a receiving set will anticipate the possibility of cognitive change; consequently he will order his cognitive structure to make it more susceptible to change. Second, it is assumed that a highly unified structure is not one that can be changed easily, because interdependence of components simply increases the forces required to induce change. It would follow that the receiver will not perceive many interrelations among the components, for in anticipating influence, he would also anticipate considerable cognitive work in reorganizing a highly unified cognitive structure.

The explanation of the difference between conditions in unity is not entirely convincing, essentially because Zajonc has assumed that the person anticipates influence from the group when he hears about the object (job applicant) for a second time and, more difficult to understand, the individual is assumed to alter his cognitive structure in order to open himself to influence. There is an argument by McGuire and Millman (1965) that people will alter their opinions prior to influence in order to brunt the devastating effect of a potentially persuasive communication, but at the same time this argument implies that people do not like to be influenced, will try their best to avoid and resist influence, and certainly would not arrange their cognitive structures to enhance their susceptibility to cognitive change. In short, we find Zajonc's explanation to be unconvincing because it assumes that people will create conditions to facilitate their own influence when they anticipate exposure to a persuasive communication.

If people do arrange to have themselves influenced, they probably do so when they know very little about the issue relative to the source of potential influence and when they are not firmly committed to any position on the issue. Had Zajonc shown the same difference between receivers and transmitters under conditions where the subjects were relatively expert and committed to their way of thinking on the issue, the application of his account would be difficult at best. In fact, many social psychologists would argue that the committed individual who expects to hear viewpoints at variance from his own will actively defend (e.g., Allyn & Festinger, 1961; Brehm, 1966; Kiesler & Kiesler, 1964), which implies that the subjects set to receive might structure their cognitions more rigidly (with more unity) than would the transmitters. We would like to propose what may be a more general explanation of the difference between senders and receivers in unity of cognitive structures. The explanation is derived from the theory of objective self awareness, and focuses on the cognitive structure of the sender.

THE OBJECTIVE SELF AWARENESS ANALYSIS: A BRIEF OVERVIEW

When someone is exposed to information about an event, he will form numerous impressions of the event that he will defend as his own. When asked to convey those impressions to an audience he will realize the possibility of constant attention from the audience, the anticipation creating objective self awareness. The immediate focus of the individual's objective self awareness should be on the correctness and consistency of his beliefs, thus the focus of his attention while anticipating delivery of the communication will be on the interrelationships of his beliefs. In contrast to the relatively subjectively aware receiver, the person preparing to transmit will be hesitant to allow simple juxtapositions of his beliefs. He will attempt to integrate and relate them so that they fit logically together, and it follows that he would have a high score on Zajonc's measure of unity, since to be consistent in his beliefs he would have to insure the inner consistency—hence interrelatedness—of his beliefs.

In addition to the motivation for internal consistency, there is another reason for Zajonc's finding, this one also implied by the present theory. If someone anticipates the delivery of a communication it will be important for him to remember what he is about to say, for once he commits himself to a presentation of the material, he can be evaluated on the basis of his coherency. Because of the objective self awareness created through the anticipated evaluation, he will interrelate the parts of his presentation in such a manner that each part is easier to remember.

Our explanation does not deny that people oriented toward reception of messages become objectively self aware, but only that the anticipated attention of an audience will effect considerably more objective self awareness with respect to the relevant cognitive structures than will the anticipated receipt of a message. We might also note that the anticipation of delivering a message to an audience is not the only variable that will increase the unity of cognitive structure, for as we have discussed before, there are numerous impersonal sources of objective self awareness, any of which should create greater unity in a person's beliefs about an object. In addition, the mere physical presence of others who might conceivably attend to the person is theoretically sufficient to cause objective self awareness and consequent critical examination and reorganization of beliefs, but the expectation of delivering a communication to them is not crucial.

COHEN

Cohen has analyzed impression formation in terms of Zajonc's distinction between two types of communications sets and has argued that the situational demands placed on a person can guide his organization of impression material   particularly if the situation is varied between one that demands transmission and one that demands reception. He argues that a person set to transmit information will polarize information, which means that he will exclude, suppress, or minimize one of the extremes in a contradiction. Further, cognitive structures will subsequently be organized around, and made to be consistent with, the pole of the contradiction that is not suppressed. When set to receive an impression, the polarization will be much less noticeable; instead of restructuring the information, the person will suspend cognitive reorganization. By suspend, Cohen means that ". . . he should bring together or see as related—or explain away—the contradictions between cognitions by entertaining the opposing cognitive elements and minimizing their contradictions."

We agree with Cohen in part. From the theory of objective self awareness it is reasonable that polarization would occur in the interest of consistency when the individual expects to transmit. But we disagree with Cohen's definition of suspension, which is to say that we doubt that there are many forces toward consistency, or minimization of contradiction, when the person expects to receive but not transmit. With a set to receive, the individual will be less objectively self aware than with a set to transmit, and we propose that greater polarization, unity, and other attempts at consistency will result given a set to transmit because the objective state will lead the person to strive after correctness and internal consistency. Before pursuing this theoretical argument we should examine the experiment by Cohen (1961).

The procedure differed markedly from that of Zajonc in that the manipulation of set to receive or transmit was introduced prior to the information, but in most other respects the experiment was similar. Cohen used a second variable in order to test an idea about the differential reaction to conflicting material: If there is generally a greater propensity among the transmission-oriented subjects to organize conflicting information around one pole of the contradiction, the difference between transmission-oriented and reception-oriented subjects should be exaggerated, the more conflicting the list of traits is. Accordingly, the internal consistency of the trait list was varied.

Subjects in the "Reception" condition were given some information about the character traits of a student, and were told that after they read over the traits they would hear others' impressions of the same student. Subjects in the "transmission" condition were led to believe that after they read the list of traits, they would have to communicate as complete a description of the student as they could to some other people. After the manipulation the subject was given the trait list, which was either mildly contradictory or replete with contradictions. After having read the list for five minutes the subject was instructed to write as complete a description as possible of the student described in the trait list.

The dependent measure was fairly elaborate, involving coding of subjects' written descriptions. First each complete thought was scored as either positive, neutral, or negative, and Cohen argued that the more the subject's remarks were exclusively either positive or negative, the more the subject could be assumed to be organizing his impression around one of the extremes. It was predicted, of course, that subjects in the Transmission condition would tend to organize around one extreme more so than subjects in the Reception condition.

Second, the stories were coded to determine the extent to which the subject organized the material to be consistent with one pole, or element, of the contradiction.

The two types of data were consistent, and supported the hypothesis that subjects set to transmit would show a greater tendency to organize their relevant knowledge around one side of the contradiction. Cohen expected that the differences would be greater when the material contained numerous contradictions, but the data indicated that the degree of contradiction had virtually no effect on polarization.

Cohen explains his results by postulating opposing motivational states created by the two communication sets. It is suggested that transmission tuning requires a "clear, transmittable" communication, hence the subject organizes around one extreme to avoid and discard contradictions. But reception sets lead the individual to a suspension of judgment rather than polarization and tolerance of contradictory cognitions.

We find the results of Cohen's experiment to be entirely consistent with our theory, since the measure was the attempt of the subject to delete contradictions, and from our viewpoint objective self awareness was manipulated through the transmission-reception variable. Just as in the analysis of Zajonc's experiment we propose that the anticipation of the audience creates objective self awareness, with particular emphasis on that aspect of one's self that will be presented—the impressions to be conveyed. To the extent that the subject focuses on himself as a conveyer of the material with contradictions, he will become aware of the contradictions and attempt to reconcile them with one another. In Cohen's study there was no obvious way for the subject to integrate the material, for the contradictions were glaring. Jim, the student, was described as conceited, kind, loyal, and insincere, among other things, and with this list the objectively self aware subject's only alternative is to present approximately one-half of the traits to the audience, either the good or bad half. One of the more interesting features of the Cohen experiment is that his subjects seemed to have performed the cutting and censoring necessary to reduce the number and magnitude of contradictions well before their presentation.

BROCK AND FROMKIN

These authors (1968) derived a prediction from Cohen's data that those set to transmit information would have a strong tendency to selectively expose themselves to information supporting their first impression of someone. An impression formation paradigm was used, just as in the Cohen study. Half of the subjects received material leading them to form an initially favorable impression of a stimulus person, and half received material leading them to form an initially unfavorable impression. Within each of these impression formation groups, cognitive tuning was manipulated so that half of the subjects expected to transmit their impressions and half expected to receive others' impressions. The dependent variable was the amount of time spent listening to each of two simultaneously presented tape recorded communications, one of which was supportive of the subject's initial impression and the other discrepant. The results were in line with the prediction: individuals set to transmit listened more to supportive information than did those set to receive. Stated otherwise, the results indicate that a person with a transmission orientation is relatively likely to expose himself to information in such a way that the impression to be communicated is internally consistent.

AN OBJECTIVE SELF AWARENESS INTERPRETATION

What is the essence of the theory that has generated these three experiments? Zajonc has distinguished between transmitters and receivers in their mode of cognitive organization and has argued that receivers will remain open to new information, suspend judgment, and tolerate contradictory material, in contrast to the transmitters who organize the material into internally consistent, communicable wholes. The mechanism mediating these differences appears to be the necessity of communicating effectively and easily. It would be clumsy and inefficient to attempt to communicate a self-contradictory and poorly organized body of information. Speculating beyond the framework of Zajonc we might also presume that people feel uncomfortable and foolish when delivering a contradictory statement to an audience, and, further, that they can anticipate the negative evaluation that might ensue upon delivery of a contradictory message. Let us explore this possibility in more detail in terms of the theory of objective self awareness.

The effects of objective self awareness are postulated to take the form of self evaluation. When a person focuses on himself, he begins to consider traits that are salient for him at the time, and an evaluation occurs based on discrepancies between the way he perceives himself with respect to that trait and his aspiration or standard with respect to the trait. The greater the discrepancy, the more negative the affect he will experience, with the consequence that he will either attempt to avoid the situation provoking objective self awareness or else alter his actual state in an effort to reduce the discrepancy. Although it is not always possible to predict which traits the individual will focus on, we can generate unequivocal predictions from the theory by knowing which traits should be salient. For example, whenever a person engages in self-contradictory or hypocritical behavior, the creation of objective self awareness should result in an awareness of the hypocrisy and subsequent efforts to reduce the self contradictory state.

How does the theory apply to communication sets? If a person is exposed to a body of knowledge, he can be made objectively self aware with respect to that knowledge through the mere anticipation of communicating it to someone. We would argue that a live presentation will commonly create a feeling of anticipated evaluation, and, as a result, the individual will become objectively self aware, self critical, and will attempt to impart consistency to his communication. The theoretical reason for this is simple: people in general including audiences, generally value internally consistent, coherent presentations, and assuming that the individual set to transmit values the inner consistency of his communications, objective self awareness will lead to the effects observed in the three studies described above. From the theory it is clear that the presence of an audience is not the only stimulus that would generate increased consistency in a communication. Any event that arouses the objective state (e.g., a mirror, television camera, tape-recorded voice) will have approximately the same effect as an audience. In short, we would suggest that the effects noted by Brock and Fromkin, Cohen, and Zajonc among transmitters are a subclass of phenomena attributable to objective self awareness.

DAVIS AND WICKLUND

The present experiment was designed to evaluate the objective self awareness explanation of communication sets. Rather than employing a reception set, as in prior research, it was appropriate in the present case only to demonstrate that subjects given a transmission set will integrate the material within a communication in direct proportion to their degree of objective self awareness. It is important to note that Zajonc's formulation would not predict differences within a transmission set condition; thus, such differences would provide the best possible evidence for the objective self awareness account. The experiment employs two modes of objective self awareness arousal—one personal, the other impersonal. The personal mode consists of an anticipated audience, and the impersonal is constituted by a television camera. Although there is no strong basis for arguing that one of these modes would be more effective than the other in creating objective self awareness, there is reason to believe that the subject's self evaluation will be more clearly focused on the communication with anticipation of the audience than with the presence of a camera; thus, the resultant integration of the communication should be greatest with an audience if there is any difference between the effects of the camera and the anticipated audience. Keeping this possibility in mind, the main hypothesis is as follows:

The amount of cognitive integration performed on a communication will be greater under conditions of objective self awareness than under conditions where stimuli leading to the objective state are absent.

All subjects were exposed to an internally contradictory list of traits describing someone and then were asked to write a one-page essay on that person. In two conditions objective self awareness was bolstered while the essay was written. In the "Expected Audience" condition the subject was led to believe that he would read his completed essay to a small audience later in the experimental session, and in the "Camera" condition the subject was told that a camera in the experimental room was operating and that a video tape would be made of his essay-writing. Finally, a "Control" condition with neither the expected audience nor camera was included. The subjects were 39 undergraduate males recruited from introductory psychology classes. One of these was excluded from the results because of failure to follow instructions.

When the subject arrived for the experiment he was ushered into the experimental cubicle, and if he was designated for the Camera condition, the experimenter said that the psychology department had recently purchased a new camera which the experimenter was supposed to test by making video tapes of several experimental sessions. The subject was told that the camera would be running throughout the session and that a few professors would be looking over the tapes at some later date. She then pretended to turn on the camera and adjusted it so that it aimed directly in the subject's face. At this point the experimenter continued with the following remarks, which were common to all three conditions and constituted the introductory phase of the Expected Audience and Control conditions:

> This is a study in impression formation. What we are interested in is how people form impressions of each other on the basis of very limited information. In this case what I am going to give you is a list of adjectives describing one of the undergraduates here in the psychology department. The list was made up by three of the graduate students who know him well. You will have five minutes to look over the list. During that time try to form an impression of the type of person he is. This is not a test of memory, so do not try to memorize the list. Just try to get a general picture of the kind of person the person described is. At the end of the five minutes I will return and get the list. Then you will be given 15 minutes to write a speech describing this person.

At this stage of the procedure two different statements were made in order to create the expectation of an audience for some subjects. The experimenter told the Control and Camera subjects the following: "I will read the speech to some people later," clearly implying that the subject would not be present while the material was read. In the Expected Audience condition the experimenter's remarks were as follows:

> After you finish you will give your speech to two students. I have a friend running subjects down the hall. When he finishes with his subjects he sends them down here to serve as an audience for my subjects.

The experimenter then asked if there were any questions, and, consistent with her previous instructions, she handed the subject the list of adjectives and left the room. The adjectives were identical with the highly contradictory list used by Cohen, and are listed below:

very friendly
extremely generous
ruthless
extremely dependable
overly conceited
very kind
scheming
very cold
highly loyal
insincere

Five minutes later the experimenter returned, collected the list, and instructed the subject to write a speech about the person described in the list. She then left the room and returned 15 minutes later to debrief the subject.

The dependent measure was the extent to which the subject integrated the contradictory list of adjectives into an internally consistent essay. This is similar to the analysis performed by Cohen. The essays were rated for integration by two independent raters, blind with respect to condition, and the correlation between their ratings was .77. The essays were rated on a three-point scale, such that "1" was equivalent to no integration, "2" indicated some attempt to integrate, and "3" was the rating for a successful integration. It might be noted that the common form of subjects' attempts to integrate was to see one cluster of the person's traits—either the good or bad one—as a superficial aspect of the person, while the alternative cluster was described as the more meaningful and "deeper" description of the person.

From the hypothesis it was expected that integration would be a positive function of the extent of objective self awareness, and, further, that if any differences were obtained between the Camera and Expected Audience conditions, the Expected Audience would be the higher of the two. The means were as follows: Control, 1.94; Camera, 2.48; and Expected Audience, 2.58. The strongest difference was between the Control and Expected Audience conditions ($p < .05$), and the Control-Camera difference was just short of significance ($p < .08$). The difference between the Camera and Expected Audience conditions did not approach significance. The data are summarized in Table 7.

The results were generally consistent with the hypothesis in that the anticipation of delivery of the speech to an audience maximized the integration of the essay. It was not surprising that subjects who wrote their essays in the presence of the camera did not show quite as much integration as subjects who anticipated an audience, and although this slight difference between the

TABLE 7

Mean Integration Shown in Essay

Expected audience	2.58^{a} $(12)^{b}$
Camera	2.48 (13)
Control	1.94 (13)

[a] The essays were scored such that 1 = no integration, 2 = some attempt at integration, and 3 = successful integration.
[b] Ns in parentheses.

Expected Audience and Camera conditions was not statistically significant, the reason for expecting the Expected Audience condition to be higher in integration should be reviewed, together with a theoretical overview of the experiment.

The purpose of the camera was to create a stimulus condition that would cause the subject to focus on himself, just as he would focus on any external event. Conceptually, the camera operates the same way as a mirror or a tape-recording of the individual's voice: Because of the camera, the subject imagines himself on a television screen, and in the present experiment, he also knew that others would examine the video tape at some later date. It was clear to the subject that his essay-writing performance per se was not being recorded by the video machine, but for the theory that does not matter. Once objective self awareness is aroused the theory implies that the person will come to examine himself along dimensions that are salient in his current situation, and in the present experiment it may be argued that he focused on the internal consistency of his essay. Assuming that a dominant value in essay-writing is that of organizing the material into a coherent and meaningful whole, it follows that integration would be bolstered by the presence of the camera.

If anything, the expected audience resulted in a more direct focusing of attention on the essay. Not only were subjects in that condition objectively self aware due to the anticipated audience reaction, but the fact that the reaction would be based directly on the quality of the essay should have aroused a relatively strong tendency to write coherently, and to present the material in integrated form. Although objective self awareness may have been created in equal amounts by the camera and by the anticipated audience, the effect on integration should have been stronger in the case of the anticipated audience because the expected audience, more than the camera, focused the subject's attention on his essay.

The results support our contention that an analysis of communication sets in terms of objective self awareness is feasible, and, further, that there are communication-set phenomena that cannot be handled adequately by Zajonc's theoretical formulation. Specifically, Zajonc speaks only of the distinction between a set to transmit and a set to receive. He does not analyze variables that could affect the person's cognitive work within one set or the other. The present experiment has demonstrated that among subjects who are set to communicate, cognitive work in the form of integration (called "unity" by Zajonc) is positively related to objective self awareness. (It should be recalled that a communication set was imparted to all subjects in the sense that the experimenter said that he would read the speech to some people later.) We have not dealt with the receiver set in the present research, since the purpose was to demonstrate that objective self awareness can operate within the communication set. From the standpoint of the theory, the cognitive work performed in a reception set would be approximately equivalent to that in a communication set in which objective self awareness were not aroused.

THE UNUSUAL NATURE OF COMMUNICATION SETS

Perhaps one of the more remarkable features of the communication set phenomena found in the studies we have described is the strong bias taken toward information to be communicated. *A priori,* we might suppose that a person who is responsible for communicating information to others would feel some obligation to present both sides of the issues. Certainly, in the case of information relevant to air raid escape routes, methods of vaccination, and other life-and-death matters, there would be constraints operating on an individual to deliver all available information, whether it is internally contradictory or not. It is conceivable that such constraints would operate against the effects found in the present research, for as a person becomes increasingly objectively self aware he would be prone to present all of the information to the extent that it is vital, such an effect operating against the value of internal consistency. Whether or not this is the case can only be settled in additional research, for in the studies described above the information was anything but vital to anyone's interests.

AN IMPLICATION FOR CREDIBILITY

The implications of the research for the behavior of public officials are ominous. If we may assume the arousal of objective self awareness through the anticipation of a live audience, a speaker given enough time to prepare a body of material certainly could be expected to reorganize it into a unified whole to the point that the original meaning vanishes. Presumably, in the interest of consistency, the speaker would simply fixate on one pole of the contradiction—perhaps the one he thinks the public will be most willing to tolerate—then skillfully weave the communication around that pole. Generally it is presumed that public exposure is a safeguard of credibility: when a man is forced to speak before the entire nation, as opposed to a small group of reporters or staff people, it is commonly thought that the truth of his statements is thereby improved and his candid qualities maximized. But if the present research has any validity, such is not the case. As the size and political significance of the audience increases, so will objective self awareness and the subsequent tendency to present a unified and biased pole of a contradiction.

PREPARATION VERSUS DELIVERY

In the chapters on subjective self awareness, a frequent example is the public speaker. It is argued that action-taking would create the subjective state, with the result that self criticism would be absent while the person speaks. The present chapter implies that the anticipation of delivering a communication can create effects opposite from those to be observed while the speaker is in progress. While in preparation, and during a pause or following a delivery, the speaker will often find himself in the objective state, but self criticism can be terminated simply by proceeding with the speech. If anything, the listener will be more objectively self aware than the speaker, provided that the speaker is actively setting forth his ideas. But as soon as the communication ceases, that difference between speaker and listener will reverse itself. In short, placing a person in a communication set will not necessarily create the effects found in the Chapter 9 experiments. It is important first to specify the stage of the speaker's progress, since the communication set effects postulated as a function of objective self awareness will occur only when the speaker's action ceases or has not begun.

COMMUNICATION SETS AND COGNITIVE IMBALANCE

Finally, it should be noted that the communication set phenomena described in the research are not conceptually different from other effects we have examined, provided that objective self awareness is taken as the theoretical perspective. The subject is made objectively self aware by the anticipation of an audience, and as a result he imparts consistency to the material to be used in his talk. In the second of the experiments by Wicklund and Duval (1971), a certain issue or body of knowledge was made salient for the subject, just as the material for the speech was salient for the communicator in the Davis and Wicklund study. When objective self awareness was created in the Wicklund-Duval experi-

ment; the subjects were found to alter their attitudes toward the position represented by a recently performed behavior. In that study a television camera
was employed to create the objective state, but in all theoretical respects that
finding and the results of the communication set studies are similar. The similarity
is almost operationally identical if we examine the Camera condition in the
experiment by Davis and Wicklund: the only difference between that and the
attitude-behavior discrepancy experiment is in the type of consistency used as
theoretical evidence.

Chapter 9

SUBJECTIVE
SELF AWARENESS

OVERT BEHAVIOR AND SUBJECTIVE SELF AWARENESS

If people had total control over their shifts between subjective and objective self awareness, we would suppose that the subjective state would frequently be preferred. In some individuals the state would be preferred chronically, and in certain situations leading to excessive discomfort in objective self awareness the subjective state would be preferred by everyone. Objective self awareness cannot long be tolerated comfortably. Given a recent success experience, a person may not experience much negative affect, but all too quickly he will come to examine himself on less successful dimensions with the result that he will attempt to turn attention to the environment, away from felt personal discrepancies. It is the chronically misfit, maladapted, and unsuccessful to which Eric Hoffer turns his attention in *The passionate state of mind* (1954). We find the phenomenon he describes to be an interesting example of the attempt of such individuals to create conditions that will allow constant subjective self awareness.

Hoffer's work is a study of those who engage in passionate activity. For our purposes this activity does not necessarily entail membership in extremist groups as he describes in *The true believer* (1951). Any intense, dedicated efforts fall within the domain of our inquiry.

Hoffer's understanding of the reason behind passionate pursuit can best be understood by an examination of several quotations from *The passionate state of mind:*

> There is in most passions a shrinking away from ourselves. The passionate pursuer has all the earmarks of a fugitive.
>
> Passions usually have their roots in that which is blemished, crippled, incomplete and insecure within us. The passionate attitude is less a response to stimuli from without than an emanation of an inner dissatisfaction.
>
> A poignant dissatisfaction, whatever be its cause, is at bottom a dissatisfaction with ourselves. It is surprising how much hardship and humiliation a man will endure without bitterness when he has not the least doubt about his worth or when he is so integrated with others that he is not aware of a separate self [1954, p. 7].

There are two ideas which seem notable. First, passionate activity has its roots in dissatisfactions, incompleteness, and insecurity; and, second, hardships and pain are better tolerated when the person is integrated with others so that he is unaware of himself as a separate entity. If a person is unaware of himself as a separate entity, he is, as we have argued, in a state of subjective self awareness, and Hoffer has anticipated our theoretical formulation by viewing passionate activity as a source of the "selfless" feeling. It is clear that Hoffer is discussing the individual who is chronically dissatisfied and incomplete, which is to say that upon focusing on himself as an individual entity, this person will almost inevitably experience discomfort, and that his discomfort will be a direct function of the extent to which he finds himself falling short of desired standards. As we have suggested previously, the uncomfortable objectively self aware person will attempt to avoid the conditions that cause attention to be focused on himself, and an effective way to accomplish this is to engage in an activity that forces attention onto the object of activity. It is the fixing of attention upon the external world that constitutes the subjective state, as we have argued in the first chapter. A clear implication of this line of thought is that the activity, rather than the end result, is of foremost importance. When attempting to move from the objective state, the means are infinitely more important than the ends, since the primary purpose is avoidance of self criticism. From this viewpoint any positive results accruing from attainment of the intended goal are a secondary consideration. Again, Hoffer concurs:

> That we pursue something passionately does not always mean that we really want it or have a special aptitude for it. Often, the thing we pursue most passionately is but a substitute for the one thing we really want and cannot have. It is usually safe to predict that the fulfillment of an excessively cherished desire is not likely to still our nagging anxiety.
>
> In every passionate pursuit, the pursuit counts more than the object pursued [p. 8].

Although we would take issue with Hoffer with respect to his suggestion that the object of pursuit is a substitute, we find his comments regarding the substitutibility of goals to be entirely consistent with our thinking.

There is an important question that arises at this point. Are the goals themselves increasingly irrelevant as the negative affect associated with objective self awareness increases, and will the activity be more passionate the greater the negative affect? Presently we do not have the answer, and we are obligated to allow for either of two alternatives. (1) Given any amount of negative affect in the objective state, the person will engage in activity, and the more negative affect, the less meaningful are the goals themselves and the more active the individual will become. In short, there is a monotonic relationship between negative affect and the two postulated effects. (2) Alternatively, the relationship could be nonmonotonic, such that any minimal negative affect will bring forth activity of one sort or another, but in such a way that the meaningfulness of specific goals and amount of activity do not vary systematically as negative affect increases beyond a minimum. Given this alternative, individuals who are objectively self aware will be found in activities ranging from cigarette smoking to running, but the extent of activity would simply be arbitrary and probably a function of whatever activities are available.

Because the idea of standard of correctness is crucial for our theory we might suppose that the life aspirations instilled in a person would have a profound effect on the extent of his passionate zeal in later life. For example, it has been argued elsewhere that the parents of authoritarians are especially prone to set high moral standards, and to instill in their children a reluctance to admit that they are wrong (Brown, 1965, p. 498). With such a background it would seem common that such children would, when objectively self aware, find overwhelming discrepancies between standards of correctness and their actual level of attainment. Thus these same products of authoritarian background should often be found in passionate pursuit of a variety of goals—sometimes apparently vacuous and unrelated goals.

Hoffer's concern is generally with the person who is chronically misfit, but we find it more useful to examine the occurrence of passionate activity through a consideration of specific instances causing objective self awareness and the resultant focusing on one's "misfitness." We suggest that the need for activity as a means of avoiding uncomfortable self evaluation will arise in everyone from time to time and that the situations leading to these "objective self awareness crises" are predictable. We have proposed that the onset of self evaluation will often be followed by attempts to eliminate the objective state.

For example, when someone enters a room full of strangers he is likely to feel that others are examining him, and the resulting objective state will motivate him to eliminate that state. He could avoid the presence of the people who cause him to evaluate himself on "precarious" dimensions, or he could reduce the discrepancy between his actual state and ideal state on the dimensions. Given that these processes are successful, the state of objective self awareness will either be reduced or at least become more tolerable. But if the people cannot be avoided, or the discrepancy not reduced, what can we then expect from this person?

If we continue to employ the example of the party, there are some fairly obvious routes to subjective self awareness, all of which entail activity. The person can initiate small talk, and provided he is successful in continuing an active conversation, the activity will circumvent any threatening self examination. It is important that the conversation be innocuous and never potentially threatening, for the person will necessarily stop talking sometimes, leaving himself in a position to be evaluated according to his prior remarks. This would lead to potentially unfavorable self evaluation from others unless the conversation were structured so that it did not lend itself to evaluation. Such conversation is not difficult to initiate—we find it running rampant at cocktail parties, and especially cocktail parties constituted of strangers. Ironically enough, such trite conversation is ridiculed away from the party by most of those who attend; those who are critical of meaningless conversation away from the party are the same ones who feel comfortable with small talk when in the situation.

Verbal behavior is not the only route to increased subjective self awareness, although we suppose that trivial conversation is the preferred mechanism at a party of strangers. Nonverbal actions such as helping the host arrange card tables, mix drinks, pass peanuts, and so forth should all tend to bring about greater subjective self awareness. In the context of these examples, an important theoretical point should be mentioned.

First, a person's attention is not always completely diverted from himself because he engages in drink mixing or chair arranging. However, the more strenuous and involved are his activities, the more stimuli there will be to attract his attention and to divert his attention from himself. In short, the stimuli creating objective self awareness and the stimuli associated with his task will be in "competition," one set forcing his attention toward the self, and other set forcing attention away from the self.

Hoffer is not the only author to note examples of what we characterize as attempted increase of subjective self awareness. While Hoffer dwells on chronic differences between individuals in their discomfort and adjustment, Goffman (1967) focuses instead on variations in "discomfiture" that are experienced by all individuals:

> . . . to appear flustered, in our society at least, is considered evidence of weakness, inferiority, low status, moral guilt, and other unenviable attributes. . . . When discomfiture arises from any of these sources, understandably the flustered individual will make some effort to conceal his state from the others present. The fixed smile, the nervous hollow laugh, the busy hands, the downward glance that conceals the expression of the eyes, have become famous as signs of attempting to conceal embarrassment [pp. 101–102].

Goffman elaborates on this theme by citing Lord Chesterfield, who argues that individuals who are ashamed in company can be counted upon to try numerous "tricks," many of which are habitual. These include putting the fingers to the nose, scratching the head, twirling hats, and numerous other awkward activities. We suggest that the activities are not necessarily as "awkward" as Goffman and Chesterfield would have them. The movements that the objectively self aware individual undertakes when the attention of others (hence self evaluation) threatens are not simply nervous habits, as Chesterfield and Goffman imply, but are useful in bringing about subjective self awareness and can just as well be coordinated actions. Ideally, the objectively self aware person would join in a strenuous game such as volleyball or touch football. The more energy the person can direct onto the environment, the less likely it is that he will focus on himself as an object.

Goffman has discussed the very phenomenon we are studying in terms of self consciousness in conversation:

> At the cost of his involvement in the prescribed focus of attention, the individual may focus his attention more than he ought upon himself—himself as someone who is faring well or badly, as someone calling forth a desirable or undesirable response from others. It is possible of course, for the individual to dwell upon himself as a topic of conversation—to be self-centered in this way—and yet not to be self-conscious. Self-consciousness for the individual does not, it seems, result from his deep interest in the topic of conversation, which may happen to be himself, but rather from his giving attention to himself as an interactant at a time when he ought to be free to involve himself in the content of the conversation [p. 118].

Goffman has stated that the person is self conscious in conversation only when he attends to himself while not speaking. The suggestion that talking about oneself does not seem to be associated with self consciousness is a rather noncommon-sense suggestion, but it is consistent with our argument that activity, regardless of the form, will heighten subjective self awareness. Perhaps the woman at the party who strongly fears self evaluation is the same one who talks incessantly and who is careful to avoid topics that would lead to a negative self evaluation.

There are situations analogous to the cocktail party that are potentially more powerful in their potential for creation of objective self awareness, and they are nearly as common. It is a common observation that a speaker's greatest nervousness occurs just prior to his performance, but once he launches into his presentation he feels relatively comfortable. The interpretation is obvious. Standing alone, anticipating his appearance before an audience, the speaker is passive and quite conscious of the potential forthcoming attention of the audience. The result is an intense state of objective self awareness that may lead to severe self evaluation that he would prefer to avoid. The desire to "get it over with" is one manifestation of the effort to attain subjective self awareness. The relatively comfortable state reached upon speaking reflects the effectiveness of exerting force on the environment in bringing about the subjective state.

Both the size and the expertise of an audience will usually be related to the objective self awareness created by the speaker's pondering his forthcoming presentation. Rather than enumerate additional variables associated with the audience, it will suffice to make a general summary statement about audiences and speakers: The greater potential the audience has for evaluation of the speaker, hence attention toward him, the more objective self awareness will be aroused prior to the presentation and at those places in his speech that call for him to pause.

We would suggest that objective self awareness in a speaking situation is by nature uncomfortable. Since the individual has not yet performed the activity, he cannot possibly find a small discrepancy between his aspiration and his actual state, and his major concern when examining himself will be the potentially large and uncomfortable discrepancy. Objective self awareness due to anticipated audience evaluation will result directly in two effects—first, an attempt to plan performance so as to minimize the possible negative evaluations, and, second, attempts to change the focus of attention from oneself to the environment. Because engagement in effortful, passionate, uninterrupted activity effects subjective self awareness, we would expect the speaker to maintain a constant flow of verbiage, with considerable passion, to the degree that he was objectively self aware before the speech and can be objectively self aware during his talk. His speech should be rapid, numerous hand gestures should be observed, and he should be reluctant to entertain questions or to grant any other form of interruption. His hesitancy to entertain questions will not arise solely from his feelings of inability to reply, but, instead, a pause for questions will allow his attention to redirect itself to his performance and appearance. Should a pause become necessary, either because of audience interference or through a failure to proceed quickly with a successive idea, the speaker can rescue himself from objective self awareness by nonverbal devices. For example, he can light a cigarette, pretend to examine his notes, or any of an assortment of behaviors that might be characterized by Chesterfield and Goffman as nervous habits. These "habits" are not necessarily the direct, uncontrollable outcome of anxiety, but they are an effort, conscious or not, to divert the focus of attention from the self. It is notable that one of the commonest sources of irritation for an audience, the same awkward and uncomfortable "aaaaaah" that serves as a connective, has probably never been explained adequately. We suggest that of all the "substitute" activities an individual might employ to avoid objective self awareness during a pause, the "aaaaaah" is among the easiest to implement. Of course, the devices of turning pages, lighting cigarettes, and adjusting the microphone could all substitute for the awkward connective, were these other activities somewhat more accessible.

A common phenomenon is the lecturer who "walks" his presentation. The analysis seems clear: if a speaker continues to move constantly, the threat of objective self awareness is diminished, for subjective self awareness is virtually inevitable, even during a pause in speech, as long as the speaker is engaged in considerable motor activity. We should use this example to reemphasize a central theoretical distinction. The speaker who walks does not necessarily focus attention on the activity of walking, for if he did his presentation would be largely incoherent. The theoretical function of his traversing the speaker's platform is not that of distraction. Walking serves to create for the person a feeling of being the subject of forces that are acting on the environment, and given this feeling he cannot evaluate himself, for he is simply unaware of the self as a distinct event to be evaluated. He is self aware only in the sense of his feeling that he is the subject of forces directed outward.

The activity creating subjective self awareness need not be something as conspicuous as smoking, nor as effortful as walking. As long as the person feels that he is imparting forces onto events external to himself, he will have the feeling of being the subject. A case in point is the speaker who keeps an iron grip on his microphone. The same effect may be attained by gripping the sides of the podium, thrusting one's hands into his pockets, or, in a more contrived setting, by squeezing a hand dynamometer.

The precise psychological causal relationship between objective self awareness and activity is not altogether obvious. There is good reason to think that the objective state brings forth activity, and although we do not pretend to understand the precise reason, two possibilities are as follows. (1) Through repeated experiences with objective self awareness and the subsequent accidental or incidental performance of activities, people probably come to associate activity with reduced negative affect. This explanation is simply an instrumental learning approach, and, as such, serves as a supplement to the present theory. (2) Looking back to the Zajonc interpretation of social facilitation, we might assume that negative affect is drive-producing, and thereby increases the organism's activities (as long as these activities are dominant). According to this interpretation, the person does not "elect" or "decide" to pursue activities nor would any specific learning experience be necessary.

These two explanations are not exhaustive, though we see them as plausible and subject to test. But for the present we will not dwell any longer on the reasons for the association between objective self awareness and activity.

RESEARCH ON PHYSICAL EFFORT, SUBJECTIVE SELF AWARENESS, AND ATTRIBUTION

Our introductory remarks elaborated on the possibility that one common function of overt behavior is that of bringing about the subjective state. Numerous anecdotal examples of the ''self conscious'' person's activity were considered, and Goffman and Hoffer were cited as supporting the proposition that the objectively self aware person, especially when he is a failure, will seek activity. Theoretically, there is no reason to suppose that this desire for busywork and the numerous "nervous" activities are necessarily consciously motivated activities. We do not find it necessary to take a stand on the conscious-unconscious issue, except insofar as the discomfort itself is concerned. (From the theory, it is necessary that the person is aware of the discrepancies for the discrepancies to have any motivational significance.) It is possible that people understand, on a conscious level, the relationship between activity and decreased objective self awareness, but the ultimate answer to this question in no way affects the theoretical derivation.

There are at least two ways to test our notion about activity. The individual could be placed in a situation where activities are available to him, and if objective self awareness were varied, we would expect the objectively self aware subject to spend more time in activity. Alternatively, some subjects could be placed in a standard activity while others remain passive. From the theory the active subjects should show less evidence of objective self awareness. It is the latter strategy that has been followed in each of the three experiments by Wicklund and Duval which are reported below.

All three of the experiments creating subjective self awareness used attribution to self or other as the dependent measure. As we have seen in the analysis of attribution in Chapter 4, the notion of discrepancy size is unnecessary when the theory is applied to attribution. To recapitulate, it is postulated that the attribution of responsibility for any event is determined by the focus of the individual's attention; thus, if attention is turned toward the self due to stimuli creating the objective state or to the absence of forces that would take attention away from the self, the individual will see himself as causal for whatever events are to be explained. Conversely, when subjectively self aware, causality will be located outside himself, in whatever object, person, or phenomenon is the focus of his attention.

Experiment I

In the first experiment there were just two conditions, one involving effort and one not, and three dependent measures were used. Each of these measures was designed to measure the subject's tendency to blame himself for certain negative consequences accruing from his actions. From the theory it was argued that a person will attribute causality to himself to the extent that he is objectively self aware, and, accordingly, it was hypothesized that forcing subjects to engage in an activity would decrease self blame.

All subjects were female undergraduates. When the subject arrived for the experiment she was shown into a large experimental room and seated in a chair with a self-contained desk. The experimenter (a male undergraduate) proceeded to say that the experiment consisted of two parts: the first part dealt with language learning ability, and the second with manual dexterity. He then explained what the subject was to do during the first part, and said the following.

> To begin with, we are compiling writing samples from average U.S. college students for the purpose of testing foreign students. These foreign students have had about one month of spoken English, which they studied in their homeland. We will be measuring the ability of these foreign students to learn the English language in relation to their cultural background. Here is a list of utensils common in our own culture but unfamiliar to the foreign students. We want you to write a sentence or two describing and explaining the use of each item. After you do this, we will read your descriptions and explanations to the foreign students to determine how much of your explanations they understand.

Then the experimenter gave the subject a list of six household items and asked him to write a brief description of each item. The items were as follows: coffeepot, flour sifter, egg beater, pliers, screw driver, and toaster. After the descriptions had been written the experimenter led into the manipulation by elaborating on the purported second part of the experiment.

EXPERIMENTAL MANIPULATION

The subject was reminded that the second part of the experiment would involve manual dexterity, and was then informed that it would be necessary to build up some muscle tension in her forearms prior to the actual manual dexterity procedure. The experimenter said that this would be accomplished by means of a hand grip of the type used for building a strong grip. In the Control condition the experimenter then proceeded with his questions, but in the Grip condition he handed the subject the grip along with a small block of wood. The grip resembled a nutcracker in shape, and required a substantial pressure to force the handles together. Because it was desirable experimentally for the subject to exert a constant pressure, her task was facilitated by the placement of the block of wood between the ends of the handles, thus a relatively slight pressure kept the handles locked around the block of wood. Once the subject in the Grip condition had a firm grasp on the device, the experimenter proceeded with the following line of questioning.

PERCENTAGE UNDERSTANDING

First, the experimenter said that he would like the subject to estimate the percentage of foreign students who would be able to comprehend the full meaning of each of the descriptions. He then read aloud each of the subject's six descriptions, and after each one he requested the subject's percentage estimate.

CONFIDENCE

Second, the subject was asked to indicate how confident she was in her descriptions. For this measure she was told to say a number between "1" and "10," such that "1" represented no confidence and "10" represented high confidence.

ATTRIBUTION OF RESPONSIBILITY

Third, the subject was asked to ascribe responsibility to herself or to the foreign students for their possible difficulty in comprehending the descriptions. Specifically, the subject was told to consider the possibility that the foreign students might not understand the descriptions, and then to indicate whose responsibility the potential lack of understanding would be by stating a "percentage your fault" and a "percentage their fault." It was required, of course, that the two percentage estimates add to 100.

After the three measures had been taken, the procedure was terminated and the subject was debriefed.

The hypothesis stated that subjects would not engage in self-blame to the extent that they were subjectively self aware. It was expected that the effort entailed by squeezing the hand grip would increase the proportion of time spent by the subject in subjective self awareness, and that, as a consequence, those subjects would show less self-blame than those in the Control condition. The three dependent measures will be discussed separately. It should be noted that five subjects from the Grip condition were deleted from the data analysis because they were unable to hold the grip steadily. They either dropped it or had to repeatedly readjust it in their hands while the experimenter asked the questions. The attribution result (below) is significant even if the five subjects are included.

PERCENTAGE UNDERSTANDING

The first measure consisted of six questions, each one asking the subject to estimate the percentage of foreign students who would comprehend the written description. The six estimates were averaged for each subject, and the means

TABLE 8

Means of Three Measures of Self-Blame (EXPERIMENT I)

	Grip condition $(14)^a$	Control condition (18)
Percentage understanding	45.81^b	43.06
Confidence	6.43^c	5.33
Attribution of responsibility	45.71^d	62.50

^{a}Ns in parentheses.
^{b}The means for percentage understanding refer to the subject's average estimate of the percentage of foreign students who would understand his six descriptions.
^{c}The higher the mean, the more confidence in the written descriptions.
^{d}The means for attribution of responsibility refer to the percentage of fault imputed by the subject to himself.

of the Grip and Control conditions are 45.81 percent and 43.06 percent respectively. The means differ in the expected direction, but the difference does not approach statistical significance.

CONFIDENCE

This item simply asked the subject to indicate on a 10-point scale her confidence in her descriptions. The Grip condition mean (6.43) was higher than the Control condition mean (5.33) as expected, and the difference was just short of significance ($.10 < p < .20$).

ATTRIBUTION OF RESPONSIBILITY

This question required the subject to imagine the possibility that her descriptions would not be understood, and to attribute a percentage of responsibility for such lack of understanding to herself and to the foreign students. Consistent with the hypothesis, the mean attributed responsibility in terms of percent the subject's own fault was 45.71 in the Grip condition and 62.50 in the Control condition, the difference being significant beyond the .02 level. The data for all three measures are summarized in Table 8.

DISCUSSION

As the results have shown, the pattern of results was not identical for all three measures. The first measure manifested only a slight nonsignificant trend in the expected direction, the second measure produced a stronger but still not significant difference, and the third measure offered strong statistical support for the hypothesis. One approach to understanding this pattern is the assumption of sequential effects. Perhaps there was something about the placement of the attribution question last in the series that rendered it the most powerful in discriminating between conditions. For example, considering the novelty of the hand grip, it is likely that some time passed before the subject felt at ease while gripping the device. In the early stages of their effort expenditure, subjects may well have been concerned about whether or not they were holding it correctly, and such concern only would have operated to increase objective self awareness. If this concern about the self was a product of the novelty of the setting, it would follow that the subject would gradually become less concerned about her with the passage of time; thus, toward the end of the questioning period the effort would have shown its greatest effect in bolstering subjective self awareness.

Alternatively, there may have been no sequential effect, and the difference in results between measures might have been due to intrinsic aspects of the questions. Disregarding the specific questions momentarily, we might consider what would constitute the appropriate question in the present paradigm. Ideally, the manipulation was so strong that all subjects who operated the grip were totally subjectively self aware while all control subjects were entirely objectively self aware throughout the procedure. This state of affairs was, of course, not achieved, but we assume that the manipulation did create differences between conditions in the direction of that ideal difference. Consequently, an appropriate question is one that neither forces the subjectively self aware subject out of her state nor brings the objectively self aware person toward subjective self awareness. The question should be balanced, such that the subjects in either condition could respond without thereby moving toward the characteristic state of self awareness of the alternative condition. It would seem that the final question, which asked the subject to distribute responsibility to herself and to the others in any proportion she saw fit, met the condition of balance—for the subjectively self aware individual is not forced to concentrate upon herself critically by the question, yet at the same time the objectively self aware subject can easily focus upon herself critically while considering the question. In this respect the other types of questions asked appear unsuitable.

The first type of question simply asked the subject how many students would understand. The question contained no hint that the subject might be at fault for the failure to comprehend, thus the objectively self aware subject's attention is drawn from herself to the failings of the others. Had this question been rephrased to include a statement focused toward self-criticism, it may have been more successful. The second item, which asked for the subject's confidence, suffered from the opposite problem. Here, the subjectively self aware person is forced into objective self awareness because the experimenter raises the question of whether or not the subjects should be confident. Given such a challenge from the experimenter, the subject squeezing the hand grip is forced, by the experimenter, to examine herself critically in order to answer the question. There is no easy way to handle the question that would allow the subject to remain in the subjective state. Of course, it should be noted that the confidence item was not totally unsuccessful in reflecting the predicted difference, which could mean that subjects exerting effort were forced into objective self awareness momentarily by the question, but because of the effort did not long remain in the objective state. The last question, which contained neither of the apparent flaws of the first two items, would appear to be the best form of question to employ in attempting to discriminate between objectively and subjectively self aware individuals, although questions that force subjects into one state or another may also suffice, as suggested by the confidence item.

Because of the strong possibility that the first item is unsuitable for distinguishing between subjects who are subjectively and objectively self aware, that type of item—which focuses the subject's attention away from himself—was deleted from the second experiment. Disregarding the differences between the dependent measures in the first experiment, the results of that exploratory study were encouraging; thus the second experiment conducted was conceptually similar.

Experiment II

The second experiment was virtually identical with the first, except for a slight change in the measurements. As we noted above, the type of question that makes reference only to other people was deleted. In addition, confidence in the subject's attitudes about various social and political matters was measured rather than their confidence in the correctness of their definitions, and, finally, the measure of attribution was a hypothetical question rather than one based upon the subject's actual behavior. There was an exploratory attempt to create subjective self awareness by means of placing the subject in a position physically superior to that of the experimenter, but because the manipulation was unsuccessful and complex it will not be discussed here.

After the subject entered the cubicle the experimenter proceeded to describe the experiment as having two parts. The first part was said to involve an attitude questionnaire while the second part was described as research on manual dexterity that entailed the subject's manual rotation of a turntable. An incomplete pursuit rotor had been placed on the table, and its appearance was that of a crude record player turntable. The subject was told that he would learn more about the manual dexterity project later in the session, but that first, some attitude statements were needed from him.

A total of seventeen atittude items, each with a confidence measure, was read to the subject. The first six items were presented prior to the manipulation, their purpose being that of allowing the subject to become familiar with the format. Before reading the items the experimenter reminded the subject that he probably had already filled out a questionnaire in his psychology class with similar items, and that the purpose of reading him some of the same items again was to obtain a more sensitive measurement that is easier to score. She told him that he would be asked to respond to the items by stating a number, in contrast to the previous group testing session in which he replied to the questionnaire by placing a check mark next to a dot. In fact, the two methods of responding to the questionnaire are functionally equivalent because the numbers the subject was allowed to use during the session were the same ones that corresponded to the dots on the earlier questionnaire. However, subjects did not understand that the two systems were equivalent, thus the rationale provided a plausible excuse for a second administration of the questionnaire.

THE FIRST SIX ITEMS

The experimenter then told the subject that she would read six attitude statements. Each of these was to be a simple statement, and the subject was told to respond to each statement with a number between "1" and "22," such that a low number would represent strong disagreement with the statement and a high number would represent strong agreement. It was explained further that each attitude statement would be followed by an item asking the subject for his confidence in his attitude—and again he was told to respond with a number between "1" and "22," where a low number corresponded to low confidence and a high number to high confidence. The experimenter proceeded to read the six attitude statements and the associated confidence measures, then she informed the subject that she would have to leave the room for a couple of minutes because she was missing the next page of questions. The sole purpose of her leaving the room was to give the subjects in the Turntable condition sufficient time to practice rotating the turntable, and in order to hold the differences between conditions to a minimum, subjects in all conditions were given the two minute pause.

CONTROL CONDITION

The experimenter simply returned to the room and read the remaining eleven attitude and confidence items. The attitude statements are not listed here, because they did not constitute the dependent measure. The confidence measure consisted of the following question and was asked after each attitude statement: "How confident are you that your opinion is correct?" Following the attitude questions the experimenter read a question based on a hypothetical situation. The question was conceptually similar to the attribution-of-responsibility item employed in Experiment 1:

> Frequently it happens that many of the students in 301 (Introductory Psychology) classes fail to complete the requirements for experiments. Should this happen to you, what percentage your fault and what percentage the fault of the department would it be?

TURNTABLE CONDITION

Just before the experimenter left the room for a two-minute break, she told the subject that because he would be working on a manual dexterity task later, it would be necessary for him to warm up. Then she instructed him to place a finger on the edge of the turntable, and to rotate it slowly and continually for the next few minutes. She told him that it would be best if the process of rotating became fairly automatic by the time the manual dexterity task was to begin. The subject was instructed to continue to rotate the device while the experimenter was out of the room, and when she returned she proceeded with the remainder of the questions, just as in the Control condition, and the entire time the subject continued to spin the turntable.

There were two theoretically relevant dependent measures: the eleven post-manipulation confidence items, and the attribution-of-responsibility item. From the hypothesis, it would be expected that subjects in the Turntable condition would be more confident than Control subjects, and that subjects in the Turntable condition would attribute blame to the psychology department more so than Control subjects.

CONFIDENCE

Change in confidence between the premeasure, administered approximately a week prior to the experiment, and the measure taken during the experimental session was analyzed to test the hypothesis. The number of subjects had to be reduced somewhat in each condition (for this analysis only) because some subjects had not filled out the premeasure and some did not answer all of the items during the session. A mean change in confidence was computed for each condition, based on each subject's change score for the total of the eleven confidence items and these means are shown in Table 9. Consistent with the hypothesis, the mean confidence tends to increase in the Turntable condition, while there is a decrease in the Control condition. The difference between conditions approached the conventional level of significance ($p < .08$).

ATTRIBUTION OF RESPONSIBILITY

The percentage of blame attributed by the subject to himself was analyzed, and the means in Table 8 are generally as expected in that attribution of blame to oneself is greatest in the Control condition. Largely because of one subject in the Control condition whose attribution score was 80 percentage points below the mean for that condition, there are no reliable differences between the conditions using the F test, but if subjects are divided at the median (see Table 8), the Fisher exact test shows a difference of borderline significance between the Control and Turntable conditions ($p = .054$).

As in the first experiment, not all of the dependent measures showed strong

TABLE 9

Confidence in Attitude and Attribution of Responsibility (Experiment II)

	Mean change in confidence	Mean percentage blame attributed by the subject to himself	Frequencies of subjects above and below the attribution-of-responsibility median	
			Above	Below
Turntable condition	17.18[a] ($n = 11$)	84.12 ($n = 17$)	5	12
Control condition	−5.77 ($n = 13$)	90.62 ($n = 16$)	11	5

[a]The means are change in confidence for the sum of the 11 confidence items.

differences between conditions. It was expected that subjects who received the Turntable treatment would show more confidence in their attitudes than would Control subjects, and the comparison between the Turntable and Control conditions revealed an effect just short of significance. Again, it might be argued that the confidence item does not allow the subject who is exerting effort to remain in subjective self awareness while answering the question, and that, as a conseqeunce, the differenece between conditions was attenuated. In any case there is reason to think that effort exertion enhances an individual's general confidence if the results of Experiments I and II are taken together.

With respect to the attribution-of-responsibility item, the present results replicate those of the first experiment, and with a different form of exertion. The results of the present experiment were slightly weaker than those of the first, but the fact of the consistent finding does lend plausibility to the idea.

Experiment III

The third experiment had two central purposes: first, it was desired to replicate the relationship between effort exertion and attribution-of-responsibility found in the first two studies, rather than to explore additional manipulations or less sensitive dependent measures again. Second, it was not clear either in the first or the second experiment whether the relative success of the attribution-of-responsibility items was a sequential effect (those items always appeared last in the sequence of questions) or an effect due to inherent aspects of the questions. In Experiment III only the attribution-of-responsibility type of item was employed, and enough of them were included so that a sequential effect could be ascertained should one appear. The effort manipulation was identical to that of Experiment II.

Subjects were led to believe that an ostensible two-part experiment would require them to reply to some hypothetical attribution-of-responsibility items and then to perform a manual dexterity task. Some of the subjects were told to rotate a turntable while the questions were asked (Turntable condition) as in Experiment II, while the Control subjects did not expect to rotate the turntable until the questions had been completed. A total of ten questions were asked, each of them asking the subject to place himself in a hypothetical situation in which a negative consequence could be attributed to himself or to another.

When the subject entered the cubicle he was seated across the table from the experimenter, and was told that the experiment would consist of two different activities. The first half of the experiment was said to consist of answering some questions from a questionnaire that was being developed by several psychologists in the department, and the second part was described as a project on manual dexterity.

CONTROL CONDITION

The subject was then shown the turntable, and the experimenter (a female undergraduate) said that later in the session he would be asked to place a finger on the edge of it and rotate it slowly. At that point she excused herself from the cubicle and said that she would return in a minute, which she did. Upon her return she asked the subject to reply to each of ten hypothetical situations, which are listed below. He was told to imagine himself in the situation, and then to assess responsibility for the unfortunate event depicted by ascribing a "percentage at fault" to himself and to the other person or institution in the situation. It was required that the two percentages sum to 100. After the questions had been read the subject was debriefed.

TURNTABLE CONDITION

The subject was shown the turntable as in the Control condition, but he was requested to place a finger on its edge and proceed to "warm up for the manual dexterity task." The experimenter told him that it was important that the turning response be fairly automatic by the time the manual dexterity task begins, which provided a rationale for his rotating the device several minutes prior to the task. She instructed him to continue to rotate, then she left the room for a minute, returned, and asked him the ten questions while he continued to move the turntable. Finally he was debriefed. The ten questions are the following:

1. You're diving off a diving board and just as you dive off, someone swims up from under water and you land on top of him.

2. You're driving down the expressway when suddenly the woman in front of you slams on her brakes and you run right into the back of her.

3. You're taking a test and you notice that the guy sitting next to you is copying every one of your answers. You don't say anything to him or cover your paper. Pretty soon, the teacher takes up both papers and gives you both an F.

4. You have to have a serious operation and the doctor you've hired is reputable, but he's never performed this type of operation before. You decide to let him proceed with the operation, but afterwards you have severe internal bleeding and you're in much worse shape than you were in to begin with.

5. You have to get to campus one night, and you could walk in about 20 minutes, but you've been working all day and you're pretty tired, so you decide to hitchhike. Instead of taking you to campus, the guy who picks you up beats you up, takes all your money, and drops you on the other side of town.

6. You pull up behind a bus that's stopped at a stop sign and you want to turn right at this intersection. After waiting for one and one-half or two minutes the bus hasn't moved. Finally, not knowing what he's going to do, you decide to pull out around him and have to cut back in front to turn right at the corner. Just as you do, he pulls out and runs right into you.

7. You bought a new shirt about a week ago. You've worn it a few times so it needs washing. There are no directions on the material from the manufacturer telling how

to launder it so you go ahead and wash it like you usually do. Afterwards when you put it on, it's three sizes too small and the colors have faded.

8. You have an 8:30 class and you're there every morning. You have a report due the last Monday of classes and you've known about it. One day you cannot possibly drag yourself out of bed so you stay home. On that same day the teacher changes the date of the assignment to the Friday before that Monday. When you return to class that Friday you don't have your assignment and your grade is lowered.

9. You have a book checked out of the library and it's due in about two days. A friend of yours wants to borrow it, so instead of returning it, you let him use it. About three months later, you receive a note that the book has never been seen and you owe a huge fine.

10. You're driving down the street about five miles over the speed limit when a little kid suddenly runs out chasing a ball and you hit him.

Once again, the subjects who exerted effort (Turntable condition) attributed less blame to themselves than did the Control subjects (see Table 10). The average attribution to the self was computed for each subject from his 10 responses, and the means of the two conditions based on these averages were reliably different ($p < .05$). In order to test for a sequential effect, the ten items were simply divided into groups of five, and the mean change from the first five to the second five was computed (see Table 10). The mean decrease in attribution to the self in the Turntable condition and the mean increase in the Control condition are consistent with what may have been a sequential effect in the first two experiments, and the difference between the means is significant ($p < .05$).

SEQUENTIAL EFFECTS

The final experiment provided direct evidence for the sequential effect that was suggested by the discrepancies between dependent measures in Experiments I and II. It would appear that the longer an individual performs a task, the greater power the task has to produce subjective self awareness. Judging from subjects' reports, at least one major reason for this effect in the present research had to do with their discomfort during the earlier stages of questioning. The combination of an unusual form of effort and unexpected questions made

TABLE 10

Mean Attribution to Self (Experiment III)

	Mean based on the sum of the ten items	Mean change between first five and last five items
Turntable condition ($N = 14$)	49.65[a]	−3.30
Control condition ($N = 16$)	57.63	9.01

[a]Mean percentage blame attributed by the subject to himself.

them apprehensive about their role in the situation, but they overcame this discomfort as they grew accustomed to the unique combination of the task and questions. Conceivably there are other reasons for the sequential effect, but we will not explore possible explanations further at this point. The finding is important because it does shed some light on the experimental paradigm, and although something about the items themselves could have contributed to the difficulty of obtaining differences with items other than the attribution-of-responsibility questions, there is good reason to presume that the temporal placement of the items in the procedure was related to the effects of subjective self awareness. Whether or not this sequential effect would be found generally is a question that should be settled through additional research. The ultimate explanation for the temporal effect, of course, has little bearing on the validity of the main results.

The Theoretical Import of the Experiments

The concept of subjective self awareness means only that consciousness is the subject of attention, rather than the object. By the "subject" is meant that consciousness is trained outward, onto any event except the self. When a person engages in an activity and his action necessarily requires his conscious attention, it is clear that he cannot examine himself. Consequently the attribution of responsibility for undesirable consequences is outside himself, and as Duval (Chapter 5) has shown, this effect operates for events with positive consequences as well.

A Contrast Between Perceptions of Actor and Observer

In a theoretical statement on person perception, Jones and Nisbett (1971) set forth the argument that there is a pervasive tendency for actors to attribute their actions to situational requirements while observers tend to attribute those same actions to stable personal dispositions. The authors cite a number of reasons for these discrepant attributions, including the following: (1) The actor and observer do not have equal information. In particular, the observer neither has the experiential concomitants of the action, nor does he comprehend the causes of the behavior to the extent the actor does. (2) The differential attribution can be attributed in part to a difference between actors and observers in the type of information that is salient for them. For example, action itself is more salient for the observer than the actor, for the responses are taken for granted by the actor while they are not known by the observer until observed.

Our presentation of Jones and Nisbett is slightly cryptic, but the reason for introducing their formulation is not complicated: they have analyzed the case of the actor and observer, given that these are two distinct individuals, and their discussion assumes among other things that the actor and observer do not have identical information. We suggest that their basic thesis is correct even when the observer and actor possess identical information, which is to say that actor and observer are one. In all three experiments discussed above, the purpose of the effort exertion was to render the subject more an actor than an observer of himself. Theoretically, the person is a self observer only when objectively self aware, and it is then that he will attribute blame to himself. As a subjectively self aware actor, self criticism will diminish and he will attribute blame to the environment.

Chapter 10

SUBJECTIVE SELF AWARENESS: A SECOND APPROACH

In addition to the action-taking basis of subjective self awareness, the theory implies an alternative approach that may be called "at-oneness" with the environment. The common spiritual and metaphysical overtones of "at-oneness" should be disregarded, for all that is intended by the term is that the person finds himself in such a position that it is relatively difficult to see himself as distinct from the environment. This basis of subjective self awareness is exactly the opposite of the methods employed to create objective self awareness in the experiments reported by Wicklund and Duval (1971) and in the experiment by Duval *et al.* The objective state was created by showing the individual symbols of himself that reminded him that he was a distinct entity in the environment. In contrast, the at-oneness approach would place the person either symbolically or physically in close proximity with some aspect of the external surroundings.

Research on Deindividuation

Festinger, Pepitone, and Newcomb (1952) conducted a correlational study to examine the relationship between the identifiability of group members and negative comments made by the members toward their own parents. Several small groups were assembled and given ample time to discuss their relations with their parents. It was argued by the authors that expression of hostility toward one's parents would be inhibited to the degree that the individual could be singled out by other group members, which is to say that anonymity will lower the restraints against expression of hostility. Within each group two important measures were computed: (1) The first was an index of identifiability. Following the discussion each person was asked to identify who in the group had made which statement, and it turned out that there was considerable variation between groups in the extent to which the members could accurately associate statements with their sources. It was presumed that a group of people with poor recall of the source of statements is a deindividuated group. (2) The measure of lowered restraint of hostility was simply the number of negative comments about parents minus the number of positive comments. As predicted, there was a positive relationship between deindividuation and amount of hostility, although the interpretation of these data should be held with some reservation in light of the correlational nature of the experiment. In addition to that major finding, Festinger *et al.* also noted that deindividuated groups were more attractive to their members than were less individuated groups, although the latter result was of questionable statistical significance. The experiment was replicated by Cannavale, Scarr, and Pepitone (1970), and their findings were similar although the data did not attain the usual level of significance.

In 1965, Singer, Brush, and Lublin reported two experiments in which deindividuation was created through the homogeneous clothing of the groups. About half of the groups dressed up in their own clothing for the experimental sessions while the remainder were dressed in lab coats once they arrived at the session. According to the authors, "A person's choice of clothing seems to be a set of cues which affect his *feelings* of identifiability without affecting his *actual* identifiability [p. 357]." The authors investigated both conformity behavior and the use of obscene language, and the results were as might be predicted: the greater the identifiability, the greater the conformity but the less frequent was obscene language.

Zimbardo (1969b) reports an experiment quite similar to the research of Singer *et al.* To effect deindividuation, some of the subjects were asked to don lab coats and hoods, thus physical identifiability was all but removed. The remaining subjects wore their own clothing in addition to nametags. All subjects were subsequently given the opportunity to shock a victim, and as would be expected from the earlier research, more aggression was manifested in terms of electric shocks administered when subjects had been deindividuated.

Baron (1971) proposes a difficulty with Zimbardo's research which lies in a confounding of anonymity and uniformity of appearance. Zimbardo's hooded subjects operated in the dark, while the nonhooded or easily identifiable subjects

TABLE 11

Mean Latencies in Seconds for Aggression in Baron's Experiment

	Visible	Nonvisible
Hoods and lab coats	5.71[a]	9.01
Nametags and own clothing	8.79	5.98

[a]The smaller the means, the greater the level of aggression.

operated in dim light. This should not have made any difference provided that the subject believed he was not being observed by his victim, but Baron suspects that subjects felt observed by their victims even though there was an experimental precaution against this possibility. In short, subjects who wore hoods may also have been relatively anonymous, in the sense that they felt they were not seen by the victim, while such anonymity would not hold for nonhooded subjects.

In order to examine this possibility more closely, Baron designed an experiment in which distinctiveness (Hoods and Lab Coats versus Nametags and Own Clothing) and anonymity (possibility of being viewed by victim) were varied independently. The experiment was in most other respects quite similar to Zimbardo's research. Consistent with Baron's expectations, the anonymity variable had a considerable impact. Among subjects who were not anonymous (Visible condition), the hoods and lab coats effected a greater level of aggression as measured by latency. This finding is completely consistent with that of Zimbardo. But in the Nonvisible condition, just the opposite results were obtained, such that hooded subjects showed a lower level of aggression (see Table 11).

The results within the Nonvisible condition show a pattern just the opposite from the effects within the Visible condition. This result is clearly not interpretable in terms of deindividuation, although its presence does not subtract from the import of the finding within the Visible condition. Nonetheless, it is intriguing, should be explained, and Baron proposes the following account.

It is possible that the presence of curtains between the subject and target, in addition to the anonymity of hoods and lab coats, suggested to the subjects that they were administering a severe level of aggression. Otherwise, why would the experimenter provide them with so much "protection?" Accordingly, the subjects in the Hoods and Lab Coats-Nonvisible condition inhibited their aggression relative to other subjects, as shown by the long mean latency of 9.01.

Dion (1970) carried out an experiment much in the same vein as the work by Baron. Subjects had the opportunity to aggress, unprovoked, by administering an uncomfortable white noise to another subject through earphones. As one would expect, no one actually experienced the white noise. Anonymity from the experimenter was varied by either telling the subject that his administration of noise would be monitored, or that he would not be monitored as an individual.

On a measure of duration Dion found that anonymity led to greater aggression, consistent with the research reported above.

All of the preceding experiments are conceptually quite similar. A behavior that ordinarily would have been inhibited before a group was disinhibited by lowering the identifiability of the subject. By our use of the preceding examples we do not by any means intend that the presence of others will commonly increase the subjective state. In the Baron, Singer *et al.*, and Zimbardo research those subjects who were dressed alike presumably were subjectively self aware relative to those dressed uniquely, but this would not be taken to mean that a person will be more subjectively self aware when in the presence of similar others than when he is alone. The theory implies that the presence of others, provided that the person feels the focus of their attention, is one of the stronger and more usual sources of the objective state, and this power of the group is not totally attenuated by similar dress.

Some Theoretical Elaboration

The exact strategies that could be used to generate the subjective state via at-oneness will be easier to understand if the idea is given a more detailed treatment. The three experiments reported above (Wicklund and Duval) were predicated on the assumption that the subjective state can result from a transfer of attention away from the self, but in the case of at-oneness the process is different. The self as a distinct entity is to some extent obliterated such that the person would find it relatively difficult to focus on himself even if conditions were appropriate for objective self awareness. To some degree the person comes to place what was formerly his distinct self into a concept that encompasses various features of the environment in addition to the self. For example, when a fraternity member becomes so totally indoctrinated that he comes to view himself as just another Greek letter and espouses ideas no different from those in his immediate social surroundings, then he has in large part been absorbed by the concept of the fraternity. Since his self and the fraternity blend into one, it would be somewhat difficult for him to be objectively self aware in the sense of the theory.

Many other examples of at-oneness deal with social institutions. Certainly any radical or revolutionary social movement requires a selflessness, and just as in the fraternity example members of such movements commonly "identify" with the movement, which is to say that their original self has been swallowed up by the movement. The line of demarcation between the person's self and the social movement is no longer recognized by him. Similarly, Ziller (1964) applies the concept of individuation to the bureaucracy, and notes that such factors as the homogeneity of members, use of titles rather than names, and pressures toward uniformity would all make for deindividuation.

It is notable that the at-oneness approach to the subjective state resembles the subjectively self aware state of the child (Chapter 3). Just as the child does not discriminate the self as a distinct entity, the person swept up in a social institution fails to differentiate a causal agent self from the remainder of the environment. The child has severe difficulty in self criticism, and so should the person who is aware of an institution in lieu of the self.

Rather than continue to cite examples to attempt to convey our meaning of at-oneness, it is appropriate at this point to make a more conceptual statement. Certainly it is not possible to place the person into a position where every aspect of the self is submerged within a larger entity, but it should be feasible to create at-oneness with respect to certain classes of dimensions of the self. In the case of the fraternity, the person is immersed in a setting where his personal values cannot be discriminated from the prevalent values around him; consequently there are no distinct personal values to be uncovered in the state of objective self awareness.

It is easy to imagine situations where the individual would not feel as though he stands out physically from his background, such that it would be difficult to arouse the objective state by showing the person physical reflections or symbols of himself. The research by Singer *et al.* and Zimbardo has been cited as an example of this physical deindividuation, and we would also suppose that the person could in some circumstances blend into the physical environment as well as into the group. A person strolling through the dense fog may well feel an absence of differentiation between his body and the immediate environment. Temperature may also play a vital role. If a room is hot and somewhat humid it would be more difficult to differentiate the perimeters of the body than under conditions of greater contrast. Finally, and perhaps more obvious, there are numerous kinds of camouflage that can give a person the status of a chameleon. In general, one's clothing, automobile, inside walls of the house, and other personal surroundings can be described in terms of the amount of camouflage that is afforded the person.

Not only are values and physical appearance subject to at-oneness, but behaviors are commonly performed within a context allowing the individual a freedom from distinction as the sole source of certain behavioral effects. Whenever action is undertaken jointly as in a lynch mob, race riot, or even productive activity, it is more difficult for the person to view his behaviors as distinct from those of anyone else. Typically, the members of a mob would not be objectively self aware while they are acting anyway, but subsequent to the action each individual's self evaluation (presuming the members become objectively self aware at some point) will be considerably less painful than if each person had performed the behavior as an individual. In short, the behavior flows through the group as a unity, and as far as the individual member is concerned, the essence and significance of his individual contribution is difficult to ascertain. Le Bon (1895) has offered a similar proposal in noting that the group is capable of savagery by virtue of the transformation of distinct individual thinking into a "collective mind."

The Theoretical Positions of Singer and Zimbardo

Singer *et al.* conceive of deindividuation as a subjective state, not directly measurable, in which people lose their self-consciousness. But deindividuation is by no means equated with the absence of self-consciousness, for the authors set forth some definite criteria for inferring that deindividuation has been brought about:

> . . . deindividuation may be inferred only if two consequences have occurred: if the person in the hypothesized deindividuated state engages in a usually undesirable act, and if his attraction to the masking group increases. This is not to say that deindividuation always produces undesirable behaviors and enhanced group liking, but rather that the emergence of these behaviors and effects provides a sounder basis for the inference of deindividuation [p. 357].

The parallel between this conception and our own is hardly obscure. First, we have stated explicitly in an earlier chapter that many behaviors are performed in the subjective state that are later evaluated negatively by the person, once objective self awareness is created. The implication is that the subjective state will lead to behaviors that are disparate from the person's standards, whether subjective self awareness is brought about by at-oneness (deindividuation), motor activity, or distraction. Second, Singer *et al.*, Festinger *et al.*, and Cannavale *et al.* have argued that the deindividuated group will be attractive to its members. From our framework this is not surprising in that objective self awareness has been postulated as a condition of negative affect and as a state to be avoided.

While Singer and his associates describe deindividuation as a state in which self consciousness is absent, we view deindividuation as one possible root of subjective self awareness. When a person is completely at one with others, it is impossible for him to take himself as an object.

Zimbardo is generally in agreement with Singer *et al.* regarding the conditions that bring about deindividuation, a point which is evidenced by the similarlity of their research. But Zimbardo more severely limits those behaviors he calls individuated:

> Virtually by definition, deindividuated behavior must have the property of being a high-intensity manifestation of behavior which observers would agree is emotional, impulsive, irrational, regressive, or atypical for the person in the given situation [p. 259].

The precise conceptual similarity of these behaviors is difficult to understand, and we wonder why the behaviors must carry such extreme characteristics.

Our own analysis presumes that a behavior that is discrepant from the person's standards will be more likely in the deindividuated state, but the behavior by no means must be emotional and so forth.

Zimbardo goes on to suggest that deindividuated behaviors must not be responsive to the situation, to the target or victim of action, or to any aspect of the self that would tend to inhibit the response. We would agree with this proposal, but we find it useful to couch the ideas in more general terms. In short, the subjectively self aware person will not respond to his standards of correct behavior, for consciousness cannot focus on the self.

THE DUAL FUNCTION OF ACTIVITY

Thus far we have dwelled upon the theme that activity serves to channel attention away from the self, and that as a person becomes increasingly objectively self aware he will show greater efforts to terminate self consciousness through engaging in motor activity. We have assumed that this activity is the direct outcome of a desire to reduce the negative affect engendered by objective self awareness, but in many cases there could be an alternative reason for the activity. When a person is objectively self aware he comes to focus on discrepancies between his present state, or performance, and his standards or ideals. If he finds discrepancies he attempts to reduce the discrepancies, typically by altering his attitudes, behaviors, or other traits in the direction of the standards. If a person's objective self awareness is increased and he shows increased productivity in a certain matter, we cannot always pinpoint which of the two possible theoretical reasons explains that increase. On one hand, the behavior serves the function of taking the person out of the objective state; but on the other hand, it may function to lower the discrepancy between performance and ideal performance.

These two reasons for increased performance could be unraveled in several ways. If performance of a behavior were contrary to a standard (the behavior might be an immoral one), or if no standards applied to the behavior, then we could better evaluate which of the two processes were operating. If a person engages in activity capriciously, changing goals intermittently and never focusing on any given end state, there may be good reason to think that his activity is serving the reduction of the objective state, rather than discrepancy reduction.

It is important to note that the question of which process operates does not apply generally to the creation of subjective self awareness. The question arises only in those situations in which the person is free to embark on a task or not, and where objective self awareness is varied. An alternative approach to understanding the bases of the subjective state is the one taken in the research we have described, where the subjective state is varied by forcing activity onto the person. In such a context, the notion of discrepancy reduction is irrelevant to the measures of self-blame that were taken in the experiments.

Even though the issue of "avoidance of objective self awareness versus discrepancy reduction" applies only to a specific class of situations, the issue itself has some interesting implications for social facilitation. With regard to the facilitative effects of other individuals, it may be that increased performance occurs because of the person's desire to leave the objective state, rather than because of increased drive, discrepancy reduction in the objective state, evaluation apprehension, or any other processes suggested in our remarks on social facilitation.

Chapter 11

SOME THEORETICAL
AND RESEARCH ISSUES

THEORETICAL ISSUES

Conscious or Unconscious?

Throughout the preceding chapters we have discussed the directionality of conscious attention as a phenomenon that is "conscious," and perhaps implied in the "consciousness" language is that the feeling states of subjective self awareness are unconscious. This is neither the intended nor correct implication, for there is good reason to view the feeling states as conscious, and just as conscious as focused attention. Both states are informative for the person, and the information is available immediately (it is not suppressed, etc.), whether the individual is in the objective or subjective state. The feelings that arise within the person during the subjective state have an immediate impact on him even though he is not focally aware of them. Similarly, the person who becomes objectively self aware is immediately aware of discrepancies within the self and begins to resolve them. In neither the subjective nor objective state is there any need to infer an unconscious condition with latent effects that would not be described as conscious within a Freudian framework.

Hilgard (1969) lists several phenomena that are typically explained in part by postulating an unconscious, and these include amnesias, tics, dreams, and various subliminal influences, none of which our theory purports to explain. And, finally, Hilgard's reading of the evidence leads to the conclusion that there is no sharp difference between what is conscious and what is unconscious nor does the evidence even appear to imply a psychic region of unconscious that is qualitatively distinct from consciousness.

The Pervasiveness of Subjective Self Awareness

One more consideration has to do with the mutual exclusiveness of the two states of self awareness. We have spoken of objective and subjective self awareness as if there were no overlap between the states, and this is correct with respect to focus of attention. In objective self awareness the focus is inward, while in the subjective state it is directed outward. But there is a common element between the two states. The individual experiences the feeling state of being the source of action and perception no matter whether he is objectively or subjectively self aware. In subjective self awareness he is the source of perception and action directed outward, and we have labeled this state as we have because the person is self aware only in the subjective sense. In the state of objective self awareness the person has these feelings as well, but the state has been labeled "objective" because he is the focus of his own attention in addition to feeling himself to be the source of attention.

What is the Difference Between Self and Nonself?

Most of our discussion has assumed implicitly that the self ends with the perimeters of the body, but it is appropriate to examine the definition of "self" more carefully. The distinction should, for the present purposes, be drawn with respect to the theory.

When we talk about subjective self awareness as a feeling state we refer to a process that takes place within the organism's body. To feel oneself as a causal agent can hardly mean that the referent of such feelings is outside one's own body. Therefore, with respect to subjective self awareness, the awareness of self must necessarily be an awareness of something within the organism, and it should be clear that the definition of the self presents no important problems as long as we are interested only in the feeling state.

The case of objective self awareness introduces a complexity. Until now we have argued that in objective self awareness the individual focuses upon actions carried out while in the subjective state, upon traits, attitudes, and so forth. But the causal agent self which is the target of objective self awareness is not simply an isolated element with perceptions and actions; it has actively moved and perceived the environment. Given that a person has had repeated intimate contact with a portion of his environment, it would be easy to conclude that these features of the external world are incorporated as part of the self. We think this is a reasonable conclusion; the obvious difficulty lies in understanding the processes by which an element once not part of the self comes to be incorporated.

In terms of the theory, what would it mean for some of the environment to be incorporated into the self? If objective self awareness can be created in any salient part of the self by causing the person initially to focus attention on that incorporated feature, then the new feature would functionally be a part of the self. Conversely, if that part of the environment functions as an aspect of the self, it should be possible to cause the individual to evaluate that incorporated feature, provided it is salient at the time, by initially turning his focus toward another aspect of the self. For example, it is commonly presumed that teen-aged boys incorporate their automobiles into their self images. If so, it should be possible to carry out one of the experiments we have discussed earlier such as those involving a mirror or television camera, by substituting for the camera the presence of the young man's hot rod. The theoretical argument would be the same as before; a dimension of self is made salient, such as the person's attitude-behavior discrepancy, then objective self awareness is aroused in another area (in this case the car), and, provided the attitude-behavior discrepancy is salient, the individual will come to evaluate himself on that dimension.

Although it is possible to conceive of arbitrary criteria by which to decide whether or not an element is a part of the self, it would be more satisfactory to specify the factors responsible for a feature of the environment becoming incorporated into the self. And at this point the best we can do is to hazard a conjecture, for the theory does not pretend to answer this question nor has anyone else provided an adequate solution to the question. We find it plausible that an environmental event is a functional part of the self if, from the person's point of view, that event operates as an extension of the causal agent itself. In general, any tools, aids, or devices that enable the person to carry out his intentions could easily come to be incorporated, for at some point in using these tools, the person may lose the precise distinction between his own faculties and the faculties of the environment. The artist's brush, the musician's violin bow, the young man's automobile, and the housemaid's cleaning implements are crucial elements for the successful accomplishment of certain endeavors. Because these elements are necessary, they would always be associated with the initiation and completion of those actions, and, as such, would become progressively more difficult to discriminate from the causal agent self. The person may have the intention and ability, but because the tool is a necessary component to the action, it could become incorporated into the self image.

Do People "Voluntarily" Become Objectively Self Aware?

Throughout the previous chapters we have argued for a general propensity to avoid the objective state. Our assumptions for this argument have been the following: (1) it is difficult, if not impossible, for a person to continually focus on just one dimension for a considerable time, even if there is no intraself discrepancy in the case of that dimension; and (2) as the person transfers his focus from one dimension to another, he will inevitably find numerous discrepancies and incur negative affect. Although we have no experimental evidence that the objective state will be avoided even when a failure experience has not recently occurred (see Duval *et al.*, Chapter 2), the theory directly implies such an avoidance. But everyone has had experiences of becoming objectively self aware without the provocation of the stimuli we have listed, stimuli such as other people and obvious symbols of the self. Such experiences have even happened to the authors on occasion. Are these experiences invalid evidence for the theory, or are we wrong in assuming the avoidance tendency? We would propose the following answer.

It is certainly true that the objective state takes place without the help of others present and self related symbols, but this is not to rule out the notion that the state is initiated by environmental provocation. In Chapter 9 and the communication set chapter it was noted that the objective state could be brought about through the anticipation of others' evaluations, and the evidence in the Henchy and Glass study of social facilitation and in the experiment by Davis and Wicklund offers good support for such an assumption. Provided that anticipation of interaction with others aroused the objective state, the question of "voluntary" objective self awareness can be answered.

When a person appears to undertake an action or pattern of thought and no readily apparent external cause of his undertaking is apparent, the observer is likely to say that the action was begun "voluntarily." Such is the case when a person contemplates himself but is not in the immediate presence of the stimulus conditions we have often mentioned. But to claim that the action was initiated voluntarily is only to admit to ignorance, and it is our contention that the anticipation of social interaction or of symbols of the self can be invoked to explain why the objective state is entered when the person apparently is isolated from immediate stimuli that would provoke introspection.

RESEARCH ISSUES

Conflicting Standards

The application of the theory assumes a certain knowledge of the individual's standards of correctness, for the direction that discrepancy reduction will take cannot be known unless the standard on the relevant dimension is located. Experimentally, this knowledge can be gained in any of several ways, and the result sometimes can be twoconflicting standards on one dimension. The conflict may be attributable to the fact that different approaches are taken in ascertaining the standards. For example, if there is an experimental attempt to give the subject a value favoring aggression, but at the same time he enters the situation with a value of pacifism, a clash of values results. The conflict might also be due to the subject's bringing incompatible standards into the experimental situation with him, or even to the experimenter's creating two inconsistent standards within the laboratory setting.

Typically the research we have performed has taken one of two tacks: (1) a standard is created, or closely related to this, a previous standard has been emphasized; and (2) the subject's standard as he brought it to the laboratory was left intact. An example of the former is the social facilitation experiment reported toward the end of Chapter 7, in which the subject was instructed to work as rapidly as possible. An example of the latter tack is the experiment on avoidance of objective self awareness (Chapter 2), in which we assumed that subjects brought with them a personal standard of high intelligence and creativity.

We should like to make the point that both of those experiments could have failed if we had seriously misjudged the standards operating. If the instructions in the social facilitation experiment had failed, and subjects took a slow-down to be a personal standard, the results should have been opposite what they were. In the avoidance experiment the pattern of results would have been much different had the subjects not brought with them high aspirations for intelligence and creativity. But there is a third possibility as well. If the social facilitation subjects had brought with them a standard of "work slowly and diligently," this would have operated against the experimentally created standard of speed, and if these conflicting ideals had been equally strong there would have been no differences between conditions. We would then have suspected the effectiveness of the mirror in provoking the objective state, or perhaps found a methodological (or even theoretical) flaw, all of which would have been unwarranted given that the subject's standards were in conflict.

Is there some sure way to ascertain that just one standard predominates in any particular setting? We can rely on our intuition about people in the situations where we look at them, we can ask them directly for their standards, and we can attempt to instill new (or at least uniform) standards into them. The latter approach should generally be the most powerful and reliable, if done correctly. Perhaps the purest test of the theory would involve creating a new dimension, on which the subject could have no value system, and impart a single value to him. Almost as reliable as this somewhat unlikely approach is the use of intuition when limited to dimensions where the standards should be obvious. This was the strategy adopted in the attitude-behavioral discrepancy research reported in Chapter 6, in which it was assumed that subjects universally place value on consistency between attitudes, or standards, and behavior.

In summary, our recommendation for research related to the theory is twofold; for the clearest predictions and most successful application, the standards of correctness should either be completely obvious and universal, or else a standard should be created in such a way that it will dominate over any possible competing standards. This leads us to the next question, having to do with self reports and individual differences.

Individual Differences

There are two questions to be raised: one has to do with individual differences in values, the other with individual differences in objective self awareness.

DIFFERENCES IN VALUES

The use of individual differences in values as a research strategy is not completely without merit, although we favor the strategies suggested above (use of universal values and creation of new values). A researcher might recruit some subjects, ask them to indicate on a form their desires for various places along a dimension, and assume that the standard by which they will operate is their favorite or preferred point on the dimension. But there is a difficulty here. The subject may well express a view that has little to do with the way he actually operates—the expressed value may simply be a response to the demands of the experimental situation rather than his private standard of correctness. Such a difficulty is obviated if a strong value is experimentally created or if a blatantly universal value is tapped for the research purpose. A second difficulty is that the subject's report, even if an attempt to be honest, may be largely orthogonal to his operative standards of correctness. This point requires some elaboration.

Many of our standards are implicit. They guide behavior consistently, and the individual can often successfully correct discrepancies between those standards and his behaviors, but this is not to say that he has ever practiced verbalizing many of those standards. For example, there must be hundreds of standards that govern the way one drives an automobile around a crowd of people, but these are standards which are neither formally expressed nor even put into words by the individual. The standard approximates a mental picture of the correct behavior, and when asked to represent this standard on a psychological scale the individual jots something down, but his response may have little to do with the operative standard. The standard and the questionnaire response would not necessarily be opposed, but simply independent of one another. Again, the difficulty is met by employing the research strategies we have proposed.

Certainly the application of the theory should not be limited to experimental research. To the extent that there are implications for applied social psychology and clinical problems, it will be necessary to assess individual standards, and our hope is that the clinician's intuition will lead him to implement the theory to his benefit. In short, we suspect that his hunches and direct observations of others' standards will be more useful to him than will paper-and-pencil tests of values.

DIFFERENCES IN OBJECTIVE SELF AWARENESS

It may be tempting to categorize people according to whether they are typically objectively or subjectively aware, and then to the more objectively self aware individuals to show more discrepancy reduction and avoidance of stimuli provoking the objective state. We view such an approach as questionable, at best, primarily for two reasons.

The first reason has to do with general philosophies of individual differences versus situational variables. Proponents of individual differences argue that situation variables are weak by comparison, transitory, and often "artificial." We would seriously question this objection, especially in the context of the theory, for we view conscious attention as predominantly under the control of surrounding stimulus conditions. Proponents of situational variables and manipulations object to individual differences on the grounds of their ambiguity. Any given scale, or other supposed manifestation of the person's psychological state, can easily represent numerous different aspects of the person, and in no way could be labeled as a pure reflection of one distinct trait. To take an example, someone who scores highly on the TAT measure of achievement motivation is not solely a "high achiever." In addition, the score may reflect his differences from others on thousands of dimensions, such as extraversion, intelligence, age, sex, hormonal functioning, ad infinitum. The experimental or situational variable approach handles this difficulty by randomizing out all other variables except for those of interest. Of course, it might be objected that a manipulation of a given variable simultaneously manipulates other variables of psychological import, and this can hardly be denied. However, what is important is that the investigator knows what he has done to the subject; but by way of contrast, the individual difference approach gives virtually no idea of the conditions that brought about the individual difference, and therein lies the important ambiguity.

The second reason operates independently of one's philosophical bent. It is a practical consideration that is possibly unique to theories about self awareness. We can think of no easy way to ask a subject how self aware he is without creating self awareness. For this reason and the foregoing reasons we have devoted none of our efforts to individual differences in objective self awareness.

This is not to deny that such differences exist, in that some people surely spend a greater proportion of time focusing on themselves than others. But theoretically these differences have as their source the person's immediate situation and anticipation of situations that arouse the state; thus, in the last analysis, it is the environment we should inspect if we want to know something about the frequency and duration of someone's objective self awareness.

APPENDIX:
Experimental Tests of the Theory

BIBLIOGRAPHY

Abelson, R. P. & Rosenberg, M. J. Symbolic psycho-logic: A model of attitudinal cognition. *Behavioral Science*, 1958, **3**, 1 13.

Allen, V. L., & Levine, J. M. Consensus and conformity. *Journal of Experimental Social Psychology*, 1969, **5**, 389-399.

Allport, F. H. *Social psychology*. Boston, Massachusetts: Houghton Mifflin, 1924.

Allyn, J., & Festinger, L. The effectiveness of unanticipated persuasive communications. *Journal of Abnormal and Social Psychology*, 1961, **62**, 35-40.

Anderson, N. H. Averaging versus adding as a stimulus combination rule in impression formation. *Journal of Experimental Psychology*, 1965, **70**, 394-400.

Argyle, M. Social pressure in public and private situations. *Journal of Abnormal and Social Psychology*, 1957, **54**, 172-175.

Aronson E. The effect of effort on the attractiveness of rewarded and unrewarded stimuli. *Journal of Abnormal and Social Psychology*, 1961, **63**, 375-380.

Aronson, E., & Carlsmith, J. M. Performance expectancy as a determinant of actual performance. *Journal of Abnormal and Social Psychology*, 1962, **65**, 178-182.

Aronson, E. & Carlsmith, J. M. Effect of the severity of threat on the valuation of forbidden behavior. *Journal of Abnormal and Social Psychology*, 1963, **66**, 584-588.

Aronson, E. & Golden, B. W. The effect of relevant and irrelevant aspects of communicator credibility on opinion change. *Journal of Personality*, 1962, **30**, 135-146.

Arrowood, A. J. & Ross, L. Anticipated effort and subjective probability. *Journal of Personality and Social Psychology*, 1966, **4**, 57-64.

225

Asch, S. E. Issues in the study of social influences on judgment. In I. A. Berg and B. M. Bass (Eds.), *Conformity and deviation*. New York: Harper and Row, 1961.

Asch, S. E. Effects of group pressure upon the modification and distortion of judgments. In H. Guetzkow (Ed.), *Groups, leadership, and men*. Pittsburgh, Pennsylvania: Carnegie, 1951.

Asch, S. E. *Social psychology*. Englewood Cliffs, New Jersey: Prentice-Hall, 1952.

Asch, S. E. Studies of independence and conformity: A minority of one against a unanimous majority. *Psychological Monographs*, 1956, **70**, (9, whole No. 416).

Back, K. W. Influence through social communication. *Journal of Abnormal and Social Psychology*, 1951, **46**, 9-23.

Barker, R. An experimental study of the relationship between certainty of choice and the relative valence of alternatives. *Journal of Personality*, 1946, **15**, 41-42.

Baron, R. S. Anonymity, deindividuation and aggression. Paper presented at the Convention of the Western Psychological Association, 1971.

Blake, R. R. & Mouton, J. S. Conformity, resistance, and conversion. In I. A. Berg and B. M. Bass (Eds.), *Conformity and deviation*. New York: Harper and Row, 1961.

Bossart, P., & Di Vesta, F. J. Effects of context, frequency and order of presentation of evaluative assertions on impression formation. *Journal of Personality and Social Psychology*, 1966, **4**, 538-544.

Brehm, J. W. Increasing cognitive dissonance by a fait-accompli. *Journal of Abnormal and Social Psychology*, 1959, **58**, 379-382.

Brehm, J. W. Motivational effects of cognitive dissonance. In M. R. Jones (Ed.), *Nebraska symposium on motivation*. Lincoln, Nebraska: University of Nebraska Press, 1962.

Brehm, J. W. *A theory of psychological reactance*. New York: Academic Press, 1966.

Brehm, J. W., & Cohen, A. R. *Explorations in cognitive dissonance*. New York: Wiley, 1962.

Brehm, J. W., & Crocker, J. C. An experiment on hunger. In J. W. Brehm and A. R. Cohen, *Explorations in cognitive dissonance*. New York: Wiley, 1962. Pp. 133-137.

Brehm, J. W., & Jones, R. A. The effect on dissonance of surprise consequences. *Journal of Experimental Social Psychology*, 1970, **6**, 420-431.

Brehm, J. W. & Wicklund, R. A. Regret and dissonance reduction as a function of postdecision salience of dissonant information. *Journal of Personality and Social Psychology*, 1970, **14**, 1-7.

Brehm, M. L., Back, K. W., & Bogdonoff, M. D. A physiological effect of cognitive dissonance under stress and deprivation. *Journal of Abnormal and Social Psychology*, 1964, **69**, 303-310.

Brock, T. C., & Buss, A. H. Dissonance, aggression, and evaluation of pain. *Journal of Abnormal and Social Psychology*, 1962, **65**, 197-202.

Brock, T. C., Edelman, S. K., Edwards, D. C., & Schuck, J. R. Seven studies of performance expectancy as a determinant of actual performance. *Journal of Experimental Social Psychology*, 1965, **1**, 295-310.

Brock, T. C., & Fromkin, H. L. Cognitive tuning set and behavioral receptivity to discrepant information. *Journal of Personality*, 1968, **36**, 108-125.

Brown, R. *Social psychology*. New York: The Free Press, 1965.

Byrne, D. Interpersonal attraction and attitude similarity. *Journal of Abnormal and Social Psychology*, 1961, **62**, 713-715.

Cannavale, F. J., Scarr, H. A., & Pepitone, A. Deindividuation in the small group: Further evidence. *Journal of Personality and Social Psychology*, 1970, **16**, 141-147.

Carlsmith, J. M., Collins, B. E., & Helmreich, R. L. Studies in forced compliance: I. The effect of pressure for compliance on attitude change produced by face-to-face role playing and anonymous essay writing. *Journal of Personality and Social Psychology*, 1966, **4**, 1-13.

Carlsmith, J. M., Ebbesen, E., Lepper, M., Zanna, M., Joncas, A., & Abelson, R. P. Dissonance reduction following forced attention to the dissonance. Proceedings of the 77th Annual Convention of the American Psychological Association, 1969, 321-322.

Chesterfield, Earl of (Philip Darmer Stanhope). *Letters to his son*. (Walter M. Dunne, Ed.) New York: Wiley, 1901. Originally published 1774.

Cohen, A. R. Communication discrepancy and attitude change: a dissonance theory approach, *Journal of Personality*, 1959, **27**, 386-396.

Cohen, A. R. Cognitive tuning as a factor affecting impression formation. *Journal of Personality*, 1961, **29**, 235-245.

Cohen, A. R. A dissonance analysis of the boomerang effect. *Journal of Personality*, 1962, **30**, 75-88.

Cohen, A. R., Brehm, J. W., & Fleming, W. H. Attitude change and justification for compliance. *Journal of Abnormal and Social Psychology*, 1958, **56**, 276-278.

Cohen, A. R., Brehm, J. W., & Latane, B. Choice of strategy and voluntary exposure to information under public and private conditions. *Journal of Personality*, 1959, **27**, 63-73.

Cooley, C. H. *Human nature and the social order*. (1st ed., 1902) New York: Schocken Books, 1967.

Cooper, J. Personal responsibility and dissonance: The role of foreseen consequences. *Journal of Personality and Social Psychology*, 1971, **18**, 354-363.

Costanzo, P. R. Conformity development as a function of self-blame. *Journal of Personality and Social Psychology*, 1970, **14**, 366-374.

Costanzo, P. R., & Shaw, M. E. Conformity as a function of age level. *Child Development*, 1966, **37**, 967-975.

Cottrell, N. B. Performance expectancy as a determinant of actual performance: A replication with a new design. *Journal of Personality and Social Psychology*, 1965, **2**, 685-691.

Cottrell, N. B. Performance in the presence of other human beings: Mere presence, audience, and affiliation effects. In E. C. Simmel, R. A. Hoppe, & G. A. Milton (Eds.), *Social facilitation and imitative behavior*. Boston, Massachusetts: Allyn & Bacon, 1968. Pp. 91-110.

Cottrell, N. B. Social facilitation. In C. G. McClintock (Ed.), *Experimental social psychology*. New York: Holt, Rinehart, and Winston, Inc., 1972, Pp. 185-236.

Cottrell, N. B., Wack, D. L., Sekerak, G. J., & Rittle, R. H. Social facilitation of dominant responses by the presence of an audience and the mere presence of others. *Journal of Personality and Social Psychology*, 1968, **9**, 245-250.

Crutchfield, R. S. Conformity and character. *American Psychologist*, 1955, **10**, 191-198.

Davis, K. E., & Jones, E. E. Changes in interpersonal perception as a means of reducing cognitive dissonance. *Journal of Abnormal and Social Psychology*, 1960, **61**, 402-410.

de Charms, R. *Personal causation*. New York: Academic Press, 1968.

Deutsch, M., & Gerard, H. B. A study of normative and informational social influence upon individual judgment. *Journal of Abnormal and Social Psychology*, 1955, **51**, 629-636.

Dion, K. L. Determinants of unprovoked aggression. Unpublished doctoral dissertation, University of Minnesota, 1970.

Dreyer, A. Aspiration behavior as influenced by expectation and group comparison. *Human Relations*, 1954, **7**, 175-190.

Duval, S. Causal attribution as a function of focus of attention. Unpublished manuscript, University of Texas, 1971.

Feather, N. T. Attribution of responsibility and valence of success and failure in relation to initial confidence and task performance. *Journal of Personality and Social Psychology*, 1969, **13**, 129-144.

Festinger, L. Informal social communication. *Psychological Review*, 1950, **57**, 271-282.

Festinger, L. An analysis of compliant behavior. In M. Sherif and M. O. Wilson (Eds.), *Group relations at the crossroads*. New York: Harper and Row, 1953.

Festinger, L. A theory of social comparison processes. *Human Relations*, 1954, **7**, 117-140.

Festinger, L. *A Theory of cognitive dissonance*. Stanford, California: Stanford University Press, 1957. (a)

Festinger, L. An experiment on exposure to information. In L. Festinger, *A theory of cognitive dissonance*. Stanford: California: Stanford, University Press, 1957. Pp. 162-176. (b)

Festinger, L. Behavioral support for opinion change. *Public Opinion Quarterly*, 1964, **28**, 404-417.

Festinger, L. & Carlsmith, J. M. Cognitive consequences of forced compliance. *Journal of Abnormal and Social Psychology*, 1959, **58**, 203-210.

Festinger, L., Gerard, H. B., Hymovitch, B., Kelley, H. H., & Raven, B. H. The influence process in the presence of extreme deviates. *Human Relations*, 1952, **5**, 327-346.

Festinger, L., Pepitone, A., & Newcomb, T. Some consequences of deindividuation in a group. *Journal of Abnormal and Social Psychology*, 1952, **47**, 382-389.

Festinger, L., Schachter, S., & Back, K.W. *Social pressures in informal groups*. New York: Harper, 1950.

Festinger, L., & Thibaut, J. Interpersonal communication in small groups. *Journal of Abnormal and Social Psychology*, 1951, **46**, 92-99.

Festinger, L., Torrey, J., & Willerman, B. Self evaluation as a function of attraction to the group. *Human Relations*, 1954, **7**, 161-174.

Festinger, L., & Walster, E. Post-decision regret and decision reversal. In L. Festinger, *Conflict, decision and dissonance*. Stanford: Stanford University Press, 1964. Pp. 97-111.

Fisher, S. & Lubin, A. Distance as a determinant of influence in a two person serial interaction situation. *Journal of Abnormal and Social Psychology*, 1958, **56**, 230-238.

Freedman, J. L. Attitudinal effects of inadequate justification. *Journal of Personality*, 1963, **31**, 371-385.

French, J. R. P., Jr., & Raven, B. H. The bases of social power. In D. Cartwright (Ed.), *Studies in social power*. Ann Arbor, Michigan: Institute for Social Research, 1959. Pp. 150-167.

Freud, S. *Inhibitions, symptoms, and anxiety*. London: Hogarth, 1949. Originally published 1936.

Gerard, H. B. The anchorage of opinions in face-to-face groups. *Human Relations*, 1954, **7**, 313-325.

Gerard, H. B. Deviation, conformity, and commitment. In I. D. Steiner and M. Fishbein (Eds.), *Current studies in social psychology*. New York: Holt, Rinehart, & Winston, 1965. Pp. 263-277.

Gerard, H. B., Wilhelmy, R. A., & Conolley, E. S. Conformity and group size. *Journal of Personality and Social Psychology*, 1968, **8**, 79-82.

Goffman, E. *Interaction ritual*. Garden City, New York: Anchor Books, 1967

Goldberg, S. C., and Lubin, A. Influence as a function of perceived judgment error. *Human Relations*, 1958, **11**, 275-280.

Hardy, K. R. Determinants of conformity and attitude change. *Journal of Abnormal and Social Psychology*, 1957, **54**, 289-294.

Hare, A. P. *Handbook of small group research*. New York: Free Press, 1962.

Harris, R. J. Dissonance or sour grapes? Post-"decision" changes in ratings and choice frequencies. *Journal of Personality and Social Psychology*, 1969, **11**, 334-344.

Heider, F. Social perception and phenomenal causality. *Psychological Review*, 1944, **51**, 358-374.

Heider, F. Attitudes and cognitive reorganization. *Journal of Psychology*, 1946, **21**, 107-112.

Heider, F. *The psychology of interpersonal relations*. New York: Wiley, 1958.

Helmreich, R. & Collins, B. E. Studies in forced compliance: Commitment and magnitude of inducement to comply as determinants of opinion change. *Journal of Personality and Social Psychology*, 1968, **10**, 75-81.

Henchy, T., & Glass, D. C. Evaluation apprehension and the social facilitation of dominant and subordinate responses. *Journal of Personality and Social Psychology*, 1968, **10**, 446-454.

Hilgard, E. R. Levels of awareness: Second thoughts on some of William James' ideas. In R. B. MacLeod (Ed.), *William James: Unfinished business*. Washington, D.C.: American Psychological Association, 1969.

Hochbaum, G. M. The relation between group members' self-confidence and their reaction to group pressures to conformity. *American Sociological Review*, 1954, **19**, 678-688.

Hoffer, E. *The true believer*. New York: Harper, 1951.

Hoffer, E. *The passionate state of mind*. New York: Harper, 1954.

Jones, E. E. *Ingratiation*. New York: Appleton-Century-Crofts, 1964.

Jones, E. E., & Davis, K. E. From acts to dispositions. In L. Berkowitz (Ed.), *Advances in experimental social psychology*. Vol. 2. New York: Academic Press, 1965.

Jones, E. E., & Nisbett, R. E. *The actor and the observer: Divergent perceptions of the causes of behavior*. New York: General Learning Press, 1971.

Julian, J. W., Regula, C. R., & Hollander, E. P. Effects of prior agreement by others on task confidence and conformity. *Journal of Personality and Social Psychology*, 1968, **9**, 171-178.

Kelley, H. H. Attribution theory in social psychology. In D. Levine (Ed.), *Nebraska symposium on motivation*. Lincoln, Nebraska: University of Nebraska Press, 1967.

Kelley, H. H., & Lamb, T. W. Certainty of judgment and resistance to social influence. *Journal of Abnormal and Social Psycohology*, 1957, **55**, 137-139.

Kelman, H. C. Effects of success and failure on suggestibility in the autokinetic situation. *Journal of Abnormal and Social Psychology*, 1950, **11**, 267-285.

Kelman, H. C. Compliance, identification, and internalization: Three processes of opinion change. *Journal of Conflict Resolution*, 1958, **2**, 51-60.

Kiesler, C. A. Group pressure and conformity. In J. Mills (Ed.), *Experimental social psychology*. New York: Macmillan, 1969. Pp. 233-306.

Kiesler, C. A., & Corbin, L. H. Commitment, attraction, and conformity. *Journal of Personality and Social Psychology*, 1965, **2**, 890-895.

Kiesler, C. A., Zanna, M., & De Salvo, J. Deviation and conformity: opinion change as a function of commitment, attraction, and presence of a deviate. *Journal of Personality and Social Psychology*, 1966, **3**, 458-467.

Kilpatrick, W. H. *Selfhood and civilization*. New York: Macmillan, 1941.

Koch, S. Behavior as "intrinsically" regulated: Work notes towards a pre-theory of phenomena called "motivational." In M. R. Jones (Ed.), *Nebraska symposium on motivation*. Lincoln, Nebraska: University of Nebraska Press, 1956. Pp. 42-87.

Koffka, K. *Principles of gestalt psychology*. New York: Harcourt, Brace, 1935.

Lacey, J. I. Somatic response patterning and stress: Some revisions of activation theory. In M. H. Appley & R. Turnbull (Eds.), *Psychological stress: Some issues in research*. New York: Appleton-Century-Crofts, 1967.

Lazarus, R. S., Deese, J., & Osler, S. F. The effects of psychological stress upon performance. *Psychological Bulletin*, 1952, **49**, 293-317.

Le Bon, G. *The crowd*. New York: Viking, 1960. Originally published 1895.

Lewin, K. *A dynamic theory of personality*. New York: McGraw-Hill, 1935.

Linder, D. E., Cooper, J., & Jones, E. E. Decision freedom as a determinant of the role of incentive magnitude in attitude change. *Journal of Personality and Social Psychology*, 1967, **6**, 245-254.

Linder, D. E., Cooper, J. & Wicklund, R. A. Pre-exposure persuasion as a result of commitment to pre-exposure effort. *Journal of Experimental Social Psychology*, 1968, **4**, 470-482.

Linder, D. E., & Worchel, S. Opinion change as a result of effortfully drawing a counterattitudinal conclusion. *Journal of Experimental Social Psychology*, 1970, **6**, 432-448.

McGuire, W. J. Selective exposure: A summing up. In R. P. Abelson, E. Aronson, W. J. McGuire, T. M. Newcomb, M. J. Rosenberg, & P. J. Tannenbaum (Eds.), *Theories of cognitive consistency: A sourcebook*. Chicago, Illinois: Rand McNally, 1968. Pp. 797-800.

McGuire, W. J., & Millman, S. Anticipatory belief lowering following forewarning of a persuasive attack. *Journal of Personality and Social Psychology*, 1965, **2**, 471-479.

Mansson, H. H. The relation of dissonance reduction to cognitive, perceptual, consummatory, and learning measures of thirst. In P. G. Zimbardo (Ed.), *The cognitive control of motivation*. Glenview, Illinois: Scott, Foresman, 1969.

Martens, R. Effect of an audience on learning and performance of a complex motor skill. *Journal of Personality and Social Psychology*, 1969, **12**, 252-260.

Mason, R. E. *Internal perception and bodily functioning*. New York: International Universities Press, 1961.

Mead, G. H. *Mind, self, and society*. Chicago, Illinois: University of Chicago Press, 1934.

Mills, J. The effect of certainty on exposure to information prior to commitment. *Journal of Experimental Social Psychology*, 1965, **1**, 348-355. (a)

Mills, J. Effect of certainty about a decision upon post decision exposure to consonant and dissonant information. *Journal of Personality and Social Psychology*, 1965, **2**, 749-752. (b)

Mills, J. Avoidance of dissonant information. *Journal of Personality and Social Psychology*, 1965, **2**, 589-593. (c)

Mills, J. Interest in supporting and discrepant information. In R. P. Abelson, E. Aronson, W. J. McGuire, T. M. Newcomb, M. J. Rosenberg, & P. J. Tannenbaum (Eds.), *Theories of cognitive consistency: A sourcebook*. Chicago, Illinois: Rand McNally, 1968.

Mills, J. *Experimental social psychology*. New York: Macmillan, 1969.

Mills, J., & Jellison, J. M. Avoidance of discrepant information prior to commitment. *Journal of Personality and Social Psychology*, 1968, **8**, 59-62.

Mills, J., & Ross, A. The effects of commitment and certainty upon interest in supporting information. *Journal of Abnormal and Social Psychology*, 1964, **68**, 553-555.

Mills, J., & Snyder, R. Avoidance of commitment, need for closure, and the expression of choices. *Journal of Personality*, 1962, **30**, 458-470.

Morse, S. & Gergen, K. J. Social comparison, self-consistency, and the concept of self. *Journal of Personality and Social Psychology*, 1970, **16**, 148-156.

Mouton, J. S., Blake, R. R., & Olmstead, J. A. The relationship between frequency of yielding and the disclosure of personal identity. *Journal of Personality*, 1956, **24**, 339-347.

Newcomb, T. M. *Personality and social change: Attitude formation in a student community*. New York: Holt, Rinehart and Winston, Inc., 1943.

Newcomb, T. M. An approach to the study of communicative acts. *Psychological Review*, 1953, **60**, 393-404.

O'Neal, E., & Mills, J. The influence of anticipated choice on the halo effect. *Journal of Experimental Social Psychology*, 1969, **5**, 347-351.

Osgood, C. E. & Tannenbaum, P. H. The principle of congruity in the prediction of attitude change. *Psychological Review*, 1955, **62**, 42-55.

Paulus, P. B., and Murdoch, P. Anticipated evaluation and audience presence in the enhancement of dominant responses. *Journal of Experimental Social Psychology*, 1971, **7**, 280-291.

Piaget, J. *Judgment and reasoning in the child*. (1st ed., 1924) Totowa, New Jersey: Littlefield, Adams, 1966.

Polanyi, M. *Personal knowledge: Towards a post-critical philosophy*. New York: Harper & Row, 1958.

Rabbie, J. M., Brehm, J. W., & Cohen, A. R. Verbalization and reactions to cognitive dissonance. *Journal of Personality*, 1959, **27**, 407-417.

Rappoport, L. H. Interpersonal conflict in co-operative and uncertain situations. *Journal of Experimental Social Psychology*, 1965, **1**, 323-333.

Raven, B. H. Social influence on opinions and the communication of related context. *Journal of Abnormal and Social Psychology*, 1959, **58**, 119-128.

Rosenberg, L. A. Group size, prior experience and conformity. *Journal of Abnormal and Social Psychology*, 1961, **63**, 436-437.

Rotter, J. B. Generalized expectancies for internal versus external control of reinforcement. *Psychological Monographs*, 1966, **80**.

Samelson, F. Conforming behavior under two conditions of conflict in the cognitive field. *Journal of Abnormal and Social Psychology*, 1957, **55**, 181-187.

Sarnoff, I., & Zimbardo, P. G. Anxiety, fear, and social affiliation. *Journal of Abnormal and Social Psychology*, 1961, **62**, 356-363.

Sartre, J. P. *Being and nothingness*. New York: Philosophical Library, 1956.

Schachter, S. Deviation, rejection, and communication. *Journal of Abnormal and Social Psychology*, 1951, **46**, 190-207.

Schachter, S. *The psychology of affiliation*. Stanford, California: Stanford University Press, 1959.

Schilder, P. *The image and appearance of the human body: Studies in the constructive energies of the psyche*. New York: International Press, 1950.

Scott, J. P. Social facilitation and allelomimetic behavior. In E. C. Simmel, R. A. Hoppe, & G. A. Milton (Eds.), *Social facilitation and imitative behavior*. Boston, Massachusetts: Allyn and Bacon, 1968. Pp. 55-72.

Sherif, M. A study of some social factors in perception. *Archives of Psychology*, 1935, No. 187.

Sherif, M., & Hovland, C. I. *Social judgment*. New Haven, Connecticut: Yale University Press, 1961.

Sherman, S. J. Attitudinal effects of unforeseen consequences. *Journal of Personality and Social Psychology*, 1970, **16**, 510-520.

Singer, J. E., Brush, C. A., & Lublin, S. C. Some aspects of deindividuation: Identification and conformity. *Journal of Experimental Social Psychology*, 1965, **1**, 356-378.

Streufert, S. Communicator importance and interpersonal attitudes toward conforming and deviant group members. *Journal of Personality and Social Psychology*, 1965, **2**, 242-246.

Strickland, L. H., Jones, E. E., & Smith, W. P. Effects of group support on the evaluation of an antagonist. *Journal of Abnormal and Social Psychology*, 1960, **61**, 73-81.

Thibaut, J. W., & Riecken, H. W. Some determinants and consequences of the perception of social causality. *Journal of Personality*, 1955, **24**, 113-133.

Thorpe, W. H. Ethology and consciousness. In J. C. Eccles (Ed.), *Brain and conscious experience*. Study Week, Sept. 28 to Oct. 4, 1964 of the Pontificia Academia Scientiarum. New York: Springer-Verlag, 1966.

Tolman, C. W. The role of the companion in social facilitation of animal behavior. In E. C. Simmel, R. A. Hoppe, & G. A. Milton (Eds.), *Social facilitation and imitative behavior*. Boston, Massachusetts: Allyn and Bacon, 1968. Pp. 33-54.

Triplett, N. The dynamogenic factors in pacemaking and competition. *American Journal of Psychology*, 1897, **9**, 507-533.

Walster, E. The temporal sequence of post-decision processes. In L. Festinger, *Conflict, decision and dissonance*. Stanford: Stanford University Press, 1964. Pp. 112-127.

Walster, E., & Berscheid, E. The effects of time on cognitive consistency. In R. P. Abelson, E. Aronson, W. J. McGuire, T. M. Newcomb, M. J. Rosenberg, & P. J. Tannenbaum (Eds.), *Theories of cognitive consistency: A sourcebook*. Chicago, Illinois: Rand McNally, 1968. Pp. 599-608.

Ward, W. D., & Sandvold, K. D. Performance expectancy as a determinant of actual performance: A partial replication. *Journal of Abnormal and Social Psychology*, 1963, **67**, 293-295.

Watts, W. A. Cognitive reorganization following a disconfirmed expectancy. *Journal of Personality and Social Psychology*, 1965, **2**, 231-241.

Watts, W. A. Commitment under conditions of risk. *Journal of Personality and Social Psychology*, 1966, **3**, 507-515.

Wicklund, R. A. Prechoice preference reversal as a result of threat to decision freedom. *Journal of Personality and Social Psychology*, 1970, **14**, 8-17.

Wicklund, R. A., Cooper, J., & Linder, D. E. Effects of expected effort on attitude change prior to exposure. *Journal of Experimental Social Psychology*, 1967, **3**, 416-428.

Wicklund, R. A., & Duval, S. Opinion change and performance facilitation as a result of objective self awareness. *Journal of Experimental Social Psychology*, 1971, **7**, 319-342.

Wicklund, R. A. & Ickes, W. J. The effect of objective self awareness on predecisional exposure to information. *Journal of Experimental Social Psychology*, 1972, **8**, 378-387.

Willis, R. H., & Hollander, E. P. An experimental study of three response modes in social influence situations. *Journal of Abnormal and Social Psychology*, 1964, **69**, 150-156.

Wylie, R. C. The present status of self theory. In E. F. Borgatta and W. W. Lambert (Eds.), *Handbook of personality theory and research*. Chicago, Illinois: Rand McNally, 1968. Pp. 728-787.

Yaryan, R. B. & Festinger, L. Preparatory action and belief in the probable occurrence of future events. *Journal of Abnormal and Social Psychology*, 1961, **63**, 603-606.

Zajonc, R. B. The process of cognitive tuning in communication. *Journal of Abnormal and Social Psychology*, 1960, **61**, 159-167.

Zajonc, R. B. Social facilitation. *Science*, 1965, **149**, 269-274.

Zajonc, R. B. Social facilitation in cockroaches. In E. C. Simmel, R. A. Hoppe, & G. A. Milton, (Eds.), *Social facilitation and imitative behavior*. Boston, Massachusetts: Allyn and Bacon, 1968. Pp. 73-88.

Zajonc, R. B., & Sales, S. M. Social facilitation of dominant and subordinate responses. *Journal of Experimental Social Psychology*, 1966, **2**, 160-168.

Ziller, R. C. Individuation and socialization. *Human Relations*, 1964, **17**, 341-360.

Zimbardo, P. G. The effect of effort and improvisation on self-persuasion produced by role-playing. *Journal of Experimental Social Psychology*, 1965, **1**, 103-120.

Zimbardo, P. G. *The cognitive control of motivation*. Glenview, Illinois: Scott, Foresman, 1969. (a)

Zimbardo, P. G. The human choice: Individuation, reason, and order versus deindividuation, impulse, and chaos. In W. J. Arnold & D. Levine (Eds.), *Nebraska symposium on motivation*, Vol. XVII. Lincoln: University of Nebraska Press, 1969. Pp. 237-307. (b)

Zimbardo, P. G., Cohen, A. R., Weisenberg, M., Dworkin, L., and Firestone, I. The control of experimental pain. In P. G. Zimbardo, *The cognitive control of motivation*. Glenview, Illinois: Scott, Foresman, 1969. Pp. 100-126.

Author Index

Numbers in italics refer to the pages on which the complete references are listed.

A

Abelson, R. P., 123, 135, *223, 224*
Allen, V. L., 111, *223*
Allport, F. H., 155, 162, *223*
Allyn, J., 175, *223*
Anderson, N. H., 78, *223*
Argyle, M., 102, *223*
Aronson, E., 125, 127, 135, 151, *223*
Arrowood, A. J., 127, *223*
Asch, S. E., 58, 62, 84, 102, 108, 109, 111, 112, 115, *224*

B

Back, K. W., 87, 127, *224, 226*
Barker, R., 80, *224*
Baron, R. S., 208, *224*
Berscheid, E., 147, *229*
Blake, R. R., 102, 110, *224, 228*
Bogdonoff, M. D., 127, *224*
Bossart, P., 78, *224*
Brehm, J. W., 125, 127, 129, 136, 144, 147, 149, 150, 175, *224, 225, 228*
Brock, T. C., 151, 173, 178, *224*
Brown, R., 189, *224*
Brush, C. A., 28, 208, 212, *229*
Bryne, D., 59, *224*
Buss, A. H., *224*

C

Cannavale, F. J., 208, *224*
Carlsmith, J. M., 125, 127, 130, 135, 151, *223, 224, 226*
Chesterfield, Earl of (*see also* Stanhope, Philip Darmer, 191, *225*
Cohen, A. R., 125, 127, 129, 149, 151, 173, 177, 212, *224, 225, 228, 230*

Collins, B. E., 125, 127, 130, 132, *224, 226*
Conolley, E. S., 110, *226*
Cooley, C. H., 30, *225*
Cooper, J., 125, 127, 134, *225, 227, 229*
Corbin, L. H., 117, *227*
Costanzo, P. R., 104, *225*
Cottrell, N. B., 151, 156, 157, 158, 161, 162, 164, *225*
Crocker, J. C., 150, *224*
Crutchfield, R. S., 104, *225*

D

Davis, K. E., 65, *225, 227*
de Charms, R., 5, 32, *225*
Deese, J., 169, *227*
De Salvo, J., 60, *227*
Deutsch, M., 102, 115, *225*
Dion, K. L., 209, *225*
Di Vesta, F. J., 78, *224*
Dreyer, A., *225*
Duval, S., 16, 35, 66, 98, 103, 105, 138, 146, 168, 185, 207, *225, 230*
Dworkin, L., 151, 212, *230*

E

Ebbesen, E., 135, *224*
Edelman, S. K., 151, *224*
Edwards, D. C., 151, *224*

F

Feather, N. F., 104, *225*
Festinger, L., 28, 60, 82, 109, 123, 125, 127, 130, 131, 136, 146, 149, 150, 175, 207, *223, 225, 226, 230*
Fine, R. L., 16, 146, *226*

233

Subject Index

237